COMMENTS ON THE BOOK FROM READERS

I found myself learning so much about so many companies. I knew many of these companies but I didn't really know them. This book is one big wonderful storytelling book and more. Every MBA student and every CMO should read it. It's creative and innovative thinking, which is sorely needed in marketing. – *Professor Philip Kotler* (US)

For any marketer this is a must-read. A glorious dance through the technology changes that are positively impacting customer experience and a guidebook for those that want to make a real difference, academic rigour meets creative thinking with compelling examples of distinguishers at work. Felt invigorated by this book, a first for a business book! – *David Wheldon*, President, World Federation of Advertisers (UK)

The authors have taken the lid off the tin containing traditional growth models, and created a sweet shop of new strategies, ideas, principles and examples that are snackable, exciting, smart and practical for the open source world. An inspiring read that will make every business leader and marketer ask themselves difficult questions about whether they are set up for growth or set up for extinction. – *Bart Michels*, CEO, Kantar Europe (UK)

The authors have scoured the world for multiple examples of distinguishers—the companies and individuals that understand what it takes to build value systems in a new global era. They've identified the four elements of the secret sauce that sets distinguishers apart from yesterday's heroes, the extinguishers. Using examples from across the globe, their book shows how winners seemingly come from nowhere to challenge conventional thinking by deploying differentiated business models that deliver value at speed and scale. The book features a treasure trove of caselets curated from multiple industries that show how distinguishers go about disrupting industries in ways that not only delight their customers but also support communities, both now and into the future. Written in an informal and engaging style, *Distinguishers* is the smart must-have for both startups and established businesses who need to evolve their assumptions about how to win in a re-shaped world. – *Professor Nicola Kleyn*, Dean Exec Education Management; former Dean GIBS (

D1665234

I think it is absolutely brilliant. Very enriching, complete and in tune with the times. What I especially like:

- The language of distinguishers and extinguishers. It's very fresh. We needed to move away from disruptors/laggards. This book speaks to both. If you are one, how can you understand better what makes you successful? If you aren't, how can you turn to one?
- The focus is not just corporates, but persons, brands and even governments.
- The opening quote from *Alice in Wonderland* is a killer.
- The concept of speed, scale and frugality: so spot on in today's times.
- The examples/case studies are very 'relatable' and a refreshing change from the typical Apple/Tesla/Amazon examples.
- All assertions are grounded and backed by solid examples and real-world evidence.
- The table on risk attitudes (distinguishers vs extinguishers) is brilliant.
- The book covers such a rich variety of topics. It doesn't just talk about how to become a Distinguisher but also, in very concise and articulate ways, helps one make sense of all relevant emerging technologies of today: from blockchain to XaaS to APIs to 3D printing.

This is not a book you will read and put down. You will keep coming back to it. It is beyond a book—it is more like a reference manual to understand today's world. – *Arpit Kaushik*, Hypha (IN)

Professor Vandermerwe's best book to date. She picked the winners in 2000 and 20 years later she was proved right. Blindingly fast-paced, reading like the new world we live in. If this book doesn't expand people's minds to understand that there is a new business paradigm in play, nothing will. – *Greg Walsh*, former CEO, Baxter Healthcare; founder, DDS Architects (UK)

This is a book that needed to be written. It has great practical use for CEOs, COOs, CMOs and entrepreneurs but should also be read by academics and those teaching strategy, marketing and entrepreneurship at all levels in business schools. There is so much crammed into this book, with a richness of concepts that I've never seen brought together in such a holistic way. This in itself is of value, but what makes the book so readable and engaging is the breadth and richness of the case studies used to illustrate each idea. Some of these brands are very well known, but other examples were more unexpected and demonstrated how distinguishers can come from anywhere and operate in diverse market spaces and geographies. – *Dr Helen Marks*, Trinity Business School (IE)

Disrupters are passé, extinguishers are barriers: Noise without notable change. The future is about distinguishers.
Professor Sandra Vandermerwe foresaw the last customer revolution and sets out here to show how the very best are taking their sectors and the world forward in the most challenging of times. In this book, the reader can learn about where the best thinking is now and where it's headed next.
It's time to exit the extinguishers and celebrate the distinguishers.
This book isn't a wake-up call. The alarm has already gone off. But most of us slept in. This is the book that explains how those who haven't snoozed are already years ahead of the pack. But it's not too late to get out of bed …
– *Justin McLaren*, CEO, Eight hours with Elvis 8hwe (UK)

The world has changed, the dramatic impact of Covid-19 has accelerated a process that began over two decades ago. This book brings real clarity to how you find the silver lining and harness the change for the benefit of your business and customers. – *Mark Bailie*, CEO, BGL Group (UK)

This is a fantastic book. Different. Meaningful. So thanks a lot for making it. Release it at scale. With speed. – *Lisa Lindström*, Chief Experience Officer, EMEIA EY; CEO, Doberman Nordics (SE)

This book is on point and reads like a novel—stimulating and fascinating, bringing a compelling case for change to refit or repurpose an enterprise. Every kind of enterprise will be challenged to its core by this book which provides a roadmap to move from 'extinguisher' to 'distinguisher' mentality—not for the faint-hearted! – *Carinda Slabber*, former GM, Transnet (SA)

Covid-19 has wreaked havoc on an already fragile economic environment and a new way of thinking is critical to ensure that we recover stronger, greener and more sustainable than before. Distinguishers realise that growth is not about pushing the next best innovation, it is about leveraging technology and data to solve human problems and meet consumer needs within planetary bounds. A distinguisher mindset is needed as the world prepares to reset, following the pandemic and global lockdowns.
– *Joanne Bate*, COO, Industrial Development Corporation (SA)

LIST OF COMPANIES USED IN CASE STUDIES
[COUNTRY HEAD OFFICES]

Aerobotics (SA)
Airbnb (US)
ALC (SA)
Alibaba / Freshippo (CN)
Amazon / Amazon Web
   Services (US)
Anchanto (SG)
Apple (US)
Aravind Eye Clinic (IN)
BBVA (ES)
Birchbox (US)
Blue Apron (US)
BMW (DE)
Bosch-Siemens (DE)
Bugcrowd (US)
Burberry (UK)
BuyMeOnce (US)
Capitec (SA)
Cemex (MX)
Circos (NL)
Cohealo (US)
Coursera (US)
DTEN (US)
DHL (US)
Discord (US)
Discovery Insure (SA)
Discovery / Vitality (SA)
Disney (US)
Dunnes Stores (IE)
EasyEquities (SA)

Eileen Fisher (US)
Epic Games / Fortnite (US)
Etsy (US)
Facebook (US)
Farmizen (IN)
Fitbit (US)
FlexClub (SA)
ForDays (US)
GoBear (SG)
GoCar (IE)
Google / YouTube (US)
Harry's (US)
Healthy.io (IL)
Helsieni (FI)
Hyperloop (US)
IBM (US)
iFood (BR)
IFTTT (US)
IKEA (SE)
Infarm (DE)
Intercontinental Hotel (US)
JustPark (US)
Kespry (US)
Kickstarter (US)
LEGO (DK)
Lemonade, Inc (US)
Livestock Wealth (SA)
Local Roots (US)
MaaS (FI)
MedicallHome (MX)

Mercedes (DE)
Microsoft (US)
M-KOPA (SA)
Monzo (UK)
M-PESA (KE/UK)
MTN (SA)
Naked (SA)
NatWest (UK)
Neighbor (US)
Nestlé / Nespresso (CH)
Nest (US)
Netflix (US)
Noom (US)
Patagonia (US)
Patreon (US)
Peek Vision (UK)
Philips (NL)
PillPack (US)
Portbase (NL)
Rover.com (US)
Salesforce (US)
Shopify (CA)
Singapore (SG)
Slack (US)
Smithsonian (US)
SodaStream (IL)
Solaris (DE)
Sonos (US)
Spotify (SE)
Starbucks (US)

Starling (UK)
Stella McCartney (UK)
Sunrun (US)
Sushi Singularity (JP)
Swisscom (CH)
Taskrabbit (US)
Techniplas Prime (US)
Tesla (US)
Testbirds (DE)
The RealReal (CN)
Thrive Agric (NG)
TikTok (CN)
Tink (SE)
Trane (US)
Transfercar (NZ)
Trustpilot (DK)
Uber / Uber Eats (US)
Unilever / Lifebuoy (UK/NL)
Universal (US)
Vodafone (UK)
Volvo (SE/CN)
Walmart (US)
WhatsApp (US)
WhereIsMyTransport (SA)
WoeLab (TG)
Y Closet (CN)
Yummy Kitchen (ID)
Zipline (US)
Zoom (US)
Zulzi (SA)

DISTINGUISHERS

WINNING CUSTOMERS AT SPEED, SCALE & LOWER COSTS

SANDRA VANDERMERWE
DAVID ERIXON

Distinguishers: Winning Customers At Speed, Scale & Lower Costs

First published in 2021 by Nowhere Publishing

© Text: Sandra Vandermerwe & David Erixon

ISBN 978-1-991202-72-7
ebook ISBN 978-1-991202-73-4

Distributed in South Africa by Flyleaf Publishing & Distribution
www.flyleaf.co.za

Design and typesetting by MR Design
Edited by Sandy Shepherd
Proofread by Anita van Zyl
Project and Production management
by Ingeborg Pelser

To each other:
the play was fun,
the pain worth it!

Contents

What can you see?
I see nothing.
Great! What does
nothing look like?

Adapted from *Alice in Wonderland*

Introduction

The not-too-distant future is already upon us. We were always headed in a certain direction, but Covid-19 has changed our course—or, rather, fast-tracked it.

It pushed us into unknown market territories faster and accelerated what was emerging but not yet fully formed or mainstream.

It accentuated millennium values and forced the baby boomers and the late adopters to take up technology quicker than they would have imagined.

It blurred the real and virtual worlds.

It drove Generation Z to the Internet for learning, watching movie premieres or just hanging out with friends. It allowed people to collaborate virtually in ways they never thought possible or thought would ever be necessary—from dating to corporate events, funerals to weddings. And it made virtual experiences a real, acceptable alternative, from touring Kyoto neighbourhoods in Japan to watching Formula One races.

It propelled the Fourth Industrial Revolution, with technology central to customer value, how it's produced and by whom. It forced industries to re-imagine who they were and what they might become.

Because of Covid-19, there is a before and after for everyone.

Business as usual might have been an option before, but it certainly isn't anymore.

What we've learnt

What we've learnt from the pandemic is that we are better off with technology than without it, if it helps us do better things better for customers at scale, speed and lower cost.

The pandemic also taught us what we should already have known—no strategy is good enough if it is not grounded in genuine humanity, doing good for all customer-stakeholders, including the country, city, community and its citizens. And because brands in the know trade in ethics (because the market increasingly values it), cause and cosmos are part and parcel of their strategy.

If indeed the goal is to win at scale and appeal universally.

The pandemic also taught this lesson—how to react, adapt and move quickly. And that those who do so during a crisis continue to leverage the halo effects.

As Stewart Butterfield, founder of Slack, the fastest growing SaaS company of all time[1] put it; 'If you'd asked any CEO with more than 100 employees before Covid-19 whether they could get their whole organisation working remotely inside of a week, the answer would have been no, yet most did it. When you're forced to do something that seemed impossible and then accomplish it, you begin to think about what else is possible for your organisation.'[2]

Months after that remark, Slack was bought by Salesforce in the largest megadeal Salesforce had ever completed. A marriage that has created a powerful new Microsoft contender. In the words of Butterfield in a CNN interview, 'What would have taken twenty years, now is possible in five'.

Distinguishers create value

Distinguishers get that something different needs to be done and they find ways to convince others to support and help them to make it happen.

They go for speed, because they know that wait-and-see is an old strategy that doesn't work anymore.

They go for high impact, not easy.

They have natural insight, an intuitive sense of what markets want, though markets may not know it or ask for it.

Distinguishers don't think in conventional industry and product silos. They have a panoptic view that connects people, and plans, processes and propositions to unlock something new.

They actively seek to change behaviour and make the world better off for it. This drives a deep-rooted purpose, which dictates their playbook.

They use technology to do this, unlike many disruptors who typically just get people to do digitally what people already do.

They break from old wisdom and methods of accounting, because they know that customers won't pay for baggage that adds no value.

They build ecosystems that grow when they grow and thrive when they thrive.

They collaborate openly and know that the value they get from sharing is more than they would lose from someone copying them.

At the beginning, distinguishers seem like outliers; then they become the new norm. But by the time they make their mark they are so far ahead it's difficult for others to catch up—they are already old news.

Extinguishers miss or destroy value

Extinguishers are traditional operators and want to stay with the old model. It makes them feel safe, and they want to feel safe, unlike distinguishers who are constantly re-imagining what things could be like, seeking what's fresh, daring, creative, compelling and new.

Being an extinguisher may have worked in the past and may even work in the short term for some enterprises, but it's not a winning strategy for the future.

Most extinguishers have no desire to change the world or be changed by it.

But the world has changed.

Extinguishers measure success by pleasing the establishment. They don't get that the power lies outside the enterprise not inside, and that what increasingly matters is new customers, their contacts, communities and the crowd.

Extinguishers play their part to achieve budgets, fixate on operational efficiency and get rewarded for being predictably on target. They enter the digital world ostensibly to cut costs, which they often don't pass on.

They are patient, they wait or go into denial when some new entrant appears on the scene. Sometimes they copy, hide behind or call for regulation or a return to old protocols. They typically would rather buy a threatening startup than rock their existing boat.

Whether big or small, they are laden with legacy systems and procedures and if they embark on something new, they invariably hang on to this burden.

They believe that being competitive means having it all and doing it all themselves, that large marketing budgets will make them competitive, and that funds spent on technology will solve their problems.

They think that the future is their five-year plan.

They believe that collaboration is getting everyone to agree.

They would have been considered good managers in an era now behind us.

The structure of the book

This book is about understanding the mind and work of the distinguisher, who could be a person, a brand, an enterprise or, in some cases, a government. We chose cases to bring to life the changes that are happening and the people and brands leading the way. That doesn't mean that all cases, all people, and all brands are at the same level or do everything right.

We compare the distinguisher to the extinguisher and show how extinguishers can become distinguishers and how they and startups with a big idea can, and do, displace the old and bring in the next, creating a new desirable normal.

With so much input and so little time, we know that you, the reader, will want to read something that's bold, not boring; intriguing; informative and solid, not airy fairy; trendy as well as timeless; and, most of all, says something you haven't heard before, but is eminently usable.

Through our work as practitioners, consultants, teachers and researchers, we have found that whether an enterprise is mature, remaking itself or a startup, there are four major steps to winning customers at scale, speed and lower cost.

We want to share these with you, and so the book is organised as follows:

PART ONE: *Shake up—Disrupt the status quo*
We give you loads of examples to see why and how it's done.

PART TWO: *Shape up—Frame the emerging future*
We look at existing and emerging global trends, and project into a future world loaded with fascinating new ideas, concepts and gigantic opportunities, to help you frame the next normal.

PART THREE: *Speed up—Make things happen faster*
We think that in a world where everything is speeding up, doing it fast is as important as doing it differently and better.

We take you through some of the trends, tools, tactics and practices being used and still evolving, enabling enterprises that already excel to do better what they can also do faster.

PART FOUR: *Scale up—Get and stay ahead*
We show you how the model and mindset that is being used to scale up at low cost gets and keeps the enterprise ahead. It is the very opposite of what made brands successful in a past, which needs to be eradicated.

Our thanks and hope

Our thanks go to the people involved in the making of this book, and friends and colleagues for their valuable input and feedback. Thank you to: Alexander Bard, Alma Miller, Arpit Kaushik, Bart Michels, Carinda Slabber, David Wheldon, Greg Walsh, Helen Marks, Jonathan Briggs, Justin McLaren, JP Donnelly, Joanne Bate, Lisa Lindström, Mark Bailie, Nicola Kleyn, Paul McCabe, Philip Kotler.

Much of what we have written is either from our personal experience, as teachers, consultants and practitioners, or from research. We have given you references and links where we can, for you to do a deeper dive. But some of what you will read is our own interpretation, framing for you what we see happening now and anticipate for the future.

We hope you love this book.

We know you won't like or latch onto everything we have said. But we hope at least we can inspire you to make your ideas and moves as big and bold, creative and canny as some of the distinguishers we have described.

Because there is a recipe.

Definition: Distinguisher

A distinguisher is a person, brand, enterprise, government who/which:	DO YOU?	
Sets him-, her- or itself apart	Y	N
Takes customers into a new market space that he, she or it creates	Y	N
Delivers new ways of doing things in that market space	Y	N
Changes behaviour in both consumption and production	Y	N
Accomplishes this at scale	Y	N
Disrupts existing industries	Y	N
... with deep purpose	Y	N
... using technology, continuously evolving	Y	N
Solves for outcomes to get quantifiable results and impacts	Y	N
... for one or more of these stakeholders: country, community, city, consumer/ citizen, cause as well as cosmos	Y	N
Forms value-creating networked ecosystems that grow together	Y	N
... to offer interlinked ever-evolving experiences to customers	Y	N
... across brands and industries, online and offline	Y	N
Perpetually learns to get and stay ahead	Y	N
Scales markets virally, externally	Y	N
Uses agile new ways of working internally, progressing their people with them	Y	N
Monetises and creates value that is mutually rewarding and distributed	Y	N
Learns to do this all at speed	Y	N

HOW DO YOU RATE?

PART ONE

Shake up—Disrupt the status quo

Distinguishers shake up the status quo.

They are determined to disrupt the old and bring in the new.

Their objective is to change behaviour, because they envision a future with better outcomes.

They really want a better world and know what their role is in it.

They create new markets and displace the old, even if this means their own.

They understand that the customer is sometimes ahead of them and their industry.

They don't need proof—they build an educated hypothesis.

They are not afraid to make mistakes (which they do), but they rectify them quickly or when they have to.

They know that if they learn from their mistakes this will help them get it right.

They know that making it happen will make it real.

CHAPTER 1

They change behaviour at scale

Love it or hate it, a year after it was launched the online game Fortnite made more money than any other game in history, with an estimated 350 million users playing it and interplaying across the planet in 2020.[3]

It brought social gaming to the forefront of young people's lives—over 60 per cent of players are aged between 18 and 24 years old.

Of course, during lockdown, people were housebound and had little else to do but go online to work and play.

But who could have known that the brand would captivate millions of people to such an extent and continue to do so? That it would radically alter what they do with their spare time and disrupt and displace so many other forms of entertainment activity? Although it's a shooting game, no one gets killed, just 'eliminated' (it's argued), and rather than the usual violence, it embodies collaboration and learning with a kind of comic mischief.

Fortnite was invented by an unknown university drop-out, Tim Sweeney, who from his parent's garage figured out a way not only to build an online game but change spare-time habits.

Who could have guessed that at such speed and scale he could create from existing technology what is now termed a MMO (massively multiplayer online game) that interconnects players 24/7, using multiple platforms across the world?

So successful has Fortnite become that it has been able to take on Apple in a court of law, challenging the giant's dominance in the market, even though at the time of writing this book the jury is still out.

The mass social experience

We could not have imagined:

- that hordes of people would flock to live or remote tournaments to watch others play games online dressed in virtual so-called 'skins' to earn big money and big kudos;
- that earners, or core gamers as they call themselves (still mostly English speakers from US, Australia, UK, Canada and Ireland, in that order), would want to make this their permanent pastime;
- that online gaming would become an e-sport that would spawn a new profession, to which many youngsters would aspire;
- that many would join competitive revenue-generating teams;
- that top players would be recruited by other players via social media;
- that this activity would become the fastest-growing sport in the world;
- that it would be copied by traditional sports like soccer and Formula One, for which e-versions would be made;
- that e-games could be credited as an Olympic event;
- and become the future of the betting industry;
- and gaming would become bigger than the music and movie industries combined.

We could not have imagined that this online game wave would pave the way for a digital-only goods market, which would spill over into industries like fashion. It has ushered in the concept of real-time virtual dressing-up, which is bound to challenge the clothing industry. (Why do movie stars, models or zoomers need wardrobes when they can be dressed up virtually?)

No one could have known, except perhaps Tim Sweeney.

From Fortnite player to heart surgeon

People have of course long interacted with machines to play games. What Sweeney radically changed is that now they interact with each other and with machines, including collaborating in teams to compete against each other. He took people from being passive watchers of, say, TV or a soccer match ('they are doing it'), to being active participants ('I am doing it'), and then a step further, into a social experience ('we are doing it together') in the virtual world of interactivity, globally.

To top it all, they say that people who do interplay gaming, especially teenagers, learn and develop all sorts of new skills and behaviours. It enhances their memory, builds confidence, teaches social skills, demonstrates best practice in working in a group (they form tribes) and increases co-ordination and concentration.

Players have to stay mentally and physically fit and active, and practise and compete as anyone would for a tournament and a big prize. They cannot do well if they've been drinking or lose concentration. And they can't be late, because if they are, their tribe will discard them.

MMOs are increasingly immersive and multisensory, and the more and more people spend their spare time playing them, the better and better they get at it.

Some of the skills that players are acquiring are transferable, we are told, into professions from surgery to flying drones. Business skills feature as well in their development. Not only do they discover how to compete and collaborate in teams, they also devise campaigns (which can last weeks or months) and strategies, set timelines and goals, and hold retro debriefs to see what can be learned and improved. They have their own virtual V-bucks, which they trade across games for skins (outfits) and resources (weapons). And they combine virtual and physical voice, chatting on the phone to discuss tactics.

Tim Sweeney didn't invent online games. He invented a way to change how people connect. He merged entertainment, skills development, sport and costumed persona and embedded a social component to help people build a network of friends and comrades, across cultures and creeds.

Around this idea and ideology came an empire.

Probably he will have a lot to do with how the next generation thinks and behaves, not only at home but at work as well.

Has he also created the building blocks for our future workforce?

CHAPTER 2

From nowhere, they come

From nowhere, distinguishers come.

They can of course come from inside an existing industry.

Nespresso, which transformed coffee culture and changed market habits, is an example.

The idea of Nespresso was developed in 1976 by Eric Favre, an engineer at Nestlé who would later become president of Nespresso. The concept was then tested in Italy, Switzerland and Japan. But because the insider sceptics were afraid of cannibalisation, it was delayed for 10 years. Favre persevered, and in the early 2000s Nestlé made the daring jump, opening a concept store in Paris. After that things went quickly upward.

The objective was to enable customers to make a good cup of espresso without a skilled barista, i.e., a person operating a coffee machine at a café or bar. It was also to keep customers away from Starbucks, a rising star on the high street, as well as to dissuade them from roasting or grinding coffee at home themselves, which was labour-intensive. And (and this was the brave bit), it was to offer them an alternative to instant coffee, Nestlé's mainstay product.

This new way of doing things meant consumers could make premium single-serve coffee consistently well in their home (B2C) or office (B2B), which—as the numbers show—they definitely did and still do. Today, more than 400 Nespressos are drunk every second around the globe. Some 14 billion Nespresso capsules are sold every year, an important point because the business model was designed to make money out of them, not the machines[4] (which imitators have capitalised on by making Nespresso-compatible pods).

Another example of a distinguisher brand coming from inside an enterprise is Unilever's Lifebuoy soap. In 2010, before Covid-19, a distinguisher coup was mounted by the brand, which changed handwashing behaviour on a large scale and set its Lifebuoy soap brand alight.

Aimed at South Asia (it started in India), sub-Saharan Africa and South America, the goal was to get kids, mainly those at pre-school and primary school, as well as adolescents, parents and mothers-to-be, to wash their hands at critical moments. This was to avoid premature death, below five years of age, from diseases like diarrhoea, eye infections and respiratory diseases like pneumonia, which were all on the rise largely due to poor hygiene and, in particular, inadequate handwashing.

And so good has Unilever become at changing handwashing behaviour en masse that, during Covid-19, leveraging years of expertise and consumer insight, it quickly cracked into action working with governments to get people at scale to wash their hands.

The handwashing goal was noble, to improve personal hygiene and germ-free living, but more soap usage and sales became part of the prize. Although, to Unilever's credit, during the pandemic it asked people to use any soap, not just its own, something it had never done before.

Now that is distinguisher thinking.

They are often ignored at first

Mostly, distinguishers start as a dot and become a phenomenon. No one quite notices them or takes them seriously because, to the uninitiated and those of the extinguisher mindset, they don't look like 'real' competition. They fall outside traditional product and service categories.

Then, suddenly, from a dot they become a seriously disruptive phenomenon.

Jeff Bezos, the ex-Wall Street investment banker and engineering and computer science graduate, believed that if he could reach customers directly, obtaining data about them and their preferences, he could provide a service no one else did: help them choose and order a book, and get it to them in record time, irrespective of where it was being warehoused.

And he realised that once trust in his organisation was cemented, he could guide customers into an infinite number of other revenue-generating territories, at a rapid clip and low cost.

This is blasphemy to traditional thinkers, who strictly stipulate that one must stick to the core business. To get bigger, they argue, businesses should sell more of these core items, books or whatever, by stealing share from competitors and doing what they are doing, but better.

That, as we know, is shorthand for getting better buys in bulk, shouting louder through paid forms of advertising to get rid of rivals, pushing goods through long linear channels, incentivising staff and customers through promotions to sell and buy like hell, dropping the price if all else fails or adding features in the hope that no one else will copy them.

Getting beyond just technology disruption

We have to give him credit. What Bezos, founder and now chairman of Amazon, taught us, was that people's behaviour can be radically altered, even in the fairly traditional book industry. And if done well, though he was probably experimenting at the time, a new way of doing things can emerge and grow to become the next normal.

He showed us that this new way of working could and would morph into many directions and opportunities, because while products invariably lose value over time as competitors move into the market, customers—once you've got them 'locked in' (i.e. when customers want the brand as their first or sole choice)— gain value for a brand over time.

This is quite different from the customer lock-in where customers can't get out even if they want to (as with mobile subscriptions) or have no better alternative (as happened with old-style banking).[5]

Extinguishers confuse this customer inertia (not moving brand because they have no better choice, because 'they are all the same'), with customer loyalty. That is, until a better alternative comes along, and the extinguishers are caught unaware.

Distinguishers know that technology is the enabler for this alternative, i.e. it can make something bigger and better for customers.

Banks have been hit by fintechs for one reason and one reason only. Not because they have the technology that can disrupt and do what's being done anyway digitally, but because they know how to use that technology to do a better job of getting superior value to customers.

In his own words, Bezos says that technology should be invisible to the customer. The Kindle e-reader was designed to create a superior customer service experience, not to invent a new product. That meant ensuring that millions of customers could access and read hundreds of millions of books wherever they were and that the highlights, notes, bookmarks and everything else they created on their books could all be interlinked, used interchangeably across devices and even readers.

His model wasn't a variation on an old theme, it was a different approach to value, namely:

- Value is what customers get *out* of a product or service, not what goes in. Anything that goes in and is not valued or used by the customers is 'junk design DNA', i.e. waste.

- The point of incurring technology costs is to turn them into customer value—any other spend is waste.
- Big is good only if it produces customer value—otherwise it carries costs and baggage that give outsiders an opportunity to attack.
- Using technology to deliver a frictionless personalised experience for a consumer is not negotiable—nothing is more important.

This was the thinking that built the online giant that would alter the way people bought books, first, and then so much more, and meant that by 2020 Bezos would be the wealthiest man in the world.

Let's not oversimplify what was a complex system of inter-related factors that contributed to Amazon's success at winning customers. On the other hand, let's be clear. Jeff Bezos's great forte was that he changed the way people bought, read and had books delivered, using technology.

And he keeps repeating that pattern.

While Apple moulded the mobile age, it was Amazon and Bezos who ushered us into the cloud era and took centre spot, changing forever the way business uses technology, not some of the more obvious, biggest-ever names in tech history, like Microsoft, Google, Oracle and IBM.

Bezos effectively started the online revolution. And he hasn't finished yet.

Note, it was he, not really the travel industry, who during the pandemic launched virtually what couldn't be done physically, making valid an alternative form of travel. The Amazon Explore platform offers virtual travel experiences, from cultural sites to shopping for artisanal goods in Costa Rica, from clubbing to taco cooking lessons in Mexico, a total of 86 different experiences across 16 countries, for starters.

He just thinks differently.

CHAPTER 3

They create better ways of doing things

Distinguishers are obsessed with getting people to do something differently.

Steve Jobs was typical. Although Apple would excel at product design, his real purpose was to democratise computers and put what was in the hands of a few tech experts into the creative hands of the many.

How to get more people to use computers was his question. How to enable ordinary people to use a computer for what was important to them to make their dreams tangible—at school, at work, for graphic design, photography, art, music, etc.—became his quest.

Steve Jobs imagined a computer on every desk in the world. Suddenly, a person didn't have to be a programmer to use a computer.

He created an every-person-can-use-a-computer world.

And, like Jeff Bezos, the pattern kept recurring.

Jobs then went on to do the same with the mobile phone. Although Nokia dominated the mobile phone, it only kept improving the phone, as extinguishers do. Apple kept improving what people could do with the phone that they hadn't done before.

It kept changing behaviour, and changing the world—as distinguishers do. They ask: Is there a better way of doing things for customers?

Is there an easier way for people to have a dog in their lives?, asked Aaron Easterly, founder of Rover.com. The answer became the largest pet-sitting, dog-walking network in the world, disrupting the business of traditional kennels. What began in the US quickly expanded into the UK and Europe, with a new booking every three seconds.

'A lot of smart people told us they didn't think Rover could be a big business', said Greg Gottesman in an interview.[6]

Well, a lot of smart people were wrong. A billion dollars wrong!

The risk of doing too little

When the idea of Uber was hatched in Paris, in 2008, and the following year was tested in San Francisco, no one knew that it would quickly become one of the most famous distinguisher brands of our time.

Most people felt they could never trust an unknown person (or car app) to take them to work or the opera, let alone to the airport to catch a plane for an important trip.

Lo and behold, today most of us do—and each of us keeps doing it more often.

Uber changed people's behaviour, forever metamorphosing the way we move around. It altered the transport industry and every minute derivative thereof.

But let's give the brand credit. It not only changed the way we move around. People now buy fewer cars and fewer second, smaller vehicles. They spend less on fuel, insurance, maintenance and tyres, use rental cars less, are discarding, repurposing or renting out their garages, use fewer parking bays, spend time listening to music or shopping online as they ride hands free, rent their car out to Uber drivers and crowdfund others so they can buy a car. They share rides with people they don't know heading in the same direction (this trend could reverse post Covid-19), and can spend the time and money they save on something else.

The list goes on. It's a great opportunity for some; for others not so fab.

Extinguishers are often immobilised, unable to piggyback on the new wave. They keep pushing products, better and cheaper, and that can be OK for a while, but it's a cop-out because the brand often becomes marginalised, retaining larger shares of deteriorating product or service categories.

When Airbnb's Joe Gebbia and Brian Chesky discovered that one of its host's homes had been trashed, the founders realised they needed to offer insurance as part of their value-add. They talked to over 20 underwriters and were introduced to board members of some of the largest insurance companies in the world. No one was willing to underwrite the risk. So, Airbnb ended up doing it themselves, playing with various scenarios and small sums at first, until they saw that 'the risk of doing too little was greater than the risk of doing too much'.[7]

The Host Guarantee became critical to Airbnb's success, and it won over hosts in large numbers that have kept on climbing.

Some extinguishers try to stop newcomers, hiding behind regulation, unions, inefficiencies and previously vested interests.

What we now know for sure is that distinguishers run ahead of regulation and get it changed in the process of innovating and demonstrating that customer-stakeholders are better off.

Some companies react to new ways of doing things by trying to copy them to get a foothold, or even try to differentiate or elevate the original idea.

In an extraordinary turnabout, BMW and Daimler, for instance, German arch rivals, are partnering to set up an all-electric self-driving fleet with self-charging and self-parking, as part of a single mobility proposition to counter the surging power of Uber et al cutting into their own car sales. The mobile app maps out a route for customers, who can book and pay ahead of time for car-riding, parking reservation and other mobility options.

And others … well they buy the new competition out.

Uber changes gears

Uber wants to create opportunities from 'mobility'. It's obvious now. It wasn't in 2008.

That stated (which is the hard part), it's clear that this doesn't stop at only getting people around. Like Amazon, with the investment already made in firmly entrenching new behaviour, the next move is to take customers into new competitive playgrounds.

Let's track the thinking. Since Uber knew how to get people to change how they got around (matching those who want a ride with those who've got a ride), why couldn't it change where and how they eat (matching people who want restaurant food with those who've got it)? Enter Uber Eats, growing 70 per cent year on year, accounting for 20 per cent of all Uber's bookings and 10 per cent of total revenue.[8]

Ask a group anywhere in the world today (we do, all the time) how many get Uber Eats at least twice a week or more, instead of going to restaurants or takeaway places, and you'll find that most, if not all, do. And that was pre Covid-19.

And during the pandemic, understandably, it superseded ride-hail traffic.

In the space of a few years, Uber changed consumer behaviour from preparing home-cooked meals and going to restaurants to ordering home delivery of cooked food, the new fast food, obtained quickly but of high quality, with an almost infinite choice. And in the process it created a new market, growing like wildfire.

Of course, there are many brands who have jumped onto this worldwide bandwagon, matching restaurants to customers.

In Brazil, for instance, where only 12 per cent of the population order food online, food delivery is growing at 30 to 40 per cent annually;[9] it has grown by 30 per cent across all of South America.[10] With order volumes 16 times higher than Uber Eats, iFood has six million regular users ordering over 26 million meals a month from 160,000 restaurants delivered by 170,000 couriers, in more than 1,000 cities. Customers get food fast, but with machine learning meals can be matched to precise cuisine preference.

Carlos Moyses, CEO of iFood, is another distinguisher set on changing consumer habits, from making to ordering food. He described his competition as 'the stove'.[11] Because he wants to win customers by getting them out of the kitchen, away from slogging over appliances, nonetheless eating good food, but from his online platform.

What currently puts Uber or iFood potentially ahead is superpower matching capability, i.e. knowing in real time who's got what, who wants what, as well as what's the best fit, without any vested interest in any one product or service.

With that capability, a brand can go almost anywhere fast, leaving others behind. It's the formula that has taken Amazon almost everywhere and Uber into goods, then freight, connecting drivers with shippers, with a promise to provide transparent pricing and full visibility upfront so that households and industrial customers can make better informed decisions.

The rise of the virtual kitchen … and more

Physical restaurant formats are being displaced by home food delivery, which sped up during Covid-19 and is expected to continue to spiral upwards, making way for virtual restaurants. Research shows that, worldwide, 53 per cent of global consumers are comfy with ordering from a delivery-only restaurant with no physical storefront.[12]

The move to high-quality home delivery, matching who wants great food with who has it, has led to the rise of 'ghost' or 'dark' or 'cloud' kitchens. Globally, the trend towards these new shared spaces is supposedly going to grow by USD 1 trillion by 2030.[13]

In Indonesia, online cloud kitchen catering brand Yummy Kitchen, launched in June 2019, already rents out over 70 of these shared kitchen spaces, from which it delivers tens of thousands of meals every day and has more than 3,000 menus for corporate events or for employees who select and order their meals through the Yummybox app, using their corporate allowance wallet allocated to them by their employers.

A growing number of these virtual kitchens have no physical front or dining areas and exist only on an app, like Uber Eats or Yummy. And for many physical restaurants, growing proportions of their turnover are coming from on-demand home delivery.

So not only did these brands, Uber and Yummy, create new markets by changing how people eat and where, they also changed how and where chefs train and cook, how and where restaurants function (with resultant changes to their cost and structure), the role of food and beverage companies in a changing supply chain, how and where food gets stored and delivered, by whom to whom at what price.

The ramifications are quite profound. For instance:

- What is the future restaurant model?
- How will property owners and operators renting restaurant space react?
- Where and how will top-notch or aspiring chefs train and work?
- How do food and beverage suppliers adapt?
- What do suppliers of food packaging, dining accessories and kitchen equipment do to get part of the action?
- How will supermarkets, farmers and all their supply chains (local and global) take up the challenge and possibilities?
- What does the future of home and office kitchens look like— and what's the role of appliances in them?

And apart from remaking, repurposing or possible displacing restaurants, what other food-making services could home food delivery impact? Drive-thru restaurants? Fast-food takeaways? Ready meals, packaged cooking ingredients and packaged snacks? And how many others?

CHAPTER 4

They self-disrupt

It's one thing to disrupt and change customer behaviour to make other peoples' products or services or even a whole industry redundant. It's quite another to displace your own because there is a better way of doing things for customers.

Not if you think like a distinguisher.

But extinguishers don't change their behaviour. Why did no big-name restaurant pioneer premium home food delivery instead of Uber Eats? Why didn't a big brand in the travel industry initiate the virtualisation of touring and educational experiences instead of waiting for Amazon to do it? Why didn't a corporate catering company invent a Yummy? Or a pet kennel become a Rover? Or Skype become the future Zoom? Or Vodafone, 'the world's largest mobile community', create Facebook or WhatsApp?

We rest our case.

Making obsolescence work

Disrupting itself is what Netflix did and Blockbuster, the movie rental chain, didn't. Netflix went from posting rented DVDs to customers, to getting them hooked on on-demand video streaming. Then it built its own content, which all its customers across the world could view simultaneously.

It's what customers had been waiting for cinemas to do for a long, long time, and what movie producers didn't allow due to complicated country distribution policies they concocted to protect themselves.

That was, until lockdown, when Universal put the *Trolls World Tour* animation directly onto on-demand platforms, bypassing cinemas, causing a whole new way of epic movie-watching for kids. Disney and Warner followed suit months thereafter, offering online US viewing at the same time as at cinemas. They changed the game forever.

It's what Zoom did and Cisco didn't do in time. Eric Yuan tried repeatedly to convince his colleagues at Cisco that Webex had to be updated or replaced in keeping with changes in the way people worked. He finally gave up and gave us Zoom, now a stockmarket juggernaut.

It's what Kodak didn't do (it invented the smartphone, but rejected it).

But Apple did.

Who uses an iPod today? No one. Apple killed its 40 per cent revenue-driver product when it brought in the iPhone in 2007, which had all of the music capabilities of an iPod.

It takes courage to disrupt oneself. Especially if a brand is asset-heavy and needs to cover and recover the related costs. Universities are struggling with this right now as a whirlwind called e-learning has unequivocally taken off, driven by asset-light platforms, which are fast reaching their tipping point.

Distinguishers even do this when it works against their revenue models. Uber went into bikes and scooters, even though it knew that people who used them would take approximately 10 per cent fewer car rides. No sooner had consumers got used to single-ride hailing, when the company introduced Uber Pool, allowing people to share car rides with others.

Uber has tapped into all preferred multimodal options even

though the original concept was shared cars versus taxis. It now offers boats (UK); scooters (Mexico); electric bikes (Germany); helicopters (US); minibuses (Cairo); boda bodas (Kenya); self-driving cars (Sweden); electric mopeds (Paris); and motos (Dominican Republic), to name some.

And on the cards are electric scooters and electric aircraft in some countries. And by the time this book is read no doubt all of these will have spread everywhere and displaced other brands and depressed other industries.

Undaunted, Uber has committed to convert fully to an electric fleet in the US and Europe by 2030 and worldwide by 2040.

These moves are not about diversification. They're about adding value within a chosen competitive arena, in its case mobility, in order to win over and keep customers, at scale, speed and low cost to places, people and planet.

Ask extinguishers to go from manufacturing plastics to making something else and they will probably push back, because it's not their 'core business'.

Ask distinguishers to find an alternative to plastics and they will find ways to switch consumption and production to a new, better option.

Another anathema to extinguishers is selling the opposition's goods. Sometimes, to own a space this is necessary, the alternative being losing custom (revenue) and possibly customers (numbers). This happens when brands define themselves by product and anything else is seen as outside their domain.

When competing for customer rather than category, highfliers don't say no, if the request fits their strategic space (as opposed to their 'core business'—more about this later). They will stretch over conventional boundaries and even offer competing brands, rather than lose the customer. It's what Marks & Spencer is currently doing on its website, i.e. selling rival brands as well as its own, thus keeping its 22 million clothing customers firmly in its orbit.

Distinguishers move on with the times as they create the times.

Part of the Bezos success story is that he built a state-of-the-art distribution system that matched his goal of having an exhaustive selection ('access to every book in print in stock'). Seven years it took him, and then, just when he got it right, he disrupted himself. Enter the Kindle, and a sizeable portion of his customers were suddenly using an e-reader. Even people who had bought books to read, stack in bookshelves and place beside their beds, 'who like to feel them, smell them and display them, as well as read them of course' (quote from a book-lover), now have converted fully or somewhat to reading a book from a tablet.

Amazon spent a fortune to improve warehouses and delivery infrastructures to give its Prime members one-day shipping. And then the heat was on to change logistics behaviour from people and trucks to drones.

That Bezos is hell bent on 'dronology' is a natural, bold, ever-evolving part of his distinguisher psyche. He keeps ahead even if it means displacing what his brand does well.

Reaching for the clouds

Bezos did the same with Amazon Web Services (AWS), which is why and how he became number one in cloud computing, leaving the others to catch up. First Amazon built a superior website for itself to sell books online, which helped the brand get big fast. Then, expanding beyond books, it built a more varied portfolio. That done, Jeff Bezos disrupted the entire system to bring the cloud to anyone (even competitors), now the brand's fastest-growing revenue source.

Cloud computing enables businesses of all sizes, large and small, to access massive computing power without investing in expensive technology infrastructure that only becomes obsolete. With Amazon Web Services, Bezos effectively not only changed production and consumption behaviour, but also the balance of power, giving startups a kickstart, causing even more disruption.

Though some say the cloud is still in its infancy, the writing is on the wall. All other systems and business logic will eventually become redundant, probably faster and more furiously if Amazon has its way.

It's now the new way of doing things. No one can escape it.

CHAPTER 5

There's always a trigger

Distinguishers are always triggered by something they think needs to be done differently. Whereas others may not see it or want to do anything about it, distinguishers find a good reason.

Someone has a wake-up call, or experiences a pain-point, which is invariably described as a 'moment of clarity'. Bezos remembers this being when, in a passing remark, someone said that the Internet was growing by 2,300 per cent. For Unilever it was finding out that children under the age of five were dying in emerging countries because of poor handwashing habits.

If no one in a company feels or sees a trigger, it is often because the company is doing too well—until the pain of serious displacement hits it head-on.

That people would rent out space in their home to a stranger, and that these strangers then would become friends and part of a community, is just astounding. This home-sharing revolution began when three roommates realised that there would be a serious shortage of hotel space in San Francisco during a designers' conference there, so they offered an air mattress with breakfast in their rented apartment to eager takers, to make a little extra cash. And from there the company they founded, Airbnb, went on to become the lead online marketplace for hospitality.

Inventing the future

Like Bezos, most lead players don't spend fortunes trying to do research to scope needs or prove what customers want. Because customers don't know. What customer can articulate a future that doesn't yet exist? Before these businesses existed, how could we expect customers to ask for Fortnite, an Uber, the cloud, a smartphone or Netflix, or admit that any of these would become indispensable to them in their daily lives?

What market research can uncover what we see and take for granted today?

When companies or industries don't get that something new has to happen, the change will come from an outsider, because extinguishers think their competitors are the people doing what they do. Take softdrinks. As big and as powerful as their producers are, employing big researchers with big budgets, were they prepared for non-plastic and zero sugar? How could they not be?

Pepsi cleverly bought SodaStream, the Israeli creator of a whole new genre of at-home soda-making.

The music industry was stagnating, unable to make change happen, when Daniel Ek, a young Swede, introduced a new way for consumers to listen to music without having to own anything physical. Now he is CEO of the company he founded, Spotify, which streams music to the world online. Today, in the US, music streaming accounts for 80 per cent of recorded music revenue.[14] Spotify has a monthly user base of 350-odd million (over 150 million are paid subscribers, and this number grows every day) compared to Apple's 50 million.[15]

Did music producers think that consumers would just go on buying CDs when many of them contained songs that they didn't like or want?

Failure to see that a new future is actually upon us is the ultimate failure.

Triggers are the defining moment

Distinguishers are usually triggered by one or more of the following:

1. Logical triggers (logos)

A rational reason, numbers, customer disenchantment, inefficiency.

ARGUMENT: 'It's logical, here are the facts that tell us change is needed.'

EXAMPLES:
- An ageing population (leading to robotic healthcare in Japan);
- A large, idle freelance population who could test software (hatching Testbirds);
- Duplication of computing effort, and significant e-waste (solved by Amazon Web Services);
- Congested, carbon-intensive cities (inspiring the concept of smart cities);
- Under-utilised assets, such as cars, which are generally used only 5 per cent of the time (overcome by Uber);
- Shortage of hospitality space (answered by Airbnb);
- General dislike of the insurance industry (sweetened by Lemonade, Inc.);
- High accident rates (addressed by Discovery Insure, which rewards drivers for driving well);
- Inefficiency, disconnection and high costs to customer and planet in the transport sector (creation of MaaS, integrating on-demand transport services).

2. Emotional triggers (pathos)

An emotional reason—empathy, sympathy, anger or frustration with a situation.

ARGUMENT: 'It's just not adequate and I feel it must change.'

EXAMPLES:
- Difficulty in finding and exploring music (now streamed by Spotify);
- Annoyance with existing video conferencing software (now improved by Zoom);
- Frustration with the constraints of proprietary software (driving the free software movement and open-source software);
- Unable to cheaply, simply and stylishly start a retail online store (solved by Shopify);
- Obstacles to pet ownership (removed by Rover.com).

3. Ethical triggers (ethos)
'Shamechangers' feel something is ethically or morally wrong, unjust or unfair or untrue and needs to be fixed.

ARGUMENT: 'It's wrong/unfair/untrue and must be changed.'

EXAMPLES:
- Food shortages (alleviated by crowdfarming);
- Plastic waste from bottled water (solved by at-home soda-maker SodaStream);
- False information about businesses on the Internet (now verified by Trustpilot);
- A need for inclusiveness and democratisation (met by initiatives such as M-PESA, M-KOPA, FlexClub, Kickstarter).

Classic trigger cases

Logical triggers (logos)
The demographic conundrum of an ageing population with more complex diseases and too few (young) caregivers, as in Japan, has

seen the healthcare workforce go robotic (or cobotic, the new term for workers and robots working together). This well-conceived and highly co-ordinated project is becoming a powerful economic force.

Changi General Hospital, in Singapore, is in the lead and has already automated logistics, using transport robots to move documents, drugs, specimens and linen, powered by Japan's Panasonic. Next, it will use robots to move heavier items like beds. Other roles for robots are being researched: to directly interface with patients to save doctors time, to participate in precision medicine like surgery, and to monitor care via mobile apps, for personalised rehabilitation.

Emotional triggers (pathos)
Not many people know that the move to open-source software began with Richard M. Stallman, a frustrated programmer who wanted to write a little piece of code that would let people in his organisation know that the printer was jammed and that they needed to unblock it. The printer manufacturer refused to give him the source code, and a colleague who did have it had signed a non-disclosure agreement not to hand it over to anyone. Fired up by what he saw as a lack of ethics, Stallman created his own operating system that users anywhere could get, copy, make changes to and distribute. And he made it available to them for free.

His activism in support of free software led to the open-source movement, giving small businesses access to large computing power, unthinkable in a world where proprietary was the only real competitive option dominated by a few global players. That same movement inspired other open-source inventions, without which we wouldn't have the likes of Linux or Wikipedia.

We've only glimpsed the start of what's destined to become the next new standard.

For a great example of emotion sparking a whole new wave, how about Eric Yuan whose girlfriend lived several train rides away and so he envisioned a new way to enable them to see and speak to each other. This took him to Cisco's video Webex conferencing product, and then finally to start Zoom.

Ethical triggers (ethos)

Africa became the leader in the cashless movement because the Kenyan mobile phone operator Safaricom, and the executives who ran it, acknowledged that transferring money in Kenya was complicated, unsafe and expensive, and that too many citizens were excluded from the banking system. To pay for their kids' school fees it would take rural Kenyans up to three days to secure the funds; it took more time to receive the money as cash, more time to deposit it in the school's bank account, and then more time to take the receipt to the school as proof of payment. This made transferring money time-consuming, frustrating and, if done by hand, downright dangerous.

Cash had become the common enemy. The new way of transferring money and transacting via mobile phone was cashless, and made sense in a country where over 70 per cent of the population are unbanked, but have mobile phones.

Disrupting traditional institutions like the post office, banks and money transfer companies, as well as the informal economy that transported money by hand at a price, M-PESA was first envisaged as a cashless system for person-to-person transfer. Subsequently it has evolved into a fully flagged financial service, winning over merchants and individual customers across the African continent.

It is easy to imagine today with digital banking having become the norm, but it was a real big deal a decade ago.

The venture was courageous, too, when there was no evidence to support the case.

But distinguishers are triggered, and act.

They know nothing can be proven until it's done.

CHAPTER 6

They build an educated hypothesis

What distinguisher cases teach us is that an educated hypothesis is good enough when trying to shake up the status quo.

Even before the 2020 pandemic, NatWest bank in the UK discovered—with a bit of digging—that half of the UK population had no surplus equity, i.e. did not have more savings than debt, and an additional quarter had no positive cashflow, i.e. no money left after paying bills and discretionary spending. This left most people with less than two weeks' buffer to financially sustain themselves if their income ceased suddenly, or an emergency struck, major or minor.

More interestingly, the bank uncovered that there was no correlation between a customer's financial position and income, unless that income was in the top 5 per cent bracket. Some people with a lower income could save better than those who were better off. This meant that it wasn't how much people earned that was the crux of the savings crisis, their money behaviour was.

Came the Covid-19 crisis with losses of income and even jobs, and the story quickly became worse for some.

Despite being around for centuries, banks have never really had anything to do with an individual's financial stability. As long as customers paid back their loan, banks didn't really know or care how their customers were doing or felt about their finances.

Banks are still segmenting their market the old-fashioned way: 'How old are you?', 'How much money are you making?', 'Where do you live?', 'Do you have a steady job?', they ask. But they are not asking, 'How much do you save?', and according to NatWest's data, across these segments people are not saving enough.

The key takeaway from this research was that people actually just want a better night's sleep knowing that they have an adequate financial buffer and options for the future. They want to worry less. They just don't know how to get to this position, and don't believe they can.

NatWest was determined to distinguish itself by changing, enabling its customers to gain control over their everyday spending, turning the surplus achieved into savings that would change their livelihood and lives.

And it went further, asking itself if these customers could actually enjoy the experience of saving. If they did, wouldn't they save more and be better off?

It was an educated hypothesis, but good enough to begin a metamorphosis in the bank.

Other cases illustrate the power of an educated hypothesis:

NETFLIX CASE

When Reed Hastings and his partner Marc Rudolph got the movie market to abandon DVD rental and instead switch to instant-demand streaming, there was no evidence, research or data to substantiate their feeling that it would work, let alone revolutionise the entertainment world and Hollywood for all time.

They argued that everyone across market segments globally would want to watch movies when they wanted, rather than when TV channels dictated they could. Netflix would not invest in yet another physical product. Another device was the last thing people needed, it posited. What people really wanted was a service to stream movies to them, anytime, anywhere, on any device (whether TVs, gaming machines, laptops or smartphones).

It was just a hypothesis.
And the rest is history.

SHOPIFY CASE

When Canadian Tobias Lütke, and the other co-founders of Shopify, tried to set up an online store selling elite snowboards, they couldn't find a practical way to do this, even though Lütke was an experienced programmer in his own right. He was exasperated with e-commerce platforms that had limited design options and were hard to integrate with other services. He was convinced that if he was frustrated with the current way of doing things, others would be.

So he and his partners developed a hypothesis.

What if they could help small businesses compete with larger retailers on- and offline by building an aggregation platform, so that they didn't have to invest in the systems that large businesses had? Instead, the platform would provide individuals with digital tools and systems, including website-building, hosting, payments, logistics, fulfilment, stock and sales analysis, digital marketing, search engine optimisation, etc., in one integrated system. They could subscribe to all this for as little as USD 30 a month, which was easily affordable.

Now Lütke is a billionaire and Shopify is a multibillion-dollar e-commerce distinguisher brand.

DISCOVERY (VITALITY) CASE

When Discovery Insure proclaimed that it could do what had never been done before properly and at scale in the world, namely incentivise people to change their driving habits to reduce accidents and deaths on the road, and thus insurance claims, it was no more than an educated hypothesis.

There was no model to follow or specific playbook for Anton Ossip to copy. Yet today, Discovery Insure boasts a quarter of a million customers, a number that is increasing constantly, with an annual revenue growth in double digits.

It had been a way of thinking at Discovery some time before, when CEO and founder Adrian Gore launched Discovery Life, which encouraged people to be healthier so that more sustainable life insurance could be offered to them.

The Virgin Active gym chain had offered to cross-sell Discovery's health insurance to its own members, but Gore wouldn't have it. He turned the idea around to ask, 'What if customers bought Discovery insurance and then could use the gym, earn points by exercising and convert them into a discount on premiums paid?'

'That idea was the catalyst for everything, which I think is true of (all) innovation', said Gore. 'It (happens) in a moment in time. Behavioural science tells us that people need incentives to make a change. But that wasn't universally known at the time; we were just a startup acting on a hunch.'[16]

It was a hunch that made Discovery the world's largest behavioural platform, turning actuarially driven insight into behaviour change; a hunch that none of the insurance incumbents around for hundreds of years before had had!

CHAPTER 7

They grow with the flow

Part of the shake-up is getting away from the old notion of a value chain.

Extinguisher viewpoint: Value happens in a linear distribution chain as a product or service moves from its origin to the customer.

But that's a cost chain. Because costs have been accumulated, it doesn't mean that customer value has accumulated.

Distinguisher viewpoint: Value happens only when it lands in the customer's space, emanating from one part or more of a brand's ecosystem.

In the extinguisher's model, the next in line is often regarded as the customer in the value chain, invariably requiring margin negotiations between players, which often end up in a win/lose situation.

Distinguishers form and perform in an ecosystem with the express intent to get increasing value to customers, with each piece of the ecosystem playing its part. As the brand scales up thanks to its greater value, so the ecosystem grows, providing opportunities for even more value.

Ecosystems are not static, like linear supply chains. They are constantly evolving in a network that consists of partnerships (formal or loose) or acquisitions, and includes others who come into the system, like entrepreneurs or developers, who spot an opportunity to grow with the new flow.

Not to harp on Uber

No business is perfect, we acknowledge, but Uber is a good example to demonstrate the infinite opportunities that can flow to and from an ecosystem.

Here are a few:

- FlexClub, a South African startup now also in Mexico, together with Uber enables people to invest in driver vehicles. Its purpose is to democratise car ownership for drivers who want a car as a work investment instead of an expense. This is an alternative way for them to get access to finance, whereas previously they may have been considered too risky by bankers and kept out of the system. Some 70 per cent of Uber drivers fall into this category and have to rent cars, which is expensive. With FlexClub, drivers go onto a 'drive to pay' subscription plan, where they earn credits for various activities, which—together with the cash they earn from driving—funds the purchase of the car 12 months or later down the line.

  Investors, on the other hand, purchase a car which is managed and serviced by FlexClub. That car is connected to an Uber driver, whose weekly rental charge from earnings goes to the investor. Effectively, the car has been turned into an asset class, in which anyone can invest.

- BBVA, the Spanish bank, has tapped into the Uber ecosystem by building a special financial system for Uber drivers in the form of an app. It means they can get instant payments for rides instead of having to wait to get paid, and can use the app for debit and credit spending for themselves and their families.

- In Sweden, Uber partnered with Volvo (a brand notable for its safety and which promises to go fully electric by 2030) to build autonomous ride-sharing at scale, ostensibly to increase safety on roads. An idea which is not without its challenges, it still promises to be a revolution in the driving space. In the first versions, safety features will take over mundane tasks from drivers; thereafter the cars will be fully autonomous, without supervision.

- The ramifications for urban planning, parking spaces, to say nothing of the municipality revenue model, the future of buildings, on-demand spaces, office repurposing, smart cities and roads, etc., will be far-reaching. Combined with accelerated online shopping, new delivery systems, smart keys that allow drones or drivers to deliver securely into homes or the boot of a car, the opportunities begin to boggle the mind.

- And on the subject of driverless cars, another Swedish giant, IKEA, in its Danish co-space and brainstorming lab, Space10, is asking: 'What sort of opportunities can open up if autonomous cars were thought of less as cars and more like 'spaces on wheels', i.e. extensions of our homes or other places?' 'Why not', they say, 'allow consumers to use them as mobile offices or meeting areas while the cars are either stationary or on the road?' 'How can they be configured for better shopping experiences?' 'Can they become (either part- or full-time) farms, hotels, healthcare clinics, cafés, pop-up mini IKEA stores or farmers' markets? Or public facility spaces? Or even places to sleep that could be just as appealing as hotel rooms?'[17]

- And like them, Toyota is repurposing vehicles to be used as mobile food preparation spaces, for example, to make pizzas for Pizza Hut. In an autonomous car, pizza can be made while on the way to deliver it.

Wait till that scales!

Uber has enabled many local businesses to innovate, developing apps, products and services. There are loads of examples. South Africa-based startup, WhereIsMyTransport, provides travel information for commuters planning journeys, including time-tables, traffic incidents and places of interest. In India an app was designed like this for low bandwidth and phones that have less memory and less speed.

The urban mobility era is inspiring entrants beyond the Uber camp to innovate daily. This ranges from Elon Musk's promise to launch a shared autonomous robotic taxi fleet to drive urban autonomy, to the entry of driverless trucks, which will metamor-phose the freight industry.

And from car rentals came the likes of Transfercar, which began in New Zealand as an alternative to shipping new fleets of rental cars by truck or train between cities.

With a twist.

It's expensive for rental companies to relocate their fleets based on shifts in demand. What if they could match people who want to go somewhere with cars that need to be driven to a pick-up location nearby? The drivers could be students or seniors, families or singles, backpackers or event-goers. Sending these drivers from one branch to another saves rental car companies the costs of train- and truck-driving, while the drivers get a free ride to their destination.

The business later rolled out in Australia, South Africa and North America to become the new rental fleet relocation ser-vices model.

Small goes big

Shopify has created a new way for small retailers to go big because loads of players wanted to grow with the flow.

A Canadian invention, Shopify now has more than a million small retail subscribers linked to its platform in order to build or grow their retail business. Its gross merchandise value makes Shopify the third-largest online retailer after Amazon and eBay.[18]

Its offering is completely white-labelled, which means each retailer can customise their own branded website but within Shopify's system. Using the computing power of an Amazon, a million-plus independent e-commerce merchants are built into a system which enables them to retain autonomy and individuality but leverage from something much bigger.

Shopify offers a fulfilment logistics networked service with partners all over the world, with a multiple currency global payment service. By aggregating small retailers, the platform can offer merchants better shipping rates, capital and distribution capabilities.

In other words, it brings them the advantages of being big without the costs.

On- and offline sales are combined into an omnichannel system, so that retailers can sell their branded merchandise—fashion, clothing, food, art, home decor, electronics, etc.—from their own physical stores and online platforms ('bricks and clicks') as well as others, such as Facebook, eBay, Amazon or Alibaba, and all the sales are connected. The platform offers its own point of sales and integrated inventory system (to avoid users overselling), enabling Shopify to own (and displace) both the front and back end of the omnichannel.

On-demand manufacturing has increased as entrepreneurs from all over the world take orders and use Shopify to sell them directly to consumers. Costs in the supply chain are radically reduced, and manufacturer partners can aggregate many small orders in a new make-to-scale model.

As each opportunity opens and is taken up, so Shopify becomes ever more indispensable to small retail customers and ever more prosperous.

Its serial innovations continue, and include a move into banking to give merchants access to financial vehicles to start and operate their businesses, as well as rewards programmes and

Shop Pay Installments (buy now, pay later) to attract customers to boost their sales.

Zoom goes hard

For many individuals, whether they are part of a business, government agency or school, working remotely means Zooming more. Zoom meetings take place increasingly from home but also in many other venues, such as an office, classroom or hotel room. For world-class virtual video conferencing and social communication, home or any other venue needs not just the software but also the hardware.

Old extinguisher logic would mean providing customers with the hardware, say a screen to work on while video conferencing on Zoom, but it would also mean doing this as a third-party initiative, which would mean that the hardware would likely not be interoperable with or part of Zoom's overarching proposition.

Distinguishers, however, deliberately form and grow ecosystems that provide customers with interlinked value. A communications technology third party, DTEN, saw an opportunity to make its play by partnering with Zoom to provide an interactive device that enables conference-quality communication for its customers wherever they are. The ecosystem delivers an all-in-one kit specifically designed to share information with many people (using high-definition sound, light, smart camera, touch screen, smart display, interactive whiteboard and shared annotation that can be saved), installs it and maintains it.

Zoom for Home is a new addition to the Zoom Meetings licence and includes a personal collaboration device, so that teams communicating from home can elevate their environment and experience to that of a professional meeting room. This hardware as a service can be paid for monthly together with the software on a single invoice, which saves upfront costs and duplication of effort.

CHAPTER 8

They get beyond the consumer

Part of shaking up the establishment is making clear that gone are the days when a commercial result for shareholders was enough of a triumph. Today, distinguishers have a positive impact on a larger customer-stakeholder group.

To be a distinguisher is to align thinking and strategies to the needs, values and concerns of this broader customer-stakeholder group, namely: the consumer/user, citizen (who may or may not be a paying customer), the community (virtual or physical), the city and country, the causes (what people value as well as active movements reflecting these values) and the cosmos (environment/planet). (See Table 8.1 for a summary and universal concerns.)

Because it's good for business.

The examples that follow illustrate how some well-known brands have made their case for and to a wider customer-stakeholder group.

Relaying examples like these helps to make the case for change stronger, and makes it easier to get thinking to shift from extinguisher to distinguisher logic.

UBER: *consumer, citizen, community, city, country, cosmos*
Uber argues that fewer cars on the road leads to less carbon

TABLE 8.1: *Customer-stakeholders*

Focus	Major universal concerns
Consumer/user	A better result, a better individual experience, personal development, wellness, optimisation of resources, productivity, optimal decision-making, risk reduction, self-enhancement, social connectivity, ability to build community, access, inclusiveness
Citizen	A better environment, sustainable regenerative living, accessibility, ease of movement, participation, smart services, happiness
Community	Safety, health, quality of life, for more people, employment opportunities, new friendships, community (like-minded/like loving), connection and support, inclusion, investment in local facilities, upliftment, advancement
City	Self-regenerative development & infrastructure, better liveability, attract tourism and business investment, ecological and sustainability with more/open/green spaces, lower cost, lower poverty, crime, etc.
Country	Prosperity, competitiveness, sustainability, renewable, new services, digitisation, talent development and attraction, less waste, better use local resources, reduced cost infrastructure, investment attraction
Causes	Zero waste, zero damage, resource replacement, minimalism, ethics, fairness, equality, diversity and inclusion, decentralisation, a voice, non-proprietary and open source, caring, sharing
Cosmos	Environmental, no use of plastics, minimal use resources, repurposing waste, ecological, frugal, biodiversity, circular/alternative energy, replenishment dams, quarries, etc., zero carbon

emission, less waste (some say cars are used only 5 per cent of the time) and less wasted time, creates better movement and living for citizens, boosts communities joining the driver force, reduces city traffic and adds to smart impacts for countries by working to rebuild infrastructure, such as roads, and influences future green urban planning.

AIRBNB: *consumer, community, cities, countries*
Travel and tourism represents 10 per cent of global GDP and Airbnb is determined to take its share of that and more. But in return it maintains that its brand must benefit the consumer (whoever is looking for space) as well as the property owner, and enrich the surrounding community. Added to this is that it avoids the downside of mass tourism by spreading it out geographically. And owners retain over 90 per cent of every dollar spent, whereas for hotels it would be considerably less. With this money, owners can reinvest in facilities, like upgrading, further benefitting the community. Further, Airbnb professes to build new communities of friends and friendships between hosts and guests, and connect individuals in different countries to bring countries closer together—for example, encouraging US tourism to Cuba.

SODASTREAM: *consumer, cause, cosmos*
Increasingly, people want sparkling water (since 2015, water has taken over carbonated softdrinks).[19] However, sparkling water still comes in glass or plastic bottles.

It's quite fitting that SodaStream should come from a startup in Israel, a desert land excelling in water desalination.

What started with a fizz in the 70s, and had been limping along ever since, suddenly became a distinguisher brand when SodaStream marketed itself as a way to improve the planet, changing people's behaviour to make carbonated water at home instead of buying cans and glass and plastic bottles from a store.

Only five years ago, SodaStream produced more sparkling water than any other brand globally, including Perrier and San

Pellegrino (owned by Nestlé).

Making drinks from a SodaStream means less single-use plastic and can waste (estimates are that around 150 billion plastic bottles and cans are not recycled a year) and that each family with a SodaStream can avoid using and discarding thousands of cans and plastic bottles annually. SodaStream says that its users drink almost 50 per cent more water than other water drinkers; the preservative- and sugar-free carbonated drink is therefore better for the body as well as the planet.

M-PESA: *consumer, citizen, community, city, country*
M-PESA is famous for a lot of things. Not least of which is that it transformed Kenya and its economy, inspiring young people to do things they would otherwise have deemed impossible. It not only brought entrepreneurial spirit to the country, it got micro businesses started, spawned a whole lot of startups, raised income levels for households who adopted it and improved urban and rural lives.

Retail operators have been able to move to cashless, enabling them to earn more, and develop themselves and their communities. During the lockdown, M-PESA increased wallet limits for its customers and reduced and even waived fees for shops, to deliberately enable cashless, contact-free, no-wait shopping.[20]

Generally speaking, M-PESA has forced down the cost of transferring money by money transfer companies, compelling them to improve their services and pull down prices, and it has profiled Kenya's economy, inspiring young people to get out and do things.

SMART CITIES: *consumer, citizen, community, city, country, cosmos*
Half the world's population now lives in cities. Smart cities is a term coined by IBM, which was instrumental in getting the concept of sustainable city development accepted worldwide, designed to deliver better outcomes, not just for cities but for all customer-stakeholders.

The future of cities is undoubtedly digital, using technology to improve economic, social, human and environmental prosperity.

People and shared determination are at the centre of this movement. Citizens are intimately involved in the co-creating, planning and change processes, as we have seen in role-model cities like Amsterdam, Barcelona and Vienna, to name just some. Citizens in smart cities get better, faster, data-driven responses, which take into account their individual needs and save them time, money and energy.

The benefits are reaped beyond citizens, by cities, communities as well as countries, with better prospects for social and economic development. And everything is done deliberately to protect and sustain resources, the environment and the cosmos in one all-encompassing system.

DISCOVERY INSURE: *consumer, citizen, city, country*
With accident rates in South Africa among the highest in the world, Discovery Insure—part of the Vitality triad (banking/investment, health and car insurance)—decided to venture into a highly contested market, but to be different. Instead of just selling car insurance, it would change people's driving habits and thereby reduce road accidents, deaths and costs all round. Seven years later, having made its point using a never-ending stream of innovations and never having lost a driver in its top-driver echelon, CEO Anton Ossip predicts that if every driver in the country reached gold status, it could save South Africa 7 per cent of GDP (between ZAR 120 billion and 155 billion) and bring the accident rate down to that of low-accident countries.

FORTNITE: *consumer, community*
Although at first glance Fortnite looks like it's just about online gaming, Sweeney's success has in some ways been because he has understood and worked towards gaming as a positive social influence. In part it has been because he believes that online video gaming promotes interactivity, which unifies and helps build and bring together social communities within and between countries across the world. At the same time, on an individual level, it

heightens skill-building and learning for individuals and teams.

SHOPIFY: *consumer, community, city, cause*

With its competitive platform, Shopify allows independent retailers to participate in the retail market and compete with big giants. Because small retailers can run a store physically as well as virtually using Shopify's system, they can survive in a city while building volume online, at speed and low cost.

Cities benefit because they don't lose their retailers to e-commerce giants, and so they remain vibrant and diverse and prosperity spreads. A more inclusive retail environment is good for not just the small business owner, it uplifts families and communities. By reversing the era of consolidation, competition is fostered, leading to economic prosperity and capitalism in the hands of many.

ZOOM: *consumer, community*

Zoom was originally intended for large enterprises with IT backup. Suddenly, as a result of the lockdowns, it was adopted for many unexpected activities (church services, school classes, weddings, religious ceremonies, long-distance education, family events, healthcare and distance friendships), with 300 million participants meeting on it daily.[21] Its explosive growth made it the Number One free app on Apple's App Store, ahead of Google, WhatsApp and even that Gen Z favourite, TikTok, to say nothing of the millions who link up on it directly via their laptop or desktop computer.[22]

Notwithstanding its appeal for general use, Zoom is the go-to tool for work. Business meetings and conferences continued fairly effortlessly during lockdowns thanks to online conferencing, with Zoom in the lead, and people claimed that the remote experience had a lot to be said for it, lockdown or no lockdown.

Its vision to make it the 'video-enabled office of the future' has come as close to reality as one can get, probably having altered the way people communicate and collaborate permanently. Some people suggest that we should expect every conference room to be connected by Zoom in the future.

It certainly worked for the millions who would otherwise have been unable to function (and earn) during the pandemic, and it continues to shape and accelerate a work-from-home or 'you don't have to travel to communicate to do a deal' movement, already well in the making.

ROVER.COM: *consumer, community, cause*
Rover.com is not just a platform linking dog-lovers to dog-owners who are looking to have their pets cared for when they are working or away. It has and continues to deliberately bring together communities of people to enable more people to love and have dogs in their lives. Says CEO Aaron Easterly, 'It's not about building a transactional relationship (although numbers of sitters and their revenues have increased exponentially, as has Rover's), it's about sharing happiness through pet ownership.'[23]

A higher cause indeed.

TABLE 8.2: *Summary of Extinguisher vs Distinguisher Behaviour*

Extinguishers	Distinguishers
Invest in understanding existing behaviour to meet demand	Invest in changing behaviour to shape and reflect new demands
Improve products & services (replace)	Find better ways of doing things (displace)
Focus on next in distribution chain	Has a customer-stakeholder focus
Are afraid of cannibalisation—wait to be disrupted	Disrupt themselves and others
Fight to retain market share for themselves	Open up growth and revenue opportunities for others in new spaces
Are afraid to take risk	Are afraid not to take risk
Are either commercial or social	Combine commercial and social
Are hard asset heavy	Are hard asset light
Build obsolescence into products to replace them for customers	Build in their own obsolescence and make products last
Use technology primarily to reduce their efficiencies & costs to deliver stuff	Use technology to make new customer experiences frictionless at low cost
Hide behind regulation	Challenge, are ahead of and inform changes in regulation
Use triggers to change the way they get more value	Use triggers to motivate a change in the way customers get more value

PART TWO

Shape up—Frame the emerging future

Once distinguishers are determined to shake the status quo and drive change, this opens the way to build customer value, based on an already emerging future.

They build propositions that meet new needs, shape aspirations, break old boundaries and create the new normal.

They know they need to be at the cutting edge to inspire conversations, creativity and collaboration, but still be close enough to reality to make it happen.

It's not the technology that makes them smart. Everyone has it. It's how they use technology.

Here are some of the trends, tactics and tools that form and inform some of the best-known distinguisher strategies that is shaping next new practice.

Any inspiration gleaned from the ideas and imagination of these distinguishers will of course produce unique versions for every individual and help define the piece of an emerging puzzle she or he wants to own.

CHAPTER 9

Leveraging T to the power of 3—trust, transparency, traceability

Distinguishers understand how important trust is in winning customers.

Without it there is no possibility of building a reputation and taking customers to new places. And there is no foundation to build momentum for new ways of doing things.

Trust is about the transparency and traceability that allow customers to know more about who they are dealing with, what they are getting, and the processes and practices by which what they are getting has been produced.

Even more post Covid-19, customers have a heightened sensitivity to things being safe, hygienic, healthy and sustainable, and greater levels of awareness calling for a collective voice to demand accountability.

Don't tell us, show us

The baby boomers were talked to and at by brands and didn't really have the information to make considered decisions. The only data they had was on products (labels often didn't help) and they based their decisions on this, on advertising and on their own experience.

The only way they could respond was to buy or switch. There was no Internet where they could hear or be heard.

Today's consumers, especially the tech-savvy millennials, loaded with information and knowledgeable, rely increasingly on social media for advice from other consumers. Plus, many of them want information that is based on truth and science.

Pandemic reports were that as much as 90 per cent of all consumers check reviews before they buy goods and this includes choosing a professional, like a doctor or surgeon.[24] Half of all consumers are influenced by reviews, with a good chunk of them preferring to get advice from an Internet boffin than from an employee in a store.[25]

This massive switch to peer-to-peer advice has significantly altered the balance of power. And it's happening quickly at scale thanks to trailblazers like Trustpilot, founded by Danish distinguisher Peter Muhlmann. He was determined to put integrity into the Internet, which previously had been plagued by distrust, and his invention has become the trusted service platform for user-generated reviews.

For consumers, both B2C and B2B, this is a new way to get information before making a buying decision, because they can see the experiences other people have had with companies, credibly and reliably. For suppliers, it's a way to safeguard their reputation and win customers by building trust with and through users, with authentic feedback on which they can base improvements. And brands and reviewers are allowed free and direct access to the platform to discuss comments and interact.

This is destined to disrupt and take over from customer satisfaction surveys, which may contain bias and often report averages, which can be distorting.

Now in several countries, Copenhagen-based Trustpilot drills down to different locations, claiming that 90 per cent of all customers check reviews before choosing a local store.[26] It's a way for them to make better choices but also for multi-location stores to see what areas are getting what responses.

Trustpilot allows no incentives, removes false reviews and provides warnings through public alerts of fake claims and fraudulent behaviour, which is crucial to their agnostic positioning. In 2020 it removed 2.2 million fake reviews, including brands boosting their own profiles, paid-for reviews, reviews containing damaging or illegal content, and reviews not based on an authentic user experience.[27]

And its transparency is working, because Trustpilot has won millions of customers reviewing millions of products, growing at the rate of one million a month. And it covers hundreds of thousands of companies and brands over 60 countries in several languages, with an average of three billion reviews monthly.

The advertising industry will no doubt be learning an existential lesson from this emerging trend and decide if they will extinguish or distinguish themselves, as transparency, trust and traceability replace the any-claim-will-do-if-it's-clever-enough mentality.

And brands will have to do what they say they will do, in order to win and hold on to customers.

Making supply chains honest

Palm oil is used in the manufacture of many products, from chocolates to shampoo. High demand has led to the destruction of forest and wildlife and has diminished local communities. Unilever, a 400-product company, is using cutting-edge technology to make its palm-oil supply chain more transparent and traceable, to ensure that this devastation does not take place, or if it does, it knows about it and can prevent more damage.

Unilever uses mobile geospatial analytics across thousands of supply chains spanning millions of hectares, consisting of farms, refineries and processing plants, tracked using satellite imagery, drones and balloons to collect geolocation data via a digital ecosystem. Tens of thousands of satellite images are combined with artificial intelligence, giving the company insights into the supply-chain linkages at scale to ensure that its stated 'sustainable living' purpose is being honoured.

The first pilot test took place in Indonesia and was then taken to South Asia. The same is being done in Brazil, scaling the technology to track the supply of other raw materials.

Getting 'first mile' transparency to achieve sustainable supply is in line with pressing end-user demands for verification from grocery stores and brands that products are sustainably sourced.

Blockchain is significant in this contemporary better normal supply-chain setting. Among other things, it safeguards transparency by storing information in a way that cannot be manipulated. Because data is contained in a distributed uber ledger, no one can change it—and therefore it can be trusted.

This technology architecture allows entire ecosystems to get data in real time, to use as they wish, knowing that the data is correct.

Part of why blockchain is taking off in supply chains is because customers want to know the story behind products. They increasingly want more than sustainability—they want authenticity and verified traceability. And if these expectations can be met, winning and keeping a lead is that much easier.

This massive shift in consumer behaviour to traceability through transparency is transforming many industries, including luxury fashion whose customers want to know how and where garments were made.[28]

In food, more than just nutritional value, customers want to know the details: how the animals were treated, how the plants were grown, where the food was produced, with what ingredients and storage practice.

They want to know the composition of what they put into their and their loved ones' stomachs. Their buying is more aligned to products that they feel aspire and live up to their values and micro needs, like the specific ingredients and attributes of the product. Research reveals that this trend is global and that around 70 per cent of consumers verbalise this and are prepared to pay a premium for it.[29]

The entire food industry is being repurposed for this change by first-mover distinguishers who are using blockchain to make the food supply chain more open and honest, opening the data book to all.

In essence, instead of a linear food system, which is transactional, disparate, costly and time-consuming, with visibility only one up and one down the chain, and often with players at odds with each other, blockchain-driven supply chains are collaborative, ensuring that the whole system, i.e. each player, knows simultaneously the upstream origins (who made what, when, where, the quality and cost of it) and the downstream destination (where it's headed, for whom and even for which purpose).

IBM Food Trust, a forerunner in this space, has addressed the issue of food safety and security using blockchain. Its various ecosystems consist of producers, suppliers, retailers and logistics, who have joined this nothing-short-of-a-revolution to ensure the safe and authentic supply of food across the world. Documents on regulatory requirements and customs can be shared in real time. And data can be used to generate insights like roadblocks or fraud or contamination, to ensure safety and eliminate recurring problems and food waste. It makes food recalls easier, faster and cheaper, which protects consumers from bad food and producers from cost and reputational risks.

Ports are rising to the challenge as well. Amsterdam and Rotterdam have both gone paperless and digital in the wake of new supply-chain business processes. This means that Dutch logistics solutions providers like Portbase, powered by a trusted blockchain technology, Tradelens, can provide total visibility across the entire supply chain from origin to destination, transparently offer data to companies and authorities, and act as a single point of contact and truth-teller in the trading of goods internationally. Around 110 ports and terminals, 15-plus customs authorities around the world and 234 marine gateways or seaports on five continents are connected, reducing the administrative costs and transit time of a shipment by 40 per cent.[30]

From fjord to fork

Consumers today care about the sustainability of fish. And no one knows this better than Norway, the second-largest fish exporter in the world. It is working with IBM to build a sustainable blockchain-based ecosystem, distinguishing itself as a high-quality integrous supplier of fish to the world.

A good two out of three consumers say that traceability of fish is important to them and they are prepared to pay more if they are told which fjord the fish is from, when it was fished and whether the producers are farming it sustainably.[31]

Tracing food across the supply chain can take days or weeks, costs a fortune and is happening much more than the average person realises. A new way of managing supply chains with total traceability of the fish's journey enables the industry to avoid waste and fraud. The industry's move to a transparent system in which, in addition to the supply chain, the retailer and shoppers in the store have all the relevant information, is giving Norway's fish the edge it deserves.

Truth-telling in pharmaceuticals

Trust is an issue in pharmaceuticals. Consumers generally don't trust pharmaceutical enterprises because they think that they are overcharging. People also don't trust the generic alternative of what they consider to be the real thing and pharmaceuticals are heavily investing in marketing dollars to keep this perception alive.

Consumers also have a sense that too many drugs are being consumed—that rather than curing people, pharma wants to keep people on medication.

For a long time, governments, consumers and even pharmacies have been calling for the pharmaceutical industry to increase transparency across its supply chain, in order to lower the cost of drugs and prevent price hikes, price inflation and manipulation (allegedly common in the industry), in order to establish where the costs are going and whether they are fair.

But as long as the cost for making drugs remains opaque and competition weak, pricing will be solely in the hands of suppliers.

Today, a drug has to pass through at least three parties from the drug-maker to the patient (wholesalers, pharmacies and insurers). We know that this adds 40 per cent to the retail price, but we don't know what makes up the rest of the cost.[32]

One way to get drugs to customers at lower costs is to take out the middle party—which Amazon has done. It bought mail-order online pharmacy PillPack, which has a pharmacy licence in every US state. And if we know Amazon, becoming a major player in the ever-swelling move to get medical care from hospitals to homes, consumers will get more transparency on product (and service) performance, and most likely more precision and choice, just as the brand has done in other categories, from books to batteries, phones to computer accessories.

Thereby gaining more trust and more custom.

Can financial services go transparent?

This call for transparency and trust creates opportunities for how supply chains are financed. It helps banks make smarter lending decisions across the ecosystem because not only are all the records held in the blockchain, they can trust the transactions without having lengthy audits, costly financial reviews or double checks, which take time and come with cost and errors.

With blockchain, a bank can trust that a transaction is correct and that it did happen.

It also enables banks to see the ecosystem as one customer, whose goods are going to whom, and adjust risk profiles and lending accordingly, instead of doing one-on-one risk assessments for transactions. Banks can fund the entire ecosystem as a single entity with data that is transparent and trusted, to the benefit of all, especially the small guys up the chain.

That traditional banks and insurance companies haven't been transparent and don't enjoy trust on the whole means newcomer distinguishers are popping up with huge impact. GoBear is one of the fastest fintech startups in Southeast Asia. Headquartered in Singapore, its customers span Malaysia, Thailand, Philippines, Vietnam, Hong Kong and Indonesia. Its ambition is simple: to help people who don't have credit histories (they only use cash) get access to responsible financial products, through its aggregation comparison platform.

Swiftly, the brand accumulated over 55 million users to whom they provide transparent comparisons for over 2,000 different financial products, and its impact and footprint continue to explode, changing how people find banking products, make decisions and buy.[33]

Insurance has gone transparent

It is possible for distinguishers to break into existing markets, even if they are well entrenched, if they change the business model to one of transparency, trust and traceability.

It was exactly this that made Lemonade, Inc. one of the most prized startups in financial services. Backed by Softbank, the New York-based enterprise's new way of insuring property and rentals is rocking in 23 states in the US, and the brand is expanding its wings into Germany and the Netherlands, with its rate of new users doubling every 10 weeks.[34]

Lemonade was able to turn the insurance industry on its head because it found a model that appealed to consumers no end.

Firstly, it's not incentivised to hold on to income rather than pay out claims, as the insurance industry has been able to do for much too long. It uses 20 per cent of its flat fees to get reinsurance and pay claims, and the rest is put into a pot to distribute to charities. Secondly, this pot is treated as if it belongs to the customer base and is distributed to their favourite charity.

It has eliminated bureaucracy and brokers and mastered behavioural economics and AI to assess customer applications and claims, dramatically cutting costs and loss ratios (its loss ratios are already below industry standard in certain areas).[35]

People join Lemonade digitally, using a camera. The customer experience is not compromised—they get a 24/7 bot service, and it takes minutes to make an application and seconds to get claims paid.

Because it uses anti-fraud AI algorithms, it can detect dishonesty instantly. But, says the CEO co-founder Daniel Schreiber, fraud is not reduced because of the technology. It goes down because people behave differently if they know they could be taking something away from a cause or community they care about, instead of an insurer they don't trust.

This blend of sharing, collaboration, giveback, trust and tech-savvy delivery is resonating particularly with millennials and Generation Z, and is far-reaching because once the brand has won over customers it can easily and cost-effectively extend them into new areas.

And here's the other important bit. As it gets more customers and more intelligence, its algorithm gets smarter, which means it can get more customers. Using its distinguisher sentiment and model, is how Lemonade gained over one million customers in the first four years at a five to ten times faster rate than other leading brands have been doing.

Will customers go transparent?

Transparency also works the other way around. Customer transparency helps enterprises make better credit assessments for people who have not had access to the economy. GoBear's service platform targets unbanked and underbanked people, of which there are some 300 million across the seven markets it currently serves, and many more to come from the half a billion in Southeast Asia.[36]

Because the unbanked have no credit history, the only way to make banking inclusive is to invent new ways to rate credit-worthiness using alternative sources of data. For example, data points from smartphones assess purchasing behaviour to tell if a customer may get a loan in markets like the Philippines, where less than 10 per cent of the adult population have a credit card or any other way of building a credit profile, but nearly half own and use a smartphone.

Data points that feed into risk assessments include behaviours like what time a person puts in an application or how long customers take to apply, which GoBear has down to a fine art. Applications made during the day are less risky than those done at night, for instance. Or if a loan application is filled out in less than a minute it's more likely to be fraudulent.[37]

What research shows is that when distinguishers are transparent about the use and protection of customer data, this reinforces trust. But that consumer trust is extinguished if this data is sold on, in which case customers resent it.

If the data is converted into value for customers, to make their lives easier, more entertaining, educational and/or save them money, they are willing to share it. The more critical the service provided, such as healthcare, the more sensitive the data they would be prepared to open up to providers.

Research also suggests that two-thirds of customers globally are willing to share predictive application data, provided they gain.[38] Google's predictive application, Google Now, uses customer data to create a virtual assistant for them. Taking data from emails and other locations it can predict when a customer needs to be notified or alerted.

DISNEY'S MAGIC CASE

Capitalising on insights gained from data and technology has scaled Disney's magic wider and been a winning pull for its customers.

While visiting Disneyland, people get a MyMagic+ wristband, which contains a sensor that streams real-time data to hundreds of systems to improve the experience of both young and adult in the park. The idea is transformative and smart because it enables the distinguisher to anticipate customer preferences and adapt accordingly.

No more one size fits all, by a long shot.

The MagicBand gives customers access to the park, faster check-ins to attractions, unlocks the hotel door, serves as a credit card for food merchandise, and so on. The system monitors where customers are and is present throughout the park journey, ensuring frictionless, elevated enjoyment.

Reservations for rides can be pre-booked, helping customers avoid queueing but also enabling improved staff scheduling as well as re-routing customers with incentives. Food can be pre-ordered at restaurants to get rid of delays. And via sensors in peoples' shoes and real-time customer recognition, Disney characters, many of whom are now robots, can greet children by name and talk about their interests.

In the past, Disney would alter movies post-production based on focus-group reactions, which were really about average responses and so not very effective. Now, using Big Data machine learning and neural sentiment analysis, Disney's systems can reshape movie content in real time based on individual preferences and reactions, such as offering multiple possible endings to a film.[39]

And for this convenience, customers continue to provide information in the form of data, about what they do—for how long, where they eat, what they buy, etc.—which is tracked and harvested by the brand transparently.

Obviously, people are not looking to be upsold and cross-sold, but they are looking for better experiences, and when they get them they will trade privacy for surveillance, provided that they trust the brand.

Not wanting to oversimplify, as we have all witnessed some of the challenges that data privacy and security can bring, the principles are these:

- The more transparent the enterprise is about using the data, the more the trust, and the more data that will be shared.
- The more data customers provide, the better the system can be at delivering value to them, which in theory should incentivise customers to provide more data.

If a virtuous data cycle between knowing more and doing better for customers is the object, all parties are winners.

CHAPTER 10

Completing the customer experience

Extinguishers feel safe in their product or service silos. They innovate by improving these products and services and they keep them separate, to keep the silos specialised, autonomous (sometimes even competing with each other for customers), contained and most of all accountable.

Distinguishers are connectors by nature. They join silos, products and industries to provide unified experiences within and between enterprises and brands.

And that's what makes the brands desirable.

Distinguishers look for pain-points and disconnects and they set out to use the technology to fix them. And they take customers into new 'high-ground' experiences they haven't had before, because they actively seek out what needs joining up where.

We call this the complete experience.

Not that it's ever complete (it's always evolving and expanding), but at least directionally it's an important framing concept for distinguishers wanting to oust old ideas and players.

By nature, experiences are unified activities when they cross over product, service and industry silos. Brands that are genuine connectors do so within their own organisations and also with third parties and partners, by building value-enhancing ecosystems. They may even do so with would-be competitors rather than have disjointed touchpoints and disgruntled customers.

Startups today get straight to it, unencumbered by legacy box mentality or structure, and some deliberately find a gap when enterprises or industries fail to do so.

Here's one. A South African startup, Zulzi, which began as a students' food and grocery delivery app, then went broader into households and now is taking what it knows, going national at speed and scale, including into townships and remote areas.

What the founder, Vutlharhi Donald Valoyi, discovered, was that 60 per cent of the time people don't receive what they order online.[40] Now, through Zulzi's in-app messaging, customers have a direct link to the brand's shoppers in real time and can track what has been bought and where they are. The shoppers can message customers if items can't be found so that they can choose replacements. Orders and shopping are multi-store and not just for food and groceries. It combines shopping from pharmacies, hardware shops and many others so that customers get the complete experience.

Importantly, the opportunity to complete the experience wasn't just about substituting a store with an online delivery service, it happened because so many customers had items missing when they bought online from the large legacy supermarkets, creating a value gap, which Zulzi filled and fulfilled and continues to do.

Getting systems to talk to each other. Hurrah!

First comes the mindset to unify the customer experience and make it complete.

Then comes the enabling technology, which is where Application Programming Interfaces (APIs) take centre spot.

Whereas, previously, disparate product silos or systems were unable to talk to each other, or give information to people to talk to each other, today they can because software can be layered or built on top of each other to make this possible.

We can only wonder if Roy Fielding knew, when he first worked on the modern API standard for his doctorate in 2000, that what he was about to create would take brands like Salesforce, Slack, Google—and many others—into a new paradigm, because it would enable long longed-for linkages between brands.

Salesforce was the first brand to use APIs at scale to offer enterprise clients interconnected systems, which now generate 50 per cent of its revenue.[41] What the brand does is to link data, previously not combinable, to help businesses do different things as well as work differently.

So, for example, if a bank's customer starts an application for a loan and then stops, Salesforce can connect to the bank's system, register that a customer has left the process, and remind the person to go back, prompting the next step and the most suitable channel. When the customer has finished the application, the bank can link its system to Salesforce so it can add that customer to an audience type which will inform the bank how that person is likely to react to what media.

Systems that already exist suddenly come alive when they are interconnected. Google Maps wasn't a lucrative asset until a third party showed how it could be used to locate real estate on a map, which lifted the brand to become the new norm. With other Google data built on top of the system, people can assess how far they are from public transport, schools, restaurants, bars or their favourite retailers. Then nearby restaurants can be linked, with opening times, menus, photos of meals (taken by other customers), reviews and matches that fit the customers' profiles to help them make decisions about what to do in that area. So Google Maps is a macro tool to get to a place and a micro tool to navigate within that place.

And the layering is available for anyone to benefit from and build onto. That is what makes APIs so smart.

But joining up for better experiences is not just about technology, it's about the new mindset. Google's aim is to make all the information anyone may need, even competitors' data, available in one place so that customers get the benefit. If a customer searches for a Nespresso machine it might show results from Amazon, even though Amazon is Google's biggest competitor for product searches.

PHILIPS CONNECTING HEALTH CASE

What better industry to have one unified system than healthcare, which is typified by disconnected, time-consuming duplication and endless waits and paperwork.

After a sleepy period, Dutch giant, Philips, decided to distinguish itself and reposition from being an electronics brand to a world leader in value-based healthcare. Today, Philips Healthcare provides scaleable precision medicine that uses technology to build global intelligence delivered locally to suit unique individual experiences for chronic and acute diseases.

A single cloud-based platform connects entire health communities to data that is used by patients and practitioners in a new way to improve diagnosis, treatments and compliance, and thereby ensure a higher quality of care. It's the interconnecting thread of data pertaining to a patient (with security, privacy and authorisation built in) that provides the edge. Data can be built up from each machine, as patients move around from diagnostics, imaging and monitors, which over time gives the patient, the doctor or hospital real-time medical records and insights. These can be accessed from any device, including the Web, social media or mobile phones.

A major coup for Philips is its high-quality homecare system, shifting masses of patients away from hospitals back to their homes, a trend accelerated by Covid. Teams of nurses, therapists and paramedics report to doctors remotely, adding layers of data that are unified in real time to bring patients a superior experience in their homes.

With savings of up to 40 per cent already achieved, demand is growing from all quarters as new interest in wellness and advanced scaleable technology collide to bring about endless possibilities, especially in markets with burgeoning ageing populations.

The 'health at home' principle holds for dental care, too. Philips is empowering individuals by providing smart electronic toothbrushes with sonic technology. These feed data and high-resolution imaging to a teledentistry platform that enables dental professionals (so far, in the US) to engage with their patients via a secure app, performing hygiene checks to assess common oral-health issues, such as gum disease, cavities, inflammation, etc. and to give oral care advice.

BUILDING AN AUTOMATED NEST CASE

There is no value proposition today if consumer experiences aren't unified. Bits and pieces that don't connect, talk to each other and, worse still, are not interoperable, aren't good enough.

But it's what everyone got. Until there were APIs.

The beauty of the new home automation technologies, also known as 'domotics', consisting of interconnected products, services, sensors, data, mobile software, commands and preferences, is that they are state-of-the-art because they communicate with and learn from each other, interbrand and intrabrand.

Although each system or brand may in and of itself be proprietary, the systems are open and therefore from the users' point of view are working together to produce for them a single, complete experience that neither could do on its own.

Nest has changed how people control the security and energy in their homes. It not only allows its own bits and pieces to communicate (Is the person home? Does the temperature need changing?, Is there a fault in the generator?, etc.), it also allows other products to talk to its products and they learn from others. Which means everything is part of the same system constantly growing, improving and adapting, providing the home dweller with a unified experience.

Amazon's Alexa can talk to Philips's advanced technology and instruct lights to go on or off. Google can notify the owner if there is something wrong in the house, say a fire, and can tell a Nest device to do something about it, like call an appropriate service.

And all of this can be controlled remotely by the home dweller or the virtual assistant.

From the customer's Google Calendar, Nest knows when a customer is leaving the house so it can adjust the temperature there for more energy efficiency, at different times of the day.

While this may sound like old hat, it's not. It is only possible because APIs allow systems to build other systems on each other, so developers can constantly be inspired to add value with new applications that keep on coming.

IF THIS, THEN THAT (IFTTT) CASE

Global phenomenon IFTTT (If This Then That) is a freeware distinguisher, with 20 million users in 140 countries, serving more than 90 million active connections.[42] It allows consumers to make their own mini applications on top of the APIs they have in their homes or online, via simple scripts or instructions: if this (happens), then (do) that.

The point is that it makes things work together.

More than 600 brands are connected via IFTTT, giving anyone the opportunity to create and share those unifying instructions for making modern life easier and more connected, so-called 'life hacking'. And consumers can construct and share their own scripts. And they do, en masse (see Table 10.1, page 87).

Here are a few examples, which demonstrate how linking things together form a huge change in how consumers and the products around them behave:

THE EMAIL KILLER SLACK CASE

Distinguishers look at how APIs can pull together people and their work across organisations. Email, says Slack, is a really inefficient way to communicate. It is linear and unconnected and therefore wastes people's time, energy and money if they are trying to collaborate, or are working on or across projects. With Slack, instead of an endless back and forth, people are free to use their intelligence and creativity and have one unified conversation.

How to get people to use one centralised internal communication tool instead of each person going in and out of their many emails and apps and then sending them on, is changing the way people work in organisations. Slack is the glue that binds a virtual office of people in different locations and countries. It's one place to put and access everything.[43]

This was the big idea behind Slack, basically a team messaging unifier and archiving app to disrupt emailing. The fast-growing business app was started by game developers so they could communicate better with each other while they worked. Their gaming venture failed, but Slack quickly became a global phenomenon.

Using APIs so that an enterprise can connect all its various tools—Google, Zoom, MailChimp, Trello, Skype, Salesforce, etc.—across macOS, Windows, iOS and Android, and access them through the same interface, is why they call it the better alternative. Instead of switching between different software and channels, team members in an enterprise can get to the people and the content they need from one place because Slack gathers messages and discussion into channels.

Instead of data and discussions being scattered in different email inboxes (or across multiple communications channels, including intranets), all communications are now in one place, easily scrolled through, timelined and searchable. Groups big or small, inter or intra company, who are working on a particular project or business, can be that much more productive.

It thus encourages real-time conversations and brainstorming through short messaging as opposed to the longer email, which prevents flowing dialogue. This keeps discussions going, constantly updating with comments and reactions in real time.

Which is why Slack has got 75 per cent of the top Fortune 100 companies using it, to the tune of 12 million active users a day.[44]

TABLE 10.1: *If This Then That (IFTTT) Consumer Scripts*

Brand	Interaction
Uber	• If my Uber arrives at home, then stop the music playing on my Sonos. • If I leave from home in an Uber vehicle, then turn off my Philips Hue lights. • If I'm on my way home in an Uber, then set my Nest thermostat to 'at home' mode.
Whirlpool	• If CO_2 intensity is low, then start my Whirlpool Washer. • If my washing cycle is complete, then boost my home's hot water. • If my fridge door is left open too long, then send a notification to my iPhone.
Google	• If I add a new meeting to my calendar, then create a new document for meeting notes. • If I add a calendar event marked 'Garden', then make sure my lawnmower remains inactive for the duration of the event. • If the stockmarket closes, then update my Google spreadsheet with closing price.
GE Appliances	• If I say 'turn off my oven' to Amazon Alexa, then turn off my GE oven at home. • If my washing cycle ends, then send a notification to my iPhone. • If I ask Amazon Alexa to 'turn on Sabbath mode', then set my GE fridge to Sabbath mode.
Microsoft Office 365	• If I have a meeting, then automatically silence my phone. • If I add new files to Dropbox, then automatically add the file to Microsoft's OneDrive. • If I receive an email with an attachment, then upload the attachment to my Google Drive.
Amazon	• If I add things to my Alexa To Do List, then automatically update my Google Calendar. • If my Alexa alarm goes off, then turn on my Philips Hue lights in the bedroom. • If I take a photo on my iPhone, then post it to my Amazon Cloud Drive.
Slack	• If I create a new team task in Google, then let everyone on Slack know. • If I add a new file to Dropbox, then post it on Slack as well. • If my company's share price changes, then post it to Slack's Finance channel.

Brand	Interaction
Monzo	• If I make a card purchase, then update my Google spreadsheet. • If it's a Monday morning, then pay myself a weekly allowance. • If I visit the gym, then put some money into my savings account.
Fitbit	• If it's midnight, then post today's Fitbit activity into a Google spreadsheet. • If I wake up, then turn my Philips Hue lights on. • If I hit my Fitbit target, then add some money to my weekly allowance.
Philips Hue	• If an Uber arrives at my house, then blink my lights twice. • If energy prices or CO_2 levels are high, then turn my lights red. • If I put my lights to 'relax mode', then start my 'relax playlist' in Sonos.
Sonos	• If I leave the house, then pause my music. • If I reconnect with my home WiFi, then resume my music. • If someone rings my doorbell, then reduce the volume.
Whistle	• If my dog hasn't met his exercise goal by 4pm, then add a walk to my calendar. • If my dog is not feeling well or resting more than usual, then email my vet. • If my dog leaves the house when no one is home, then text my phone.
Salesforce	• If a Salesforce opportunity is won, then tell everyone in my Slack group. • If I add a new contact into Google, then let sales leads on Salesforce know. • If I get a new follower on Twitter, then add it as a lead to Salesforce.
Husqvarna Automower	• If I leave home, then cut the lawn. • If the weather forecast predicts frost or heavy rain, then park the mower. • If Automower has a problem, then send an email to my neighbour.

Opening up banking

Because extinguishers are legacy-structured with IT designed for only one silo, it's been difficult for them to give customers a complete, unified experience. Much of the frustration about getting seamless, frictionless outcomes from organisations stems from this because customers have to go from one department to another.

With APIs, not only can this be rectified inside an

organisation, experiences can be extended across products, brands and geographies.

The big breakthrough is when customers have access to their own data, which has happened with open banking, and they can connect it as they see fit.

This allows them (individuals and businesses) to make better financial planning decisions. They can also execute those decisions themselves because open banking enables customers to transact outside of the bank's proprietary interfaces.

Open banking is mandatory in many countries in the EU, as well as in Japan, Canada, New Zealand, Australia, Israel, Singapore, Mexico and India. And in these markets, open-banking related services already account for 7 per cent of total banking revenue.[45]

To bank or not to bank

Open banking means that financial enterprises and third parties exchange data. New propositions quickly unfolding are questioning the need for traditional types of banks, but by no means the need for banking.

Here's what it makes possible:

- New banking entrants can access customer data from legacy banks and add service on top of them, to create a new value proposition, typically what financial aggregators do. They can take any type of account (current, credit card, mortgage, loan, investment, savings, insurance) from any bank, put it together and optimise otherwise poor or suboptimal decisions for or with customers.
- Product switching to cheaper alternatives can be done either by appointed new third parties or customers themselves, for example, for utilities or insurance.
- Bank outsiders can take over payment and transactions. Individuals or businesses that want to pay an invoice, can automatically action a payment via an app or accounting software

without it having to go through a separate banking transaction.

- Accounting software reconciles the payment in real time (bank APIs talking to accounting APIs), speeding up the whole process and allowing the accounting software to become the main interface for the banking transaction.
- Global small-business platform, Xero, allows small-business subscribers to get a NatWest invoice finance service, 'Rapid Cash', when they raise an invoice and get immediate payment to help them manage their cashflow more efficiently.
- New players can collect data from people's bank accounts, which previously only the bank had access to, to provide better credit scoring in real time, speeding up loan or asset-finance applications, at a greatly reduced cost. And widening the pool of people getting financial products by including those who have been excluded.
- APIs enable better and quicker advice and purchase of a new-to-market product or switching more complex financial products like long-term retirement, because of all the data that can be pulled together from multiple sources and countries in real time.
- Deposits and savings investments can be automatically managed, including hedging interest, currencies and inflation. Automated with 'if this then that' instructions can be done by the customer or a third party: for example, 'if the stock falls below a certain price, then buy this number of shares'; 'if stock grows more than 2 per cent in a week, then sell half of the shares'.

TINK CASE

Swedish Tink started on this quantum leap to open banking in 2012. In the words of Daniel Kjellén, co-founder and CEO, it did this to 'bring people financial happiness'. The brand achieved this by giving customers a holistic and better understanding of their money and better insights and tools to help them make superior banking choices, which should become the role model for next best-practice banking. Tink's user base is now 250-million strong across Europe.[46]

The underlying premise here is twofold.

- If customers are to get the best results, they must be able to move from one bank to another seamlessly to pick the best offerings for themselves.
- If banks are to win customers, they must create multi-bank products for customers, which means connecting and aggregating data across multiple provider services.

Now integrated with over 2,500 banks and fintechs, Tink aspires to become the Pan-European provider of future multi-bank financial services, breaking through old barriers to build bridges with its 7,500 developers using APIs in open-banking formats. Using Tink technology, the customer bases of the Dutch bank ABN AMRO or the Portuguese Caixa Geral de Depósitos, for instance, can now see all the accounts with all the banks they use for savings, investment, mortgage, loans, and debit and credit cards.

Tink's Mortgage Match means customers can compare mortgage rates and terms across markets and create an automatic switching offer to get the best deal for themselves at any time, triggered as often as they like.

In savings and investment with Avanza, in Sweden, when customers want to engage, they just authenticate themselves (instead of having to manually input everything), and Avanza fetches and prefills all the data necessary to make the transaction quick and easy instead of taking weeks.

Tink is excelling at banking without being a bank. That's what APIs have done. As its CEO put it: 'Low competition and high barriers to switching have limited incentives for banks to produce the best products. For the first time I think anyone who produces fantastic products at low cost will have tons more customers.'[47]

It's a good example of what's next now.

CHAPTER 11

Making anything 'as a service'

The 'anything as a service' (XaaS) wave is gathering momentum and promises to skyrocket, winning customers in accelerating numbers at speed globally.

It's a lightning move away from the transactional economy in which brands make and move stuff, which customers buy, pay for and take care of until the next time.

In some cases, brands actually relied on things going wrong with the product, so that money could be made from spare parts and replacement. And their timing was precise—they knew exactly when this would happen, and banked on it, quite literally.

Away from ownership

The major shift is away from ownership on the part of consumers, with consequent savings in time and hassle. For the brands that are into it, it's a game-changer. They now own the hardware and software (they are on their balance sheet) and are responsible for making it work when, where and how customers want it, which is what they get paid for.

As well as replacing goods when they need updating, in a proactive seamless fashion, which means they are incentivised to make things that last longer and are easy and not costly to fix, rather than the reverse.

The sector that has embraced 'anything as a service' is mostly IT. The positive for producers is that they have an ongoing relationship with the users, get recurring revenues and predictable billing cycles. The users don't need upfront investments in IT, maintenance and upgrades, scaling up is much quicker, downtime is reduced and security is improved, all at a predictable and significantly lower cost.

Contained in this IT contingent are: Infrastructure as a service (IaaS), Hardware as a service (HaaS), Platform as a service (PaaS), Software as a service (SaaS) and Content as a service (CaaS), to name some. And by the time you read this there will be countless more to add to the list.

- IaaS: Instead of enterprises investing in and building their own servers, systems, broadband and IT infrastructure support, which takes money, time, people and space, IaaS delivers it all as one service. Customers set up an IT infrastructure in hours if not minutes, and scale up capacity for storage, computing processing and bandwidth, when and as they need to.

- HaaS: Why buy hardware when you can access what you need via HaaS when you need it, and have it replaced or repaired without it sitting on your balance sheet or in a warehouse? This is particularly popular for those enterprises looking for flexibility and reluctant to commit to a specific product or brand, or not wanting to or able to afford the upfront cost.

- PaaS: The fastest-growing part of the cloud, PaaS is a service for software development where customers can build, run and manage applications via the Web, without the complexity of also having to build and maintain the environment needed, which includes operating systems, updates, storage or infrastructure. This means reducing the amount of coding needed, simplifying development and deployment, making it cheaper and more efficient.

- SaaS: Instead of boxed licensed software, SaaS means consumers can have access to cloud-based software on a monthly subscription, which is the preferred choice for 84 per cent of the software sold today.[48]

- CaaS: With CaaS, enterprises large and small can use a single repository for content in the cloud, where they can access it from anywhere, manage it, categorise it, make it available to others, search for it or do whatever they wish with it. It manages licensing, usage rights and any other commercial terms, with scale and ease. It also means that content can be accessed and used by others in real time, enabling new next models for integration, aggregation and on-demand delivery.

It costs less to have more

The benefits of the above are in the economies that are obtained through aggregating and jointly sharing assets.

This levels the playing field, because barriers to entry for new or smaller players disappear.

It is scary for large incumbents who have relied on infrastructure to keep competitors out, but heaven for those who believe in open collaboration and jointly creating and sharing value.

As Figure 11.1 demonstrates, these 'anything as a service' IT pillars enable industries and brands within them to create their own version of XaaS and reap the benefits.

Banking as a service

Banking in a box doesn't have to be bought, it can be subscribed to, which means anyone can provide financial services, pay per user and scale up as quickly as they like.

Solaris in Germany, Starling in the UK and BBVA in the US are emerging distinguishers in this regard, allowing other brands to offer banking on top of their own infrastructures. Their banking licences, regulatory obligations and risk management are sold as a service. Solaris, founded in 2015, has 60 global corporate clients using it for digital banking, card management, identity verification, consumer and SME lending, account aggregation and account settlements, powering brands such as the first app-based German broker, Trade Republic, the social enterprise bank Tomorrow and the Pakistani digital bank, Al Baraka Bank.[49]

FIGURE 11.1: *Anything as a service*

New IT Enablers … as a service					Industries as a a service FOR EXAMPLE
Infrastructure as a service	Hardware as a service	Platform as a service	Software as a service	Content as a service	**Banking** as a service
					Logistics as a service
					Drones as a service
					Goods as a service
					Entertainment as a service
					Mobility as a service
					Communication as a service
					Retail as a service
					Manufacturing as a service

Logistics as a service

Providers of logistics as a service manage transportation net-works, including truck, rail, ocean and air freight, and inbound and outbound logistics from factories to warehouses, retailers to end users, for a fee. More than 50 per cent of logistics providers use cloud-based services today, so the integration of all of these players is no longer a problem.

A modern company doesn't have to do its own logistics with all the CapEx associated with it. Logistics can be outsourced for a monthly fee. For example, DHL can take the orders, do the billing, deliver and provide track-and-trace services from one platform. Similarly, Singapore's Anchanto offers pay-per-use logistics models to help small and medium-sized enterprises compete with giants such as Amazon. Customers pay only for the services they actually need and use, instead of having to invest in a fixed-capacity IT infrastructure or warehouses.

Drones as a service

In the business world, drones (flying vehicles) are not weapons or toys but advanced data-capture devices, able to build and track a digital copy of the physical landscape. Data is captured, viewed and analysed in real time so that customers can take and alter decisions there and then.

Drones can help measure and inspect, give early warning signals and provide accurate feedback and visual data, which surpasses anything we have had before. From livestock to agri-cultural fields, real estate, city planning, mines or security, they provide more accurate and timely information. In construction, complicated ground-control points and survey-grade field data can be collected for an entire site in as little as 30 minutes by drones that monitor and supervise where people fear to tread. And new micro drones are connected to cover wider ground for more complex, multi-dimensional problem-solving.

For a fixed monthly fee, frontrunner Kespry, in North America, Europe and Australia, with around 300 customers flying around

50,000 missions annually, offers a complete drone-based aerial intelligence solution available as a subscription for all of the above. Customers get a central data platform, with various drone options for frequently collecting site data that can be combined with data from the customers' own drones or third-party suppliers, integrating them with drone networks managed by people on the ground.

Goods as a service

Goods as a service means that customers, mostly B2C, purchase a result rather than the stuff that delivers that result. For example, in the US, instead of buying solar panels and battery storage, a customer can subscribe to a solar panel service from Sunrun that delivers energy that saves on costs and is greener, even during grid blackouts.[50] Sunrun owns and manages the goods, the customer pays only for the power it produces. The same principle is used by Bosch-Siemens, for white goods. With goods as a service, the consumption of materials, energy and cost is reduced, resulting in less waste. And it reduces investment, hassle and risk for the customer.

Entertainment as a service

From music to movies, TV series, games, books and magazines—all that stuff that customers used to own and store at home—entertainment is now being accessed from anywhere. Distinguishers such as Spotify, Netflix, Amazon and Disney have reshaped how we find and consume entertainment.

They are changing user mindsets about ownership universally: from building a library of books, records or CDs, or listening to music from a radio, to buying or renting videos, or going to a movie house, to streaming on the phone, tablet or laptop.

Now, getting access to exactly what consumers want, when they want, is taken for granted.

Mobility as a service

Shifting away from personally owned or discrete modes of transportation, towards mobility provided as a service, customers access what they need through apps on their phones. The move from ownership to share-ship is earmarked to escalate to USD 600 billion in the next half decade.[51]

MaaS, the tech-enabled Finnish mobility brand, optimises plans for the customers' day, taking into account their preferences and agenda. Customers use one app and one monthly payment system to search, book and pay for all and any transport modes in one place, managing access and connecting their transport across borders, through a single portal globally. Its card is entirely virtual and open-loop, acceptable by mobility wallets such as Google and Apple Pay.

Uber now offers a monthly subscription service, Uber Pass, across the US over 200 cities. The brand gets predictable annuity income, and customers get convenience (one transaction a month) and affordability (lower total costs), because even if prices go up during a surge, the monthly subscription remains unchanged. It also includes free Uber Eats deliveries. In taxi-dense South Africa, it combines eats and rides for consumers at low rates with incentivised discounts.

Communications as a service

It used to be that consumers got phone and broadband, fixed and mobile, but all from different providers. Now brands like Vodafone provide it all through one subscription, which can include hardware like smartphones, boosters and TV consoles and access to other brand services like Spotify and Netflix.

Simultaneously, giants like Facebook and Google, with apps like WhatsApp and Google Hangout, are converging different ways of communicating into one app. WhatsApp consumers can chat, make voice calls, video calls, video conference and send voice messages and pictures all from a single communication service. With Google Hangouts, customers can decide how to communicate with other people from any type of device when working in the G-suite, which holds email, calendar, cloud storage, tasks, etc., and is charged for as one service.

Retail as a service

Providers of retail as a service are in both the online and offline space. Shopify has fortified its position as the one-stop shop of choice for small and medium-sized retailers at a low monthly fee. Its platform provides a complete retail system with templates for storefronts, content, mobile-friendly built-in commerce features and customisations, so that different brands can tailor their customer experience to suit their own positioning.

Shopify holds the upfront investments and scales and shares benefits with smaller and single-product vendors who would otherwise be unable to afford the previously high legacy entry costs.

Manufacturing as a service

Manufacturers always owned everything and did everything. Now they don't have to. They can outsource to a network of people who do various things they are good at, in order to make up the final delivery.

The network is joined by one integrated platform technology. Enterprise resource planning systems (ERP) hold this together, operating on a shared database so that everyone has all the information they need. Once one unit makes its thing, the next person takes over. The network shares the cost: manufacturers don't have to own machines or carry them on their balance sheet, these now sit with multiple vendors.

It's a distributed system—the client or one of the nodes in the system pulls it all together depending on circumstance.

Swiss Techniplas Prime has an e-manufacturing platform as well as its own manufacturing facilities. It also has dozens of manufacturing partners who work in its network. The network makes anything from pre-production prototypes or tools, to the entire fully functioning object. From a car developer it can upload designs and give a price quote in minutes, followed by the total production solution, i.e. cars delivered to the buyer's doorstep. It uses additive manufacturing with goods 3D printed to save time and money. AI optimises capacity across the network, while sensors and analytics gauge progress and movement, managing errors, with the entire system living, of course, in the cloud, for all to see and share in real time, saving hugely on cost.

CHAPTER 12

Subscribing the customer

The convergence of streaming (getting what you want), on demand (anytime you want or need it) and subscription pricing (pay per use, pay per period or use, pay as you grow) has led to a generation of consumers switching from buying stuff to paying only for what stuff does for them, how and when they want it.

This trend started in B2B around 2013, when Adobe—the frontrunner—repackaged its suite of software, desktop publishing, graphic design, video editing and Web development as Adobe Creative Cloud. This transformed its model, from a unit price per software package bought to an online subscription.

And the designer community loved it. They finally got what they needed with low upfront investment, without all the headaches of ongoing fixing and funding. Since then, Adobe has grown its revenue from USD 200 million to USD 5 billion, and its stock has gone up nearly 300 per cent in five years.[52]

Pricing for use

The appetite for this model of pricing is growing in leaps and bounds among consumers, particularly but certainly not exclusively among the newer generations.

This finally moves behaviour from buying products to getting services.

Consumers don't need to:

- buy stuff
- stock it
- book it
- queue for it
- wait for it
- have it on their balance sheet
- pay upfront for it
- manage it
- depreciate it
- maintain it
- risk repair costs and hassles
- discard it
- update/replace it
- be out of stock
- spend time dealing with problems
- support waste.

Distinguishers have turned the old extinguisher model upside down, changing production to embrace long life and residual value, with disassembly, remanufacture and recycling attributes, and the use of less material, cutting out middle costs and margin-based pricing, obliterating sales push and short lifecycle models, and generally enabling time-constrained consumers to get on with life instead of having to manage endless quantities of stuff. (Estimates are that the average household in the US has 300,000 possessions.)[53]

Here are some brands as a service that distinguish themselves: (See Figure 12.1 for a summary.)

✘ Buy and own goods
✔ **No ownership of goods**

BOSCH-SIEMENS
Bosch-Siemens Hausgeräte (BSH) in the Netherlands doesn't sell its goods. Customers get and use its household products at an

FIGURE 12.1: *Anything as a service—IT, industries and brands*

New IT Enablers ... as a service					Industries as a service FOR EXAMPLE	Brands as a service CASES
Infrastructure as a service	Hardware as a service	Platform as a service	Software as a service	Content as a service	Banking as a service	Solaris, Starling, BBVA
					Logistics as a service	DHL, Anchanto
					Drones as a service	Kespry
					Goods as a service	Sunrun, Bosch-Siemens, Circos, Harry's, Birchbox, HP, Trane, Y Closet, ForDays
					Entertainment as a service	Spotify, Netflix, Amazon, Disney+
					Mobility as a service	MaaS, GoCar, Mercedes, Volvo
					Communication as a service	Facebook, Google, Vodafone, Zoom
					Retail as a service	Shopify
					Manufacturing as a service	Techniplas Prime

affordable subscription rate for a period of time. When the item needs to be replaced or upgraded, Bosch-Siemens supplies a new one. If the machine is still usable, the company maintains it in order to keep it running well for as long as possible. The consumer is free of all the hassles associated with managing the asset.

There is no incentive to build in obsolescence that would force the consumer to replace items after some years, so all the materials used in the machines are high quality, durable and eco-friendly, meaning they last longer and can be repurposed or re-used. Rather than selling a product transactionally at a margin, the supplier is selling a service (use), retaining and constantly refreshing the assets, which are built to survive many reincarnations.

Rather than buying a washing machine, the consumer is buying washing cycles, says the brand.

FORDAYS AND Y CLOSET

Even in fashion we see this move. ForDays, a US brand, rents out t-shirts on a subscription basis. It reckons that, with good care, a t-shirt can be re-used, repaired or recombined to dramatically extend its life, and its components eventually can be recycled.

Beijing-based Y Closet, China's largest fashion rental platform with 15 million registered users, and Alibaba as its main investor, is catering to young urban working women hungry for fashion. Rather than ending up as waste, clothing and accessories are rented out. Being part of the Alibaba empire, customer credit scores can be accessed and used to allocate numbers of items to consumers, waive deposits and make subscription payments. Customers can buy the clothes if they want to after they have rented them.

In a major turn of strategy, H&M, the Swedish and the world's second-biggest fashion retailer, is joining forces with Y Closet using COS, their upmarket brand, to get Chinese consumers rewearing rather than buying new. And at home, H&M is offering evening wear for rental from its flagship Stockholm store.

✘ Pay per unit of product, service and delivery
✔ **Pay for access to product, service and delivery**

SPOTIFY

No more paying for whole CDs containing only a few tunes you like, or for that matter having to download what you like onto an iPod. With a click on Spotify, the world's largest music-streaming service sensation by number of subscribers, customers can choose specific pieces of music. And customers (70 per cent of those with the Internet listen to music)[54] love it because they have access to the bits they want when they want them.

This new form of consuming music is captivating people all over the world.

The Spotify formula is this. It puts as much music on its platform as possible so that whatever consumers want to listen to can be found there. It has no allegiance to any content. And this is happening fast, with Spotify expanding its geographical spread—it's now in 92 countries, with active monthly usership at 345 million, consuming music via its online streaming sites and apps.[55]

AMAZON PRIME AND WALMART PLUS

With Amazon Prime and Walmart Plus, customers can, for a fixed fee, get unlimited delivery.

Rather than customers coming in for repeat purchases, like food boxes or flowers, subscription buying—previously common for newspapers or magazines—is popping up everywhere.

ZOOM

No more looking for conference venues, with endless briefings, bookings, trips, costs for things not wanted, negotiations for and disappointments with things needed and not supplied. Zoom smartly connects people one to one and to teams in a virtual shared space on demand for conferences and meetings. In just four years, it went from being an upstart to an indispensable collaborative communication tool. Not only that, but the company also achieved profitability very quickly.

Neither do customers have to buy Zoom software; instead, they pay for access to a service.

The pandemic helped this groundswell, of course, but the new ways of meeting and greeting through subscription are here to stay. It costs less, takes less effort, and can be infinitely productive. Even Alcoholics Anonymous (AA) has members migrating from room to Zoom. People can join clubs anywhere and they say they feel at home, instead of having to go to a fixed physical venue close to home.

✘ Customer manages inventory (monitoring what they have or when it needs to be reordered)

✓ **Supplier manages inventory (supplier monitors what customer has and needs)**

HARRY'S, BIRCHBOX AND HP INSTANT INK

Shaving isn't what it used to be. Men shave less but want more. Harry's, the New York startup, has put firepower into a mature market with its more than 2 million repeat customers.

Razors are often difficult to get in supermarkets, expensive, and tend to run out just when they are needed. So it was a no-brainer opportunity for Harry's, which found a way to work out how quickly a person goes through a razor and delivers a replacement just in time, avoiding unshaven days.

Its monthly plans or six-to-twelve-month subscriptions have flexible, easy-to-get-out options offering a full range of men's grooming products.

Birchbox is another subscription brand that jumped into the male grooming space. It combines brands for a hair, shower and beauty regime with shaving accessories and necessities in one box, always stocked up.

Not rocket science you say? Then why didn't one of the big incumbent three razor manufacturers do it? (PS: Harry's was bought by Edgewater Personal Care, the parent company of Schick!)

HP Instant Ink did it for printer cartridges, scaling in 14 countries. Running out of ink is a big issue for customers but now they can pay a fee based on the number of pages they print a month, not cartridges, to avoid downtime and having to make a trip to buy a new cartridge. Now, connected printers send out reports. Customers pay 50 per cent less than if they had bought the product; HP Instant Ink gets a fee for cartridge recycling and shipping, as well as data on printing behaviour to manage relationships that keep customers longer and help improve the design of new products.

✘ Customer takes whatever is offered (choice limited by segmentation channel, supply, stock, promotions, etc.)

✓ **Supplier finds the best match or solution for customer**

SPOTIFY AND NETFLIX

Spotify started to seriously match people to music based on accumulated data that profiled customer preferences and listening habits, a lot like the Amazon model, which took the world by storm because rather than just taking orders it became good at discovering what people liked. Every Monday, Spotify's subscribers get Discover Weekly, a playlist matching their taste to tunes. So popular was the idea of getting personalised listening via subscription that it attracted 40 million new users almost immediately.

Music energises and inspires people. So, it's not just the accuracy of the suggestions offered by the algorithmic playlist that make Spotify so well received. It's that by bookending recommendations for playlists, tracks and artists at the beginning and end of each week, the brand effectively made itself indispensable to weekly music pleasure.

Netflix dispenses with old segmentation ideas based on demographics and psychographics because it knows people belong to social communities and will take the lead about what to watch from people they know. Customers also fall into different taste and micro taste categories (such as nature documentaries and birdwatching), which cuts across the traditional criteria.

With its 345 million (plus) consumer base, Netflix can smarten up and dig deep to find the correlation between people and content. For example, some of the nature/bird-watching groups may also like drama and war dramas, creating micro communities of interest. Netflix can identify these social networks to make sure their matching works.

✘ Incentivised to buy often
✔ **Incentivised to use when wanted or needed**

CIRCOS

One way or another we are saying goodbye to throwaway economics. Getting customers to rebuy to make sales targets just isn't cool anymore. Better, says Circos, a Danish origin clothes service, get them to pay a subscription to receive what they need when they need it.

On average, parents buy nearly 300 items of clothing for a child in the first two years of its life, most of which are worn for a maximum of only two or three months.[56]

Kids grow, clothes don't. So why throw clothes away that someone else can use once children outgrow them?

With subscribers from 16 countries, Circos is changing the way parents buy, from the time mothers fall pregnant to the child's third birthday. Its online shop rents high-quality design clothes that are durable and fit different tastes, needs and budgets.

This 'clothes as a service' concept means that people have access to a range of items, which Circos launders and renews. As a child gets older, items are exchanged for bigger sizes, and as the clothes wear out, they are recycled or reclaimed for other uses.

The brand says that renting instead of buying, albeit designer wear, costs parents less and saves the cosmos in water, cotton and CO_2 emissions. In addition, their packaging is biodegradable and compostable. And of course, when consumers do the maths, it's just more affordable.

✘ Lifetime cost unpredictable, upgrades and other services expensive, customer manages asset

✓ **Lifetime cost predictable, upgrades and other services built into subscription, supplier owns and manages asset**

TRANE TECHNOLOGIES

Trane, a dealer in climate control technology, has found that, ironically, the total cost of ownership of high-value assets is often higher than when an asset is rented. Commercial customers who buy an asset have to depreciate the asset and incur maintenance and other costs, including upgrades, with all the associated expenses and hassles, including training staff to use it. They may also have to wait longer for repairs or upgrades to take place.

Rather than spending the upfront capital on climate control equipment, industrial and commercial consumers—including those in healthcare, data centres, industrial, hospitality and commercial buildings, like hospitals, schools, hotels and factories—are renting instead. They spend the savings from the chilling machines on planned events and emergencies. Enterprises like Trane (present in 28 countries) are selling less and less equipment and therefore using less material, while enjoying new subscription revenue opportunities. In Trane's case its earnings are up by 20 per cent annually.

ZOOM

Zoom for Home offers subscriptions for extra hardware and software. A single invoice for end-to-end procurement of anything needed to enhance the meeting environment is available.

Zoom retains the equipment and refreshes and changes devices so that customers stay current with the latest technology. This enables customers to get a superior experience without having to lay out huge amounts of cash, and Zoom elevates its revenue stream.

✘ High upfront investment, recurring when upgrades are needed

✓ **No upfront or recurring investment**

GOCAR

Two-thirds of the Irish population believed that there were too many cars on the road and half felt dissatisfied with the alternative transportation option, which dissuaded them from getting rid of their cars.

It was exactly the trigger GoCar needed to introduce a pay-as-you-go model that would allow customers to book and use a car after a one-off joining fee, and get charged according to kilometres driven. Instead of owning the car the customers own the trip (use) and have no upfront or recurring investments to lay out.

The brand also has vans in its fleet. Most of these soon will be electric, and the company is making a large investment in electric recharging infrastructure.

Vehicle renting follows the same logic as a non-ownership alternative, and is offered by many auto brands as part of the new now. It takes out the large upfront cash or debt requirement and has many benefits. These include putting the contract on hold when the vehicle is not being used; the ability to change cars usually every 12 months (Volvo); access to different cars for the week and weekend; hassle-free ownership and hyper-convenience at lower cost. Luxury is not excluded from the subscription. Mercedes-Benz has a fleet of fancy cars for its customers to choose from, including a 'personal concierge' to assist with decisions, insurance, roadside assistance, service and maintenance.

✘ Value proposition is silo-driven with vested, sometimes competitive, interests

✓ **Value proposition is cross-product and cross-industry to optimise customer experience**

MAAS

MaaS (mobility as a service), which surfaced in Finland in 2015, stated its purpose to eliminate as many cars (and congestion) as possible from roads.

What emerged was a single digital interface, multi-modal service, integrating private and public transport into one seamless travel experience. Now in several countries (including public transport leaders Japan and Singapore), MaaS is planning to go even further afield. Its Whim app monitors customer habits, preferences, routines and plans, and co-creates an optimum daily route for individuals, depending on circumstances, weather, congestion, hold-ups, etc.

MaaS has no vested interest in the mode of transport except to minimise time, energy and costs per journey for citizens and workers.

It is particularly popular with millennial and Generation Z consumers, for whom managing their lives through smartphone apps comes naturally.

Another bold move is to cross borders with one ticketing system, to facilitate a single smartened open market in Europe and beyond, so that commuters can move from one country to another uninterrupted. A roaming app combines cities and countries into a single ticket on a subscription basis and, depending on where they are, customers can either pay as they go or buy a subscription in their own currency.

SHOPIFY

In the business-to-business space, Shopify is transcending the old silo approach by offering a value proposition that enables retailers to get everything they need to set up and run a store from one platform. It manages retailing on- and offline, integrating the physical and digital store.

It also integrates the digital store with marketplaces such as Amazon, Walmart and eBay, so that vendors can sell their goods on their own sites and on others.

And it connects the vendor's store to digital channels like Instagram, Facebook and Google, to help them promote and optimise their digital marketing and sales.

✘ Customers get goods when available
✓ Services supplied on demand

UNIVERSAL, DISNEY

The cinema model is broken. And it broke because the film distribution ensemble made people wait, forgetting that we live in a real-time, simultaneous, global world.

A quantum move was made when Universal allowed customers during the pandemic to stream their brand-new, animated *Trolls* movie from on-demand platforms, driving traffic exponentially onto the Internet. The initiative made Universal more in five months than previous versions combined did in cinemas.

At first, cinemas threatened to ban all Universal's movies because it had unilaterally abandoned the windowing protocol by not waiting for a movie theatre release, which is short for 'customers can only get movies screened when theatres have had an exclusive period of months to show it'.

Cut to, and a deal was struck whereby Universal agreed to a 17-day period for cinemas to show a movie before it went onto an on-demand platform.

This hasn't quelled consumers' appetite for getting movies when they want, as we see from the Netflix paid-customer base, which is growing every day (at 200-million plus) and is integral to daily life for most households. And Disney, which owns Universal, has now launched its own version of Netflix—Disney Plus—streaming brands, like Star Wars, Pixar, National Geographic and Marvel (the greatest stories all in one place) in a digital-first exclusive offering of series and movies to its subscriber base, which surpassed 100 million by early 2021.

In the music industry in the old days, the business of making and selling albums meant money had to be made in the first nine months of their launch. For most artists there was no long tail. What Spotify has done, by giving customers access to more than what's current and in store, is resurrect past albums and give them currency, by allowing customers to rediscover and effectively recycle them.

Thanks to music streaming, consumers can now listen to the new and the old. And as back catalogues gain in value, this becomes another incentive to make high-quality products that last, not just one-hit wonders.

TABLE 12.1: *The Transaction Model vs The Subscription Model*

Extinguisher's Transaction Model	Distinguisher's Subscription Model
Buy and own goods	No ownership of goods
Pay per unit of product, service or delivery	Pay for access to product, service and delivery
Customer manages inventory (only customer knows what they have or when it needs to be reordered)	Supplier manages inventory (supplier knows what customer has and needs)
Customer takes whatever is available (choice limited by segmentation, channel, supply, stock, promotions, etc.)	Supplier finds the best match or solution for customer
Incentivised to buy often	Incentivised to use what when wanted or needed
Lifetime cost unpredictable, upgrades and other services expensive, customer manages asset	Lifetime cost predictable, upgrades and other services built into subscription, supplier owns and manages asset
Investment upfront high and recurring when upgrades needed	No upfront or recurring investment
Value proposition is silo-driven with vested interest	Value proposition is cross-product and cross-industry to optimise customer experience
Customers get goods when available	Service supplied on demand

CHAPTER 13

Connecting the everywhere consumer

The world changed in 1996 when Amazon sold a book on the Internet.[57]

Now, almost everyone is online. From playing bridge to banking, from training to telemedicine, there's not much people don't buy or do on the Internet.

But that's old news.

By 2020, gaming and entertainment had been growing year on year for quite some time, driven by digital natives who have always communicated through apps, and interacted and bought online.

What caught us unaware was how much steeper the adoption rates of Internet use would be across the board as a result of Covid-19. Globally, rates for consumers and businesses jumped five years ahead of what was expected within the first three months of lockdown.[58]

Digital immigrants, the last cohort to migrate online, born pre-Internet, have now bought in, and having bought in are likely to stay in. The combination of them with the younger tech-savvy markets makes the online numbers staggering.

With customers stuck at home during lockdown, e-tailers globally were catapulted into the online world as they watched these adoption rates grow. Some rose to the occasion and got huge rewards. Many didn't.

Logistics took on a new meaning as suddenly things had to get to customers instead of the other way around. Digital delivery became essential. The last mile became the sexy part of the supply chain.

Drones and robots became a commercial reality overnight as faster and safer movement of goods became the pressing priority. Using drones has sped up transportation by 50 per cent, feeding into the need for fast, from a breed of customers who do and want things from everywhere.

Online everywhere

But what distinguishers did during lockdown and continue to do is reshape online customer experiences and deliver outcomes they would otherwise not have got.

This has resulted in changed behaviour, some of which we have never witnessed before.

Take Discord, a social networking tool with a user base of 300 million people (and growing every day) popping in and out of each other's virtual lives for a chat.[59] What started as a voice, video and text gaming forum where people could go to watch games, meet gamers, discuss matches or arrange competitions, morphed into an online platform for people from everywhere to just 'hang out'.

What this effectively means is that we now have an online hangout generation, including teens (the official starting age is 13 plus), who used to meet physically with friends to chat or have fun, doing this from wherever they are online. Friends with common interests form groups, and are invited to join a social gathering, coming and going, depending on whether the people they want to be with are available.

Online business-to-business is catching on. Whereas before, sales representatives would visit corporate clients or have them come to their factories to see and buy, now they are creating virtual venues to showcase and sell their goods.

ALC CASE

Came Covid, and ALC, a South African packaging materials company with customers importing from them from 45 countries, built a film studio in which professionals produce and manage content in real time. Customers have a live rather than staged experience in an authentic setting, where various packaging applications are shared and processes co-created and adjusted to suit individual users.

ALC's customers have learnt to interact differently and 'are not going back', says CEO Bester Pansegrouw. There are many advantages to connecting customers from and to everywhere online. This includes the obvious, travel, being able to connect anytime and in real time, planning and adjusting appointments rather than being confined by transport schedules and delays, getting reactions and answering questions there and then, with the help of translators who speak the vernacular of far-off users, a feat that can't be accomplished with other social media, like YouTube.

In these live demonstrations, interaction is not restricted by what can be experienced only in the host infrastructure. ALC and its customers can see each other's plants, view packaging in use, as well as test and share alternatives to reach optimum results.

And all the everywhere importer customer needs is a smartphone.

What experience has taught businesses, is that interacting online is not just about buying from the Internet what they bought in stores or factories before. That's just e-commerce.

It's about imagining and manifesting ways for customers to do things differently and better online from everywhere.

IKEA CASE

Take the Swedish giant IKEA, which was unhappy with the status quo, despite decades of success as a furniture store giant. Changing its claim to fame, its flat-packed furniture kits, which customers previously had to find in stores, carry to tills, transport and assemble, are now ordered and paid for online.

Three hundred stores (many franchised) and 38 countries later, as IKEA becomes a digital powerhouse, its customers are being challenged to change their behaviour and go online whenever they are ready to furnish and decorate their homes.

With some smaller store formats as showrooms to complement this.

The cumulation of IKEA's design know-how is now being harnessed and taken to customers in a platform combined with 3D and AI technology, so that they can re-imagine in true-to-scale augmented reality how their homes could be made over. A smartphone app enables consumers to browse catalogues online, to find what they like from the many options, and try it out virtually in situ before ordering online.

And through the acquisition of Taskrabbit, a gig-economy start-up platform that matches freelancers to jobs, customers can now get the goods they have bought delivered as well as assembled at home.

No doubt Covid-19 has made people rethink the design of their homes for multipurpose living and work. IKEA's audacious and brave but on-the-button move to online started before the pandemic, and now is getting a positive response from millions of consumers everywhere.

Additionally, IKEA has an open-source mentality. Third-party online retailers like Amazon and Alibaba are selling their goods on IKEA's platform as it reconfigures its stores to become fulfilment centres. Thinking like a software company, mimicking open source, it is allowing customers as well as other suppliers to morph and modify its products. Instead of a bed being only a bed, for instance, its basic chassis can become a sofa and customers can choose upholstery from another supplier instead of having to buy it ready-made only from IKEA. Or they can get their kitchen cabinet fronts from a third party who has a better fit for their taste and style.

Progress indeed.

Mobile gone mad

'Everywhere' is about consumers engaging with brands from wherever they are.

Mobile makes this possible.

Mobile usage is escalating worldwide as a percentage of online activities. Two in every three people in the world are actively using smartphones and this figure is expected to grow rapidly with 5G connection and speed.

People may be different culturally, but if there is one thing they have in common, it's mobile smartphones. And this is making the 'everywhere' customer experience a global phenomenon, for music, movies, games, books, schoolwork, social events, church, sport, paying for goods with one tap, just hanging out with friends and just about everything else.

China is home to the largest number of smartphones right now, followed by India, the US and the EU.[60] India is emerging as a 'mobile-first' country with one of the fastest-growing smartphone penetration rates in the world.[61]

There are more mobile connections than people in Japan. High percentages of mobile uptake are found in other countries, too, such as Australia (84 per cent), Norway (91 per cent), South Korea (89 per cent) and the Netherlands (87 per cent).[62]

In Latin America, 90 per cent of all Internet connections are expected to be made through mobile by 2022, with Brazil in the lead followed by Mexico in terms of take-up.[63] (More people in developing countries have a mobile phone than have access to clean water.)[64]

And as data costs come down and Internet availability goes up, sub-Saharan Africa—a region of 23 countries, from South Africa and Nigeria to Angola, Cameroon and Mali—is the fastest-growing mobile market in the world. It is expected to have 790 million active users by 2025,[65] largely in the hands of the youth, which amounts to nothing less than the largest young digital population in the world.

Across the board, consumers in urban and rural Africa use mobile and some have thus become included in economies and significant markets for the first time. Half the world's mobile money services are in Africa. With brands repurposing mobile SIM cards and phone accounts into virtual currency, people can now pay bills and trade through a mobile phone.

M-PESA, the Kenyan phone-based money transfer distinguisher, single-handedly ramped up the inclusion rate in Kenya from 27 per cent in 2007 to 82 per cent in 2020.[66] Now Africa's largest payments platform, with some 40 million users in Kenya, Tanzania, Lesotho, Democratic Republic of Congo, Ghana, Mozambique and Egypt, it processes over a billion mobile transactions every month.[67]

'Everywhere' is in the pocket

Because mobile is in the customer's pocket, wherever customers go so too goes the Internet.

Their mobile phone is always on, it's the one thing they don't leave at home!

The question therefore is, if the phone is a permanent fixture in customers' daily existence everywhere they go, what else can it conceivably be used for in order to ease and please them? The list of possibilities is endless. Here are some interesting examples:

- Israeli Healthy.io turned the question into a startup. Smartphone cameras have become diagnostic tools to test for chronic kidney disease by uploading photos of urinalysis dipsticks, ushering in mobile devices as point-of-care testers.

- Peek Vision was started by the Englishman, Andrew Bastawrous, who wanted to bring ophthalmology to Kenyans. Basically, he made it possible to use a smartphone as an eye examination kit, 50 times cheaper than the bulky clinical equipment. Easy to use by a health provider in homes, schools and communities, it is an 'eye clinic in a pocket'. The quality of the images is so good they can be used for future diagnosis and treatment.

- In China, where old methods of soil analysis in agriculture are time consuming and costly, smartphones are being transformed into portable reflectometers, which, together with test strips, analyse soil samples to give fertiliser recommendations to farmers there and then.

- Two and half billion people in the world don't have a credit rating as a result of archaic methods and risk practices used by banks and credit bureaus. Outsider third parties have jumped into this gap. Instead of looking at credit history, or outdated criteria, or excluding people with no credit record (as has happened with the gig economy and the poor), they use smartphone data points which can produce behaviour indicators algorithmically, and with AI and machine learning, these give credit scores anytime everywhere.

  Research reveals that using mobile phone data to find good prospects from the population of unbanked who have no credit listing, as well as to predict the likelihood of repayments from those who have credit, works.[68] Hundreds of thousands of data points from mobile phones everywhere reveal behaviour: what consumers do (activities), who they know (network), what they earn (income) and spend (transactions), and how they handle their debts (payments).

  Fintech distinguishers like GoBear are scaling up this new behaviour in Vietnam, Philippines, Thailand and Indonesia, turning anonymous digital footprints into the next credit score norm. In various parts of Asia this has morphed into a Financial Health Index, to score people on their financial health.

- The Fitbit health and fitness tracker uses a smartphone to capture data, which it couldn't get from just a wearable. A tracker doesn't know, for example, where a person is, whereas a smartphone does. And this is how the brand knows the activities a customer is doing and can help maximise that person's physical performance and wellness.

- Uber has developed a joint app with the Hilton chain of hotels and others, which enables customers to organise a complete travel experience on their smartphone, from selecting a hotel and room of their choice depending on their preferences, and getting to and from airports, to circumventing the hotel check-in process by going directly to their room and opening the door with a smartphone instead of a key. The phone also converts into a mobile concierge and digital tour guide, with which customers can choose and book a variety of visits to suit tastes and interests.

Using mobile can have a positive impact on customer outcomes. For example, the Lifebuoy Mobile Doctarni service in rural India gives mothers free, easily accessible advice about their child's health adapted to the child's age. Results from the pilot test have shown that the frequency of handwashing has gone up by 50 per cent, demonstrating the power of mobile. The brand is on the cusp of replicating this in other areas in India, where it hopes to reach 2.7 million rural mothers.[69]

And the applications keep growing.

Instant and in real time

With mobile always on, almost anything can happen in real time everywhere. In India, for instance, where data costs are among the cheapest in the world, people use 70 per cent of their mobile data to watch entertainment on their smartphones. One may easily assume that, increasingly, content will be watched and services received from everywhere on that continent.[70]

UK-based challenger bank, Monzo, which attracted over four million customers in less than five years, distinguished itself by providing real-time digital banking with instant spending notifications, so that customers can see what they have spent even before the card machine has printed the receipt. They can also see their account balances immediately on their smartphones without the time lags that increase overdraft fees.[71]

Because a smartphone can identify the customer's location and the location of the purchase, Monzo can pick up fraud without delay. The impact is immediate.

Discovery Insure can tell where a customer is (70 per cent of the time through a mobile, the rest of the time through a device in the car) and therefore can be the first responder to an accident. It also knows if a car is being used or not. Based on that data, during Covid-19 lockdowns, it could offer its customers rewards for driving less.

Of all smartphone users globally, 67 per cent say they use Google Maps, making it the most popular map app, five times more popular than its nearest competitor.[72] Evidently this is because it provides better directions, particularly for non-drivers (pedestrians, too, need directions to people or places). It is also more user-friendly, has the best coverage of street views and venues, like where restaurants are and whether or not they are open or full, and is infinitely accessible.

The brand has changed how customers access and use cities. No longer do they need to battle with a paper map or drive around aimlessly until they find their way. And they can now use the app to make decisions about where to do what, based on reviews and recommendations, wherever they are.

Mobile is also an easy way of collecting data and converting it into customer value in real time. For example, customers in a Freshippo store (a grocery chain owned by tech wizard Alibaba) can use their smartphone to scan the barcode on the goods they want, and instantly receive product information, recipes and reviews. This data, together with an inventory of purchases, preferences and frequency of use, enables Freshippo to keep an ongoing profile of customers for future queries, requests and deliveries.

Increasingly, apps connect with other apps on mobile to facilitate the consumer being attached to a brand from wherever they are.

In India, Google Pay is the leading mobile payment app with 75 million users, followed by Walmart-owned PhonePe. Built for India, Google Pay enables its users to send and receive money, without fees, directly from and to domestic bank accounts. They can top up their phone (or pay for their mobile subscription), pay for groceries or donate funds (as many did during Covid-19),[73] all from their mobile phone. And by the time you read this, Facebook-owned WhatsApp Pay should have been launched in India, projected to introduce another 200 million users to paying by mobile.[74]

Mobile payments in India have been facilitated by UPI (Unified Payments Interface), a real-time payment system developed by the National Payment Corporation of India.[75] Regulated by the national reserve bank, UPI transfers funds between multiple bank accounts, with 150 banks connected.

Not only can customers gain access to brands from everywhere with mobile, brands can also get to consumers everywhere, to help them make better decisions in real time.

In Brazil (as elsewhere), mobile banking is exploding and Bradesco bank, known for its emphasis on women, is using WhatsApp to get customers to consult the bank's AI-powered chatbot. Millions of customers are interacting with the bank this way, with over 100 million chats managed yearly.[76] WhatsApp is now in the final stages of launching its payments features,[77] helping users to send money directly through its chat interface, making money transactions 'as easy as sending a photo', it says.

Smart cities have millions of sensors. More importantly, they are inhabited by millions of citizens with smartphones who can participate in improving city services by sharing information.

For example, in Barcelona, tourist footprints are tracked to help enhance public services. In Singapore, geospatial databases enable citizens to augment maps to add information like traffic incidents or animal sightings, where to buy things or get a good cup of coffee.

Mobile has taken existing services like healthcare to service-scarce, remote parts of the world, a movement that has been accelerated by Covid-19. Millions of people in rural and deprived areas can't get medical care or they need to travel for days to get to a clinic at enormous cost just to get diagnosed. Telemedicine, which connects patients to healthcare providers in two-way interactions, with virtual visits and remote patient monitoring over the phone, is being used increasingly for diagnosis, treatment, prevention and rehabilitation of diseases and injuries, supplemented by drug access through pharmacies or mobile clinics. Telemedicine has been around for years and has had its fair share of ups and downs, but post 2020 it will be firmly entrenched as an increasingly appealing real-time alternative to traditional models.

M-health, as it is called, which works with synchronously interactive information and communication technology like videoconferencing or chats via mobile phone (at its most basic), is known to reduce errors, numbers of referrals, repeat visits, overmedication and costs by 70 per cent in some areas. It exposes local health workers, pharmacies and patients to global experts, and enables virtual upskilling of practitioners in the field.[78]

Wearable devices are at the forefront of self-enhancement. They go wherever the wearer goes, and linked to smartphones they give and get feedback in real time. The wearables market is set to reach over USD 60 billion by 2025.[79] Carried in a pocket, worn on the wrist or on other parts of the body (for example, smart earwear, eyewear or footwear) or as patches, wearables transmit vital data directly to the user via apps in real time, helping consumers make decisions, influencing how they act and react.

Smartphones and wearables have built-in sensors, such as an accelerometer (sensing movement, vibrations and acceleration), a gyroscope (determining orientation and angular velocity), a magnetometer (measuring the Earth's magnetic field, calculating orientation and direction) and a barometer (monitoring air pressure). Recent innovations include more complex sensors, such as proximity and light sensors, fingerprint scanners, heart-rate, blood-pressure and hormone monitors, taking data from and to anyone everywhere.

And instructions can be obeyed from everywhere. With a sensor on a wrist, sleeping systems respond to an individual's needs and automatically change room temperature and light levels, cancel noise or increase the volume of white noise, to help create better sleep cycles and increase the quality and quantity of resting time.

Merging online and offline

People can be online everywhere if the Internet is everywhere (which it isn't yet, but soon will be). Firstly, Elon Musk's SpaceX project will make Internet access ubiquitous, hyper-centralising and bypassing other known infrastructures. Secondly, peer-to-peer technology is enabling a new Internet structure to emerge, which is hyper-decentralised, removing any barriers to going online.

As a result, how, when and where people shop is changing and will continue to do so rapidly. They won't go to where things are or happen, things will come to them. Or they will go to stores to experience the brand, but not necessarily to buy there.

The store is not and no longer will be an outlet or channel, but a destination, an extension of the 'everywhere' experience.

Already, customers search on the Internet before they buy, in order to learn from reviews and feedback, compare other products, check specifications, decide on options and then make their choice.

As much as 70 per cent of consumers who buy cars turn to search engines first.[80] They then order and pay on- or offline, collect and receive goods and services, and then do their own reviews, in a cycle of re-iterative feet and finger steps.

And they do this in what is known as 'micro moments' (time caught while doing other tasks, like exercising), and they buy a variety of things from different sites at different times, rather than doing everything in one weekly shop.[81]

Some 90 per cent of all consumers in China access the web via a mobile device and everything happens from there—the marketing and advertising communication, browsing, choosing and paying.[82]

Though the number of physical footprints is reducing, it's not to say that the physical store is dead. It just has a different role, being *one* of the channels but not *the* channel. In fact, it's been reported that having a combined presence of digital and physical stores is 50 per cent more successful than having one or the other.[83]

Retail distinguishers get this. Their value proposition is built around a data-powered omnichannel formula, which, in addition to being seamless, is intelligent and personalised. Irrespective of type or number of channels, no longer can these be run separately in silos with either/or decisions being made by customers on which one to use to engage with the brand. Consumers will inevitably engage with all channels re-iteratively, each of which needs to acknowledge, know and remember them in one technology-powered interconnected real-time system.

IKEA understood this, despite its longstanding investment in stores and well-honed franchising mastery. Now, customers can choose furnishing and decor at the shop, at home, at work, on a bus or wherever, in one interactive, digital and physical, joined-everywhere experience.

FRESHIPPO CASE

Freshippo, with over 65 grocery stores in China, a country known for its very discerning customers, has taken the lead in merging on- and offline retail at scale. As a consequence, productivity has increased by three to four times that of conventional offline stores.

The game-changing hybrid experience it delivers is totally integrated. Customers can order online or in the store, and get goods delivered within 30 minutes if they live within a 30-kilometre radius. They can select raw ingredients in the store and have them cooked by chefs while they are shopping, to eat there or as a take-away, or have them cooked and then delivered. Freshippo has also merged store and fulfilment to streamline the experience. Once orders are placed via the app or offline, goods go to fulfilment centres that are a part of the store (on conveyor belts in the ceilings), to ensure instant retrieval at cashless exits. The entire system is geared to ensure goods get from farm to plate within 24 to 48 hours.

Converging on- and offline doesn't end there for parent company, Alibaba, which is opening restaurants where food is ordered entirely by phone through an app and delivered by robots.

NIKE AND LEGO CASES

Nike believes the next better normal is a combination of bricks and clicks because people want to try before they buy high-end sportswear. But its push into digital as well as directly to customers offline in store will be equally high tech, it says. What Nike wants is for customers, who aim to be fit and fashionable, to associate a blending of various on- and offline sport activities with the brand.

In Nike's Paris store, made of sustainable material and fuelled by Spanish wind power, customers combine what they can do online and in a store in one end-to-end experience. Customers browse on the Web and choose goods, which are put into digital lockers in store for them to 'try on'. Customers tap on the goods on a mannequin and get product information. When they purchase products, they go through a no-queue system. For women, Nike Fit uses machine-learning and advanced algorithms to recommend the size and fit of bras. The store offers sports activities in physical spaces, or places to virtually watch pro athletic activations in the Shanghai or New York stores. The Kids Pod is an in-store destination where kids can engage in interactive gaming and activities to keep them on the move.

LEGO has done the same. Taking back its power from reliance on some of the world's largest retailers, it is accelerating its move into retail in addition to its online stores. It plans to have 600 stores globally, 200 of them in China. In these stores, customers will be able to blend amazing physical constructions with digital experiences, and link them to continue to build, play and buy online.

Its aim is to put effort and expense into on- and offline everywhere to enhance the customer experience.

It's the only way to keep the iconic brick high up in the game.

CHAPTER 14

Succeeding at work and learning from anywhere

With the advent of digital technology, networked and anywhere, and hybrid technologies mixing the virtual and physical, we are only just seeing the beginning of the successful shift to working and learning from anywhere, particularly home.

It's part of the growing 'at home' era.

The widespread view across industries and countries is that a lot more can be done remotely than was previously imagined. And that a large chunk of the world's population will not be going back to the office in the same way.

The highest share of people wanting to work from home is among knowledge workers, whose work is the easiest to do remotely. This is probably why, in Singapore, nine out of ten employees want to continue to work from home for the majority of their time,[84] and in the EU the figure is eight out of ten.[85]

In general, the numbers of people working at home have tripled or quadrupled since lockdown. Although these figures may change, the point is that no one expects the new normal of the future to be like the old normal. Very few people will be back in the office full time.[86]

People have learnt to think, work and collaborate in new ways. Having done so, many are finding remote work a better alternative, with unexpected benefits. They don't waste precious time travelling to and from work, and have more time to devote to meetings and tasks. Working at home costs less for both employee and employer. Pollution from commuting is down, some mental health problems (like stress and conflict) are down, and life balance and interest in teamwork is up.

Additionally, when choosing a job people are saying they want this option and that it would influence their choices, and employee turnover is lower with flexible working arrangements. Reports say productivity has gone up. People have just learnt how to work better away from the office. 'Especially if no one feels left out because everyone does it,' said one executive in Silicon Valley.

And from an executive in banking in the EU, 'It forces people to get to the point quicker, and document better in order to be able to share on collaborative tools such as Slack and Microsoft Teams.' The people who report to him directly are scattered around Europe, which he says is irrelevant because the team works so much better remotely.

One may argue that if people no longer have to come to one central space to work, there will be a move out of cities into the countryside or relocations internationally to interest-specific cities and high-quality lifestyle/work destinations, broadband permitting.

Enterprises are already beginning to see the physical migration of workers. Facebook, for example, announced that if employees move out of crazy high-rent Silicon Valley, their salary will decrease.

Long before Covid-19, Amazon decided that in the next decade it would double its workforce (in 2020 it was 1.3-million strong)[87] and that the only way to do this in a financially sustainable way would be by taking out the cost of new office space. There are several advantages to this, says one Amazon executive in the know: among them, better use of time zones and shifts. Instead of having people come in for eight hours a day, stop work and take it up again the next day, the job book can be distributed over time zones to get a workflow of 24 hours a day. This opens up more possibilities for flexible working hours to a bigger pool of talent than was previously tappable, like working moms or the disabled.

With content easily created, recorded and communicated on social media, on-demand viewing can complement remote meetings for freelancers. Additionally, tools are emerging every day in order to facilitate better collaborative working from anywhere. Zoom's move to become a platform for other apps (such as Slack, Salesforce and Dropbox), known as Zapps, will allow people to organise and share ideas before a meeting and follow up thereafter.

Many other enterprises are following suit to promote working from anywhere where an in-person presence is not required, such as Shopify, Twitter, Microsoft and Facebook (Zuckerberg says at least half of its staff will be working remotely within five to ten years).[88] This will mean permanent or semi-permanent remote work options, depending on individual circumstances, with compensation for offices at home, and working part-time hours.

Of course, the proviso is always the ability to retain high levels of engagement and preserve the culture of the organisation remotely.

New ways of talent selection and management will also evolve, with a good culture fit being a priority, which according to Zoom's CEO, Eric Yuan, is important in a growth spree, but also in times of crisis or controversy.[89]

Scaling up a remote workforce requires hiring people who are self-motivated, invested in self-learning and committed to the brand purpose. The days of supervision to ensure alignment and control productivity are over.

Giving and getting feedback will also be an issue, and some say people may need more, not less feedback when working remotely. Technology and employee recognition programmes provide frameworks for this, and can be integrated with email and collaboration tools like Slack, so that check-in meetings with employees can be scheduled, goals monitored and recognition given at appropriate times.

Goodbye overheads

But perhaps the most important point here is that, where possible, distinguishers don't expect consumers to absorb the huge office overheads dictated by old minds and models. Being big isn't smart if big means costly baggage.

Which is why asset-light, low-operating-cost distinguishers can offer more affordable price points, making heavy inroads into legacy business models to get big quickly.

That said, the social dimension of work will continue to mean offices for some, but more so hybrid home-office arrangements, blending time worked remotely with time in the workplace. People working anywhere, depending on the project, will meet at appointed times as an exception, not the rule.

Remote work habits will mean fewer and smaller office spaces complemented by hubs on demand, such as are already mainstream in Australia and other countries, and smaller and shared touchdown spaces in offices for the times that employees are there.

And at home, employees are saying they need less space than they had at their offices.

Either way, the at-home era will take its toll on real-estate developers and landlords as well as rental agents and adjacent retail and other service providers who derive their revenue from city-centre hotspots. They will have to adapt quickly to the on-demand co-working place wave for the work-and-learn-from-anywhere consumer.

It will also provide many opportunities in fashion, food, furniture, fun and the functional aspects of working from anywhere, as well as anything that enables doing multiple things at and from home.

The bike gets a spike

For people still having to do face-to-face work, but commuting to work less often, the use of bikes is expected to surge. Planners, politicians and people are expected to drive the bicycle trend, which swept the world during the pandemic and is likely to stick. What was for enthusiasts a means of recreation and fitness is now a way to get around to and from work when needed, and be anywhere fast, saving on costs and time as well as dramatically improving health, air quality and congestion.

This is especially true with e-bicycles, which are quickly evolving to becoming mainstream for work commuters.

Asia-Pacific countries, particularly China, Japan, Australia, India and South Korea, are the fastest-growing bike markets. The US has seen the highest sales ever and these are expected to continue post pandemic. In point of fact, the number of Americans who use a bike to get to and from work increased about 60 per cent over the past decade.[90]

Across the globe, cities are redesigning streets, building extra cycling lanes and infrastructures like bike parks, to support and spur on the upward swing in bike ridership.

Some countries are actively providing funds, infrastructure and incentives, like the UK's GBP 1.2 billion long-term plan to get bikes (and walking) the preferred option for short journeys,[91] or France's 'bicycle repair boost' and tax incentive programmes for travel costs of staff who commute by bike. Italy has a similar programme. New York City plans to create a seamless 685-kilometre bikeway network.[92] Other countries, such as Finland, are giving an e-bike subsidy to citizens so that biking journeys can be lengthened to cover what was previously restricted to cars.

Enterprises are becoming bike-friendly as well in order to accommodate and encourage bike-commuting when employees come to the place of work. Facilities like bike parking, electric-bike charging stations, showers, lockers, bike repair shops, etc., are now all the rage.

Learning from anywhere

Technology is no longer a luxury in education, it's essential, another lesson learned from Covid-19. During the pandemic, over 1.6 billion children in 190 countries were out of the class-room.[93] Education has never seen anything like it in its entire history. Through digital platforms, learning apps and software, students began to learn differently fast. And so did teachers.

But even before the pandemic, the adoption rates of 'learning from anywhere' were climbing, with the global online education market projected to reach USD 350 billion by 2025.[94] Students were already studying entirely online, especially in the US, or enrolling in one or more online courses while staying and study-ing on campus.

E-learning is expected to increase rapidly in emerging countries as well. The so-called 'digital divide' is diminishing as smartphone uptake increases and broadband technology quickly penetrates remote rural regions, to provide Internet access.

E-learning is a fast and cost-effective way to scale up educa-tion where an alarming number of children have none, a problem exacerbated by growing populations.

The anywhere student

Learning from anywhere is becoming part of everyday life, mainly because students report getting a superior experience, provided of course they have a remote setup. They can work at their own pace and generally they learn faster online, taking 40 to 60 per cent less time than in a traditional classroom setting.

Given that social contact remains important and the rite of passage of moving away from home is still significant in some cultures, learning from anywhere is likely to be supplementary and complementary to traditional campuses. We are unlikely to go back to the old suboptimal model.

There are now micro courses, nano degrees and 'stackable' degree programmes that are self-paced and can lead to a recognised qualification. All of these offer not just choice but flexibility, which means that inter-institutional certified combinations will be the new next normal.

In this USD 2 trillion global market (compared with the global healthcare market, which is worth about USD 1.7 trillion)[95] universities have pushed pricing and discounting policies to the limit. Location-bound and classroom- and teacher-constrained, their business model is being extinguished by the zero-margin model of 'anywhere' learning platforms.

The anywhere student is seeking an outstanding digital experience, the highest possible content quality and, most importantly, an institutional reputation for better employability. Today this can be obtained from one or multiple institutions, anywhere in the world.

If geographical location isn't a factor anymore and tuition fees are coming down, why wouldn't anyone anywhere who deserves it want to study at Harvard, Oxford, Cambridge or Chicago?

And would that mean more inclusion for students who would otherwise have been excluded, increasing the numbers even more?

Virtual classrooms are made for infinite scale. But how will global institutions cater for a massive multicultural global audience?

How will faculty play their part and be ready to take on this new education tsunami? America had 1.5 million faculty members before the pandemic, of which 70 per cent had never taught a virtual course before.[96] Now, we guess, 100 per cent of them have. They are on a steep learning curve with nowhere to go except up and onward, or out.

Agnostic and global

America's Coursera, the largest online-learning platform with 76 million students and over 5,500 courses,[97] presents the promise of a new agnostic model, with others hot on its heels. With over 200 elite partners across 50 countries, it offers students access to MOOCs (Massive Open Online Courses) and enables them, at the fraction of campus costs, to tailor their own curriculum.

When more than 90 per cent of students around the world saw their schools close as a result of Covid-19, Coursera's enrolment increased to 31 million, a 520 per cent increase on the previous non Covid-19 year.[98] And with blended learning now re-shaping campus life forever, proponents believe the trend will continue.

One student reacted: 'I can still get the education (from my university), but it's going to be online. I'll get a college degree, but I'm not allowed to go to campus. Do I want to pay the same price for that? Particularly if I can get the best courses from multiple places.'[99]

Not only does Coursera offer university degrees, Coursera monitors job markets and works with enterprises to package skills in demand, in new, creative ways, making it an agnostic platform for higher education and a matchmaker for the supply and demand for new workforce talent.

Enterprises like Facebook are working with Coursera to figure out what talent it and its customers will want in the future and to design and deliver a multi-branded programme to create this talent, which it and its advertiser customers can recruit.[100]

Horizontal and tailored

In a complete turnabout from old-school silo thinking, which demands that everyone study the same traditional subjects, Finland, which has one of the top-performing education systems in the world, has already redesigned its nationwide horizontal curriculum to foster tailored learning paths to support children's interests and job aspirations.

These deliver future-facing skills for problem-solving and collaboration that cut across traditional subjects, and foster creativity, civic awareness and participation.

Learning is where the home is

Another anywhere learning trend on the up is home schooling, which began in America in the 1970s. One person, John Holt, believed that children's education should be done at home and started a liberal reform movement, which morphed in the 80s to become a legal, Christian alternative to traditional state schooling.

But who knew that over the years this system, a mixture of contact and contactless, a stronghold for countless numbers of families, would become a new education wave that would be recognised internationally as a desirable alternative to traditional education? Millions of children worldwide are home schooling (2.5 million in the US alone, with a steep rise being seen in many other countries, like the UK).[101]

From their bedrooms, living rooms and study rooms, thanks to the Internet and e-learning, kids are being taught by their parents anywhere, and evidently, they are beating schooled peers on grades, quality-of-life experience and post-school entrepreneurial success.

Micro-chunked and channelled

In the B2B space an emerging trend is micro learning, whereby people learn new things, refresh skills and reinforce knowledge in the workplace. It happens at the moment of need, on demand, which can be anytime, anywhere. It's based on the premise that people's brains think and absorb, memorise and hold attention in small units of three to seven minutes. It is supplanting more comprehensive skills and development courses, which take longer and have lengthy implementation tails.

Through any mobile device, modular chunks of learning, either structured as part of a course, or short sharp bits of content, are streamed mainly on video (YouTube being the most popular platform), sometimes supported by coaches or mentors. Importantly, this method is designed to achieve specific perfor-mance goals as a part of personalised learning pathways.

Instead of teaching by subject experts, learning is centred around identified problems. Students play an active role in creating and updating content through social interaction and exploration, via social media. Short, high-impact interventions are smartening up learning because it can be done faster, cheaper and more effectively, at scale, on demand. The old methods of job and executive training are being replaced.

Because sessions are short, employees go away with four or five takeaways around a single message relevant to their tasks, usually on 'how to do something' that can be implemented immediately.

Micro learning is gaining in popularity because it has so many advantages and can be done anywhere cost-effectively. Learners learn fast because they concentrate only on what they want to know how to do. And it gets better results. It is 17 per cent more efficient in the transfer of knowledge, reports say.[102]

Here are some of the advantages:
- Speed—course development time and update down 300 per cent
- Engagement—up 50 per cent
- Development costs—down 50 per cent
- Multitasking between various jobs on the go is easier
- Yields instant results
- Memory retention and recall levels are up
- Flexibility—it can be blended with structured courses or stand alone
- Inclusivity
- Autonomous and empowering.

Increasingly, self-motivated adults use the short sharp content to communicate ideas by video in anything from 15 seconds to 15 minutes. Once these are uploaded into the public sphere, such as on YouTube, they can be re-used for others to learn from at no cost, from 'how to grow tomatoes' to step-by-step instructions on 'how to build a tiny house'.

This has pulled in professionals, like doctors, sharing thoughts, updates, applications and procedures with colleagues to get learning and information across quickly at no cost.

TikTok, the video-creating and -sharing social media app, is perfect for the job. Up to now it has shown magnified growth in the young market, but it is growing in older-generation users in as many as 150 different countries. #EduTok was released in New Delhi by TikTok with high-impact interventions in Social Sciences, English, Mathematics, Hindi, Biology, Chemistry, etc. with an overwhelming 37-billion plus views.[103]

What more can possibly be said?

CHAPTER 15

Wishing waste away

Waste is a problem whose time has finally come and dealing with it needs to be ingrained in any contemporary business value formulation.

If the truth be said, until now it's been about consumers rather than suppliers spotting and driving down waste. But of late, with climate change palpably higher on people's agendas, most enterprises, governments and citizens fall somewhere on the continuum between two extremes of action: 'forced by litigation to do something about it' to 'dedicated to a zero-waste world'.

Stockholm (and its citizens) wants to be the first climate-positive city in the world by 2040. It aims to reduce carbon emissions with more efficient use of energy, less transport and less waste. New techniques have been designed for carbon capture and storage, combined with a district system that is fossil fuel free—no oil, gas or coal.

New waste-management systems have been devised and a method of collecting waste is under way with high-pressure tubes taking waste underground to a single collection centre. This means fewer garbage trucks and less space needed for dumping. Garbage bags are coloured differently for different kinds of waste, and through the use of optical sensors and weighing, residents receive data on their mobile phones about the amount of waste they have thrown away, for which they are charged.

The zero-waste extremists aren't just pushing for reducing waste—they want it eliminated altogether. They literally want no trash bins.

Recommerce, or ways to save resources by using less, recovering more, re-using, recycling, remanufacturing and beneficiating used materials and avoiding polluting or overusing the air, water or ground, is an emerging precept no one can avoid.

For distinguishers it is opening up opportunities.

Bring your own container

Zero-waste stores are sprouting everywhere, particularly in Europe, in countries like Germany, Italy, Spain and Norway, Sweden, Finland and Denmark, where customers come to stores or fast-food restaurants with their own packaging, weigh goods and leave with only what they will eat/use, re-use or recycle.

Enterprises are rethinking how they engage with and encourage this new behaviour. Waitrose is one of many supermarkets going plastic-free. Starting with plastic-free aisles in select stores, they intend to make 'no plastic' a permanent change in the way consumers buy.

The UK chain has designed refill stations supplied with dried goods like cereal, coffee, dried fruit, lentils, rice, etc., liquids such as wine, beer and detergents, and frozen fruit and vegetables, etc. Customers weigh what they want and take it home in their own containers. This anti-plastic move is a new way for people to shop guilt-free, says Waitrose. Refill and re-use systems are eliminating tons and tons of plastic waste which otherwise go into landfills.

Waitrose, which has dedicated roles for employees to get rid of plastic altogether, is also actively looking for alternative materials that are re-usable, easily recyclable or home-compostable for 100 per cent of its own-brand packaging by 2023, even for goods like meat, where packaging is hard to recycle.[104]

The impact of this on each and every member in the supply chain is gigantic.

Making energy circular

Data centres use a vast amount of electricity and generate a great deal of heat. To keep the servers operational, cooling systems are required, which themselves produce heat. Rather than waste the hot air, countries like Sweden and France are using it to heat apartments and homes, offices and public buildings. In Stockholm, instead of blowing heat into the air, the data centres sell the wasted resource to a heating company, which then sells it on. They say that by 2030 most of the new 140,000 apartments expected to be built in Stockholm will be heated this way. The same thing is done with the heat supermarkets generate, which is recycled back into the grid.

In many countries, energy companies will have to accept that they will be buying from and not selling to customers. Home-owners, as well as businesses, hotels and shopping centres, are installing new rooftop solar panels to produce energy, and thereby reduce their utility bills, or sell surplus heat that is released into the grid.

Storage of energy being the big obstacle, battery storage technology is taking centre stage in the fight to get ahead. Unique ideas are emerging fast and furiously. With electric cars being used more and more, they become potential storage units and, if connected to the grid, can be money-makers for owners when their cars are not being used, wherever they may be. Drivers will be able to carry renewable energy like a virtual grid.[105]

In countries like sunny Australia, homes have become the largest residential battery storage market in the world.

In the rush to balance energy demand and supply, car manufacturers like Tesla and VW are heavily invested in electric. So are oil companies like Shell, which wants to become the biggest electrical power company in the world by 2030.[106] And in ride-sharing, enterprises like Uber are planning to leverage electric fleets, creating battery storage systems that generate electricity, as a way into renewable energy opportunities.

Waste is wasted

Waste is not just the physical stuff that ends up in landfills. It's any inefficiency that wastes time, energy or resources of any kind.

Think about it. When Uber Eats or iFood, Brazil's largest food delivery platform (largely funded by Brazilians and South Africans), aggregates the kitchens of hundreds of restaurants into one central shared space, they are effectively reducing waste. Why should every restaurant have its own kitchen and carry the costs of it alone, distinguishers ask?

And why should households each have their own kitchens and appliances, etc., when brands that bulk up resources, reducing costs, energy and effort, can pass on these benefits in the form of fabulous meals on demand?

Of course, this may be an oversimplification, but the principle is what is important. New industries are developing around the notion of how to leverage wasted time, money and energy.

Why pay for waste?

In an innovative leap in thinking, South African startup, Naked, was determined to get the waste out of insurance premiums. Why, they asked, did customers have to pay for insurance when cars were stationary? What a waste!

From that single question this new distinguisher emerged to take its share of the car insurance market. With the click of a button customers can change, manage or cancel a premium. Everything is digitised and the savings are passed on to customers. Claims are instantly approved, sending the age-old haggling and small print on which the industry grew rich into the dustbin of history.

Another improvement on the system is that consumers can buy stand-alone insurance. This means they don't have to buy an entire household policy and pay extra for movables. They pay only for what they use and when they use it.

During the lockdown, Naked introduced CoverPause, which allows customers to downgrade to stationary cover on the days they are not driving, at one click. The savings can be up to 50 per cent on a premium, and the car is still covered for fire, theft or natural disasters while it's parked.

In healthcare, waste is prolific: much of the medication that is prescribed is wasted,[107] but so is medical equipment, bought or leased, including microscopes, lasers and surgical robots, because they are underutilised by hospitals, although they form a large part of the expenses.

Cohealo, based in Boston, US, is a cloud-based tracking, logistics and matching platform with the purpose of identifying lazy hospital infrastructure and cost-effective alternatives.

Through data analytics of where, when and how often medical equipment is used, Cohealo can assess equipment usage rates, pin-point equipment that is underused and save on capital expenditure and rent costs by sharing equipment across hospitals. It also compares and benchmarks between machines and facilities, and detects when equipment is overused to prevent downtime and costs.

During Covid, Cohealo's platform was extended to track ventilator availability, matching and delivering excess capability with hospitals experiencing shortages.

But Covid aside, the projected numbers make it an impressive opportunity. Machines are used on average only 20 per cent of the time. By pooling them, Cohealo can take this up to 80 per cent, saving billions for hospitals in the US and the NHS in the UK, where the pressure is on to do more with fewer resources.[108]

'Sharing medical equipment is an eight-figure per year savings opportunity for health systems,' said Cohealo's CEO, Todd Rothenhaus. 'Our 2,500th equipment share demonstrates that collaborative equipment management can be accomplished at scale, without asset damage or disruption to clinical workflows.'[109]

Surgeons get machines when they need them, and patients get on-demand access where and when they want it.

Why pay for duplication?

One of the arguments for autonomous cars is that they will be less wasteful—they are more likely to be fully utilised, a shift from one car one user to one car multiple users. Experts say they will also save millions of lives globally, eliminate congestion, reduce emissions and allow cities to be built around people, not cars.[110]

Proponents of co-living believe that each person who owns a house, laying out expensive upfront costs and paying for things that take up space and time, will be a thing of the past. Waste.

Enter IKEA and its future-living project. Space10 is a research and design lab in Denmark, where IKEA and other designers are envisioning new urban co-living. It is intergenerational (no loneliness), with modular construction (flexible adjustable spaces), and incorporates new, affordable financial models that allow co-habitants to buy shares in the community until they can afford to own their own home. Takers will have the choice of furniture that is modular (changeable/adaptable), made for small spaces and durable.

Services and resources will be shared instead of duplicated, like daycare, urban farming, local water harvesting, shopping chores, insurance, entertainment, digital interfacing and con-nectedness, dining, clean energy production, recycling, fitness, cleaning, transport and recreation. Homes can be swapped if circumstances change, and rooms can be offered out for the day if they are not being used.

Getting only what you need

On-demand delivery of good food, and the at-home high-quality cooking experience, became mega important during lockdown.

The jump in demand was quickly absorbed by meal-platform contenders such as Blue Apron. Its original market was people who like in-home cooking and making good food for the family or a special event. It's a subscription 'farm to table' meal kit concept, consisting of fresh goods, recipes and wine. Consumers choose from a myriad of recipes to make what they like to eat, for routine meals or particular eating events. It has inspired hundreds of thousands of consumers in the US and UK.

Part of Blue Apron's purpose was to eliminate food waste, because customers get only what they need to use. Not only does the meal kit eliminate wasted ingredients, it also gets rid of wasted shopping time, which appeals especially to people coping with busy modern lifestyle schedules but refusing to compromise standards. On top of that, it boasts that it elevates cooking skills and promotes family activity and better eating habits, by replacing less healthy fast food.

Throw away throwaway

France passed a law in 2015 to stop enterprises from deliberately building obsolescence into their products. That, plus the push from the minimalist movement, has influenced consumers world-wide to buy durable goods and avoid overconsumption.

The change in sentiment and behaviour, from wanting tangible stuff to intangible experiences that have more meaning, has presented brands with new opportunities. The worldwide figure for people preferring experiences over material things today is 76 per cent, said to be even higher for millennials.[111]

Among other developments, this has created a second-hand market in almost anything. Before Covid, research showed that over 50 per cent of consumers would spend more on second-hand goods in the coming years.[112]

- LEGO for instance, which makes 20 billion bricks a year, is giving them a new lease on life. Instead of being discarded once the thrill of making the model is over (or becoming landmines), the pre-owned sets are rented to customers on a subscription basis.
- IKEA is renting out its furniture to students and expatriates.

- Apple reconditions phones and takes back old versions to recycle, renovate and sell on.
- And in clothing, second-hand or worn wear is a peaking market. BuyMeOnce went viral almost immediately, which prompted founder Tara Button to give up her full-time profession and pursue the platform that pushes for throwing away the throwaway mentality. Consumers are offered a wide range of durable goods that are ethically made and come with a lifetime guarantee or good fixing services, which the brand believes is cheaper in the long run for consumers and the cosmos.[113]
- Built to last is the guiding principle for Patagonia, the Argentinian environmental activist outdoor-clothing maker. Its whole philosophy is based on the idea that clothes should be worn over many seasons. They make such good products that people don't want to throw them away, and when they do, they take them back to the seller which makes new garments from them. The company also repairs customers' clothes in 72 repair centres globally. Famously, in its Worn Wear campaign, employees went to college campuses and climbing centres to teach outdoor enthusiasts how to repair their clothing.

  The reason this brand is important is because it crosses the boundary between corporate and activist to create a new kind of brand that is swiftly changing consumption and production patterns. The number of so-called belief-driven customers buying in this way is growing fast worldwide and, in the US, it's believed to be around 60 per cent of all shoppers today.[114]

Less longer is the new luxury

Luxury fashion has been marked by oversupply, expensive celebrity shows, produce-produce production and high-budget advertising. To commit to exclusivity, stores had to buy numbers they couldn't always sell, but had to return the unsold items to vendors, resulting in oversupply and waste.

The model didn't work.

Today, even in fashion, the emphasis is on durability and making and selling what lasts. Not least because apparel and footwear account for 8 per cent of the harmful greenhouse gas emissions caused by human activities globally.[115]

Luxury brands have begun to understand that they have lost out on sustainability to lower-cost brands, and they are now making goods that are materially more durable, with a longer shelf life, to win new-paradigm customers.

But that doesn't go far enough, say durability advocates. When clothes last functionally, but not emotionally, it leads to waste. So, long-lasting has to encompass physical and emotional durability, in line with the desire of new high-income consumers for vintage, upcycled and vegan materials combined with fashion.

Also, sustainability is not just about materials, it's about eradicating throwaway behaviour. Garments have to be forged with meaning and empathy that mirrors new values so that longer-term relationships can be built with them. The object is to get customers to cherish and want to keep, care and use goods to retain their value for life.

And if not that, at least find a way to revitalise used fashion garments or parts of garments, and make the resale pre-owned market integral to fashion-brand strategies.

The alternative resell model in fashion is being taken up fast, especially online. Globally it is expected to grow three times as quickly as retail in the coming years and to stretch into other luxury areas like watches and sneakers, with some resold brands fetching more than the original retail price.

Stella McCartney and Burberry are two examples of brands that never want their items to end up as waste. They have partnered with the recommerce America-based bricks and clicks player, The RealReal, to incentivise customers to consign their worn luxury goods to it and give them a second life.

The RealReal reports that sales are increasing exponentially as behaviour shifts (so-called resale demand). To supplement closets with second-hand high brands, Levi has a range of jeans which are especially durable, made from fully recycled material and plastic bottles.

Eileen Fisher has a take-back programme, which has brought in over a million garments. Rather than the old make-buy-waste model, it makes clothes with circularity in mind—return, resell or repurpose. Worn or used clothes are refurbished or broken up and reassembled to create new unique garments or one-off pieces of art.

It's what's known in India as '*Kabaad se jugaad*', Hindi for turning waste into something useful and beautiful.

Slow fashion

Also on the rise are distinguisher brands making clothes that don't conflict with each other seasonally, which encourages waste. Instead, they intentionally make modular collections that can be built up year on year, so that wardrobes can be revitalised but have a longer life.

This move to slow fashion is a counterbalance to the fall in popularity of fast fashion,[116] with its limited editions and new collections at each season, and is radically altering the fashion landscape. Instead of fashion buyers buying collections twice a year, some of which would sell and some of which wouldn't, brands are going direct to consumers much more often (every six weeks as opposed to every six months), and are increasingly making on-demand clothes only.

There is less waste, less proliferation of product, less cost, and whoever has slow fashion feels part of a crowd in the know.

In the streetwear and middle-brand market we see the same trend. Suspicious Antwerp, founded by two 20-year-old students, is a street brand attracting models and celebs. Collections are released online, limited orders are taken directly from customers and only what has been pre-ordered and paid for is made.

More of this in mainstream markets, and the fashion model will be turned inside out irrevocably. Whereas in the past, buyers made decisions about what went into stores, which is how goods were procured and distributed (the more the better), now customers decide what they want and brands are produced in limited editions (often), with luxury created through product scarcity as opposed to price.

It's the opposite of planned obsolescence and everything else conventional minds and models believed in and built.

It's about less waste.

And less now means more.

Truly.

CHAPTER 16

Turning the invisible into assets

Instead of waste being ignored and ending up in landfills, increasingly it is being seen as a potential asset. Awesome projects are underway all around the globe. From turning plastic into 3D printing filament, ocean plastic waste into sneakers, food waste into bioplastics, or using leftover coffee grounds to grow mushrooms as a meat substitute.

Invisible waste is a little more subtle. It's there, but not obvious, and its value is increasingly being unlocked by distinguishers.

One of the ways they are doing this is by taking what was previously idle, ignored or invisible and turning it into an asset.

Individual consumers are beginning to ask, 'What do I have or know that I can monetise?'; 'Do I have spare computer processing power?', 'Do I have an idle car or tool to share, excess electricity or solar power to sell on, or capabilities knowledge or talent I can realise online?'. 'Can I trade in micro urban farming or alternative currencies?'

Elon Musk is encouraging this emerging idea, saying that customers should be able to earn a return from the assets they buy and own. His interlinked batteries, for example, are virtual power plants in and across buildings and homes (capturing energy from solar panels) in both Australia and the UK, with other countries soon to follow. These batteries can be connected to the grid as well as to Tesla cars that can be converted into auto robotic taxis.[117]

During the pandemic, enterprises like Walmart were beginning to ask, 'Why have empty parking spots at night when they could be put to use?' This is another of those next-case now epics that are likely to stick. Walmart converted 160 US stores to drive-in theatres at night, making an invisible asset multi-usable. This was a safe way for consumers to have a night out and watch their favourite movies. Picnic treats and food from curbside stops were offered from the Walmart stores, which quickly repurposed space and staff to prepare and serve meals, kicking in loads of cross-cutting synergies.

Admittedly, Covid-19 drove drive-in behaviour, but it's gone so well that it is likely to be a trend here to stay, running headlong with and parallel to the movie-streaming trend rocking the world.

In another distinguishing innovation, Walmart converted its parking spaces into mini towns across the US, complementing its supermarkets. This concept includes shops, restaurants, markets and entertainment and fitness centres.

These are just some examples of assets that have been invisible turned into a major opportunity.

Matching waste to want

Distinguishers know how to spot wasted invisible assets (not used or underused) and how to make them available to consumers. Some examples include: cars standing idle (offered to Uber drivers); unused cupboards, garages, sheds, attics (Neighbor storage); empty parking spots (JustPark); empty rooftops (urban farming); unnecessary waiting (GoCar car-sharing); too much garbage (zero waste); every business owning its own server (the cloud); too much wasted living space (IKEA's compact co-living concept).

And thanks to two-sided marketplace platforms, any invisible resource that can be spotted can be turned into value instantly, if someone can be found who wants it. With no middle people to have to pay, this materialised waste can be sold at infinitely lower cost.

So, in sum:
- Assets that have been invisible, can become money-generators for their owners.
- Brand intellectual property (IP) is increasingly about knowing who needs what and who has what, including being able to predict and pre-empt patterns.
- Customer experiences created from invisible assets turned to commercial value must be frictionless and cost-effective compared to the alternatives.
- Value must be shared in a win-win model for the brand, asset owner and user.
- Quality standards for demand and supply of assets must be maintained through reliable ranking and rating.

Here are some examples of two-sided marketplace platform distinguishers that match waste to want:

AIRBNB: *rooms, homes*
Airbnb founders needed some cash and because they predicted that people would be looking for space in hotels during the high-peak conference season in San Francisco, they rented out their room with air mattresses and breakfast.

The idea morphed into matching wasted space (rooms, homes) with a want (accommodation needed by people travelling for holiday or work). Airbnb connects hosts (now numbering nearly 3 million with 14,000 joining per month) who want to rent out space in their homes with travellers (7 million actively listed in 220 countries), creating an affordable and more sociable alternative to hotels where guests don't really need much of what they are paying for.[118]

To bring its brand into the hospitality space (instead of just renting out empty rooms), Airbnb embarked on a #OneLessStranger social experiment, in which it encouraged its host community to make hospitality gestures to their guests and other people in their community and post photographs of them on social media, which got a resoundingly positive response.

Its somewhat tarnished stratospheric popularity, during the shutdown, didn't stop Airbnb from creating virtual online matching experiences so that hosts sitting at home could be put to work and generate income. They can entertain travellers in their home virtually, by spending online time with them, giving classes like cooking or cocktail mixing. Or groups can be brought together on Zoom to engage in special events and with unfamiliar cultures, from virtual bike rides with an Olympic champion to coffee courses with a Turkish expert and meditation with a Japanese monk.

ROVER: *time and care*

Over half the people who own dogs in America say it's harder to find a good dog-walker than the perfect spouse![119] Rover.com is the online platform that connects people looking for help when they cannot be with their animals with people who have time and love pets. Rover now has 200,000 people who fit the pet-sitter/pet-walker profile in the US, and has expanded into the UK and Europe to become the number one pet-service site in the world.

TASKRABBIT: *freelance labour*

US-based Taskrabbit takes the wasted time and skill of people who are unemployed, retired or able to work in free time, and matches it to households or individuals in need of everyday household tasks or chores. These include running errands, decoration, furniture assembly, cleaning, delivery, shopping and handy work.

AI and machine learning enable precise matching of taskers with a task within a few minutes, to maximise the likelihood that a job will get done successfully and earn the tasker repeat business. From clients' 'to do' lists they can also optimise time and people. And Taskrabbit has built up sufficient learning to be able to now predict tasks that will be required in a home so it can encourage repeat business and growth for itself and its 'taskers'.

This freelance task-based platform has monetised the millions of hours of wasted skill and time that taskers have and turned them from an inactive to an active labour force in a win-win model across 70 major cities in the US, and in the UK, Canada, France, Germany and Spain.

NEIGHBOR: *storage, space*
Airbnb-inspired, just with stuff instead of people, Neighbor—based in Salt Lake City—has become an international distinguisher displacing the storage industry's mighty but mature empire, characterised by high overheads and resistance to technology.

Its online matching platform puts people who have storage, from closets to barns, garages to empty rooms or sheds, together with people who have unused stuff to store.

This more convenient, cheaper, safer and close-to-home alternative has spread like wildfire.

On this peer-to-peer network platform, home-owners can inspect the goods to be stored and set their own price, and renters and hosts can insure goods. This closes the chapter on the quote estimates, waiting for return calls, dreary facilities and contracts that the old-school self-storage companies have forced customers to accept.

JUSTPARK: *parking real estate*
With a quarter of all driving experiences plagued with parking problems that waste precious time, JustPark decided to make parking easier and quicker for customers and at the same time re-purpose underutilised real estate in homes, hotels and businesses.

With 45,000 active locations throughout the UK and 4.5 million customers paying monthly subscriptions saving costs without long contracts or commitment, this platform is matching drivers and free parking spaces in a win-win formula.

PATAGONIA ACTION WORKS: *volunteers and activists*
Patagonia has developed a digital social recruiting platform that puts together environmental activists with over 700 grant organisations, to have conversations around causes, solicit donations, post calendar events and seek out volunteers. It helps people to contribute skills and volunteer to do everything from stand for office to help build an NGO.

CHAPTER 17

Mobilising the crowdforce

Crowds are becoming more powerful. Mexico even allowed the crowd to create its Constitution in 2016.

Commercially, crowds are an important source of economic value for distinguishers. Where would Google or Wikipedia be without them?

Two sets of heads or data are better than one, and a crowd of heads much more so.

Distinguishers are using crowds in various smart ways to form an integral part of what can be best described as a part-time distributed ecosystem—a crowdforce—in a formal or informal capacity.

The crowd can help fund (as a bank or venture capitalist would do), innovate (be part of or replace R&D), produce (help make prototypes), provide data (to make products and services smarter), distribute (store and deliver), service (help other customers fix problems) and inform and influence (be part of sales and marketing teams).

The participatory culture

To understand how crowds think and work we have to understand participatory culture.

Customers were originally intended to buy, not to participate. It was us and them. Not 'we'.

Until the crowd came along.

The crowd as a political force goes back to Ancient Greek times, but it wasn't until the Internet that we really understood how much the crowd could either be enticed or voluntarily become an economic force and driver of tangible value.

Whether or not they are customers is irrelevant. What matters is that people in a crowd are a resource. They have an opinion, skill, voice, creativity and they have time that they want to use, individually, as a single member of a community or jointly as a group.

So here is a view of the new crowd-powered distinguisher factory:

TABLE 17.1: *New Factory: Major Resource—Crowd*

Labour	The crowd (working part-time, not owned nor controlled)
Material	Content, skill, money (from many)
Machine	The Internet (and, increasingly, mobile smartphones)
Fuel	Data, information, knowledge, advice, innovation (collective IQ)
Workforce motivator	Participation, status and/or currency (social or financial equity)
Marketing tool	Social media (communicate and influence)
Reward for brand	Scale and speed at low cost

To use the crowd, brands need to understand what makes this human phenomenon tick.

Clearly there has to be reciprocity. A crowd has to give as well as get back in some way. Sometimes it's by way of reward, sometimes it's just kudos and affirmation or recognition from peers, because it is the crowd that confers status and stature to those who make a contribution.

YouTube built its success on the crowd, particularly before Google bought it, when all the content was user-generated (today, most content comes from professionals) and revenue was shared with those with the most streamed content. Around 60 per cent of all Internet traffic is YouTube usage, nearly 80 per cent of Internet users have a YouTube account, 16 per cent of all video streaming is from YouTube, and it has 2 billion users.[120]

It is said that, every minute, 400 or more hours of video are posted on the YouTube site. That's a lot of content, all built by the crowd, and turned into currency.

The individuals who attract the most attention can monetise it by becoming YouTubers, TikTokers, Instagrammers, Twitterers, podcasters, advocates, bloggers, etc., because they amass followers and gain influence.

Money is not usually what drives participatory culture, but money may be an outcome. Participants thrive usually because they are making a contribution, learning new skills, meeting new people and enjoying themselves. Typically, they express themselves through memes (an image, video, piece of text, which is often funny, copied and spread rapidly), fanfiction (fiction written by a fan of and featuring characters from a particular TV series, film, book, e.g. Harry Potter), mashups (e.g. two different songs combined into one), not because these creations will necessarily be commercialised, but because they are fun to do.

Beyond these hot activities, crowd individuals also engage in deep, complex problem-solving. This is how Linux was developed and how open source happened.

The crowd is meritocratic and the quality of contribution is what matters. If individuals in the crowd are not integrous, they lose their power base. Peer recognition drives success. The more a person contributes something smart about a product, service or brand, the more stature she or he acquires and the smarter the crowd becomes. And the smarter the crowd becomes, the more powerful it becomes.

Crowdsourcing is getting crowded

Crowdsourcing is a way of harnessing and leveraging the crowd's economic value, by pulling people out there together, at scale and speed and low cost, over multiple countries and continents and timelines, ostensibly as a resource, in order to tap their knowledge and time and turn it into value. They are free, unencumbered by structure or authority, and work individually or self-organise to solve problems.

Amazon has been using the crowd for years to feed its algorithm with data, in order to better understand customers' preferences and create a competitive advantage. Apple's Siri uses the crowd to search for answers to uncommon questions it may be asked that it can't find in its database but are likely to be answered by someone on the wider Web, making the Internet inhabitants the largest crowd of all.

When enterprises solved problems in the past, they relied on what they knew, if they knew what they knew and could harness it. Now they can get the wisdom and effort of an entire crowd.

Being part of something bigger is not new. We've all been members of a club at one time, where like-minded people gather at a physical destination. Now they come together virtually, with interests that are equally social, emotional and/or financial.

Members of crowds are anywhere and everywhere, geographically and digitally, networked and connected, mixing, matching and morphing into groups depending on the circumstance.

Because they are global by nature, their value unencumbered by space, time, distance or culture, digital crowds can contain people who were previously marginalised and/or inaccessible, and they can serve a demand (e.g. crowdfunding) or a supply purpose (e.g. software development).

When crowds behave as an entity, they have a voice and members influence each other's behaviour and decision-making. We see this politically all the time, and increasingly so. Commercially, crowds can be equally forceful.

Crowds participate in and fund projects they are interested in, either as a donation or for some gain. They may produce solutions or things together, sometimes for money, other times because they want to show that they can make something work better. By sharing their intelligence and expertise collectively, enterprises can harness the collective wisdom of the crowd and make them a new powerful economic factor of production and consumption.

The crowd as an influencer

Crowds influence customers and enterprises to behave differently.

For example, crowds decide on the score of something and influence its value. And we know that apps that get higher scores get higher downloads. Of the top Apple apps, for instance, 70 per cent have four stars or more.[121]

Crowd reviews have an influence on buyer choice and where brands are placed in search listings. We know definitively that positive reviews impact sales favourably, more so than ever before. The more expensive a product is, the higher the correlation is between a high score and an actual purchase, and the same principle holds for negative reviews.

Reviews are aggregated by the brand itself, or by independents like Trustpilot. The point is that there has to be trust, which comes from both objectivity and knowledge. To maintain credibility, Amazon once fired book reviewers because they were being paid to give good book reviews.

Members of crowds give advice to each other, so raising standards and best practice. SodaStream's US Facebook page of

700,000-odd people talk to each other, give tips about healthier or more delicious ways of using the product, cleaning the equipment, what syrups to try, how to refill SodaStream tanks or get them cheaper, including using members of the crowd to deliver so as to save money.

Crowds decide whether something is good or bad. The crowd reacts, proacts and influences what brands do. For example, the 7-million-strong Nespresso Club community of coffee-lovers and connoisseurs forced the brand to start making recyclable pods. And it was the crowd who chose George Clooney as the brand ambassador, central to Nespresso's popular advertising and video campaign.

The crowd as a funding mechanism

Entrepreneurs used to rely on one source at a time to supply funds, whether it was banks, venture capitalists or angel investors, and always with complex procedures. And if one source refused or stalled, chances were the others would refuse too, or decisions would take too long and the opportunity would be missed.

Crowdfunding is an extension of the age-old practice of a friend or family member lending small bits as a decentralised way of giving or taking. Borrowing/lending or funding/investing is gaining traction worldwide, using pooled money from the crowd, on a peer-to-peer (P2P) platform.

Barack Obama famously changed the game when he funded his 2008 campaign from small amounts from many donors in the crowd, rather than relying on a few high-paying contributors.

Now, people with a story to tell about a great idea for a business can appeal to the crowd to help get it started, and members of the crowd can contribute with fractions of the total funding required for a project they are interested in or want to see work.

The entrepreneur sets a funding goal and additionally can test the demand for a product before production starts. Whereas startups might otherwise remain obscure, crowdfunding now gives them global exposure, because audiences cut across country boundaries, spanning the world.

Ask people (as we did) which crowdfund they know, and it's likely they will have heard of Kickstarter. The brand distinguishes itself by funding creative projects and therefore attracting early adopters at scale and speed. It prides itself on injecting funds into many new ventures (nearly 200,000 projects by 2020), through the billions of dollars it has raised.

The power of small, fast contributions is extraordinary. Pebble, the prototype for today's smart watch, was funded by Kickstarter and later sold to Fitbit for USD 40 million (Pebble's software is still powering Fitbit's smart watches). With Kickstarter, US-based Reading Rainbow, encouraging children to read, was brought back in digital form by raising almost USD 5.5 million from 105,857 backers. And 3D printer Snapmaker 2.0, the most-funded technology project in Kickstarter history, raised USD 7.8 million in only 30 days.[122]

Community tools enable members to see how many people have invested in the project, how many are returning investors, comments by individuals, where backers are from and how much has been pledged. And if they choose to connect with individuals they can.

Rewards can be return-bearing, but vary from project to project, like: being the first to know what's happening; being first to get a new product, or first in line for goods still to be made (i.e. becoming an early adopter); having an experience unique to that venture (e.g. holding an event in a new shop); learning how to make your own version of the goods (from chocolate to shoes); being part of the creative process; visiting new premises (like a factory, shop or restaurant); access to management, first options on products, dividends or equity.

People might donate money because they support an idea or feel it's important enough to get close to. Unlike Kickstarter, the Patreon platform is a place for ongoing crowdfunding. Patreons give money monthly to content creators who post regularly online but don't get paid for it. Typically, these people are artists, writers, podcasters, musicians, comic traders, videographers, etc.

By getting a regular monthly income from this active crowd of three million, each member of which decides who they want to support, creatives are able to stay in business and keep up their standards. Patreon processed over USD 500 million in 2019 and the numbers of receivers are going up, the highest earner earning USD 145,000 monthly![123] Patreons get the satisfaction of supporting the people whose work they like and listen to, as well as getting exclusive content that is not distributed elsewhere.

This said, and notwithstanding the fact that some backers may have many reasons for investing other than financial return, as they begin to see that some of the ideas become big and go on to be acquired or become an IPO, there is and will be increasing pressure from them to acquire equity so that they can reap the benefits that manifest in the longer term, which are likely to be substantial.

The crowd as a tester

Gaining popularity as a way of making sure customer experiences with digital products are optimised, is involving members of the crowd, particularly millennials, to provide feedback because they like to be involved and also get rewarded.

Headquartered in Germany, Testbirds, a crowd tester, tests existing and newly proposed digital products for large global corporations in real-world settings. Its online community, which stretches over 193 countries and is over 400,000 strong, consists of freelance expert testers and end users.[124] Mostly, it tests mobile apps, websites and software (like games, wearables, IoT, smart devices, etc.) in order to eliminate bugs and make sure the product is functioning optimally and meets user-friendly standards.

Google has relied on the crowd to catch bugs in its system, and its spending increases every year on its Vulnerability

Rewards Program, which attracts researchers from everywhere to look for and rectify security faults.

Bugcrowd, a US newcomer gone global security crowdsource platform, has a team of 60,000 security tester-experts working at scale and speed across several countries to make sure apps and software are free from security issues at inception and through use. A year after it was launched, Bugcrowd grew by 400 per cent, matching a freelance workforce with vendors who want to improve their security posture and prevent cyber attacks but without having to have the costs of a full maintenance team.[125]

The crowd as an innovator

The crowd is a constant source of innovation.

Members of the crowd are increasingly being used by distinguishers in a remote-worker culture, as partners, to innovate, produce or test new products, particularly digital ones. Evidently, more than half of all the companies who use the crowd use it for this purpose today, in order to tap talent at scale and speed while not having to carry the full overhead costs.

The results are majorly rewarding, particularly if the crowd is being asked to solve a specific problem. Unilever Foundry, an open innovation platform created to harness ideas from the crowd, aligns crowd input to its sustainable-living vision. The crowd is provided with briefs around specific problems in different countries and takes part in paid pilot programmes to help incubate them.

A good proportion of innovator crowds are customers themselves. On an open platform, fans and partners from all over the world develop content that make up LEGO's collaborative extended R&D team, in addition to its hundreds of in-house developers designing mind-blowing creations, like life-size pianos made from bricks, which play tunes when attached to a smartphone. And anyone in the LEGO crowd who gets a product made, gets a piece of the earnings.

LEGO's Mindstorm, a system of software and hardware for programmable robots, has a community of professionals and hobbyists of all ages who use forums and videos on YouTube to share new designs and ideas. Teams of schoolchildren are challenged in contests to design, build and program robots with educational themes, like climate control. Adults, too, are a source of inspiration and solid part of LEGO's R&D crowdforce because they are an important market in the play space, which is getting overwhelmingly competitive.

The crowd can create innovations that it shares among themselves. Using the Reddit platform, over 225,000 users of Spotify create and share software to generate charts and playlists, providing this community with constant ways to discover and recommend music from Spotify's 50-million song library. No doubt Spotify uses this to inform their own innovation roadmap.

Importantly, innovation can be scaled very quickly and cost-effectively by the crowd. So, for example, if people find a good script via the IfThisThenThat (ITTT) app to improve automation or behaviour in their home, they can post it instantly and make it part of the brand's inventory.

But perhaps what is most profound is the ongoing innovation coming from open source. Today, 98 per cent of the open-source software currently used has come from the decentralised crowdforce.[126]

That's how Finnish engineering student, Linus Torvalds, building on Stallman's work, wrote Linux, an operating system making its source code available on the Internet, so that others can contribute to it, modify it or create new software from it. And so propelled open source, which has fast become the non-proprietary alternative to creating software with communities of developers who have become a mighty crowdforce. They don't work for, report to or get paid by any centralised organisation. They self-organise and typically do this work in their spare time outside of their day jobs.

The crowd as an on-demand service provider

With the freelance gig economy growing faster than the permanent workforce in many countries, there is an excess pool of part-time skills that can become the tech-heavy but asset-light service arm of enterprises, used to smartly harness the power of the crowd.

Distinguishers use this approach as a game-changer to win and keep customers.

If a brand mobilises the crowd and thereby saves on the costs of employee benefits, warehousing, fleets, etc., which it passes on to its customers, this can provide it with a significant edge.

In food and package delivery this business model is getting huge traction, where non-professional locals are increasingly being used as couriers in fulfilment. And it won't stop there as the model scales. The more it is used, the more it becomes ever perfected and accepted.

This new way of managing a crowd-based field force is gaining in popularity for simple as well as highly complex tasks. The brand gets a broad geo-spread band of first responder freelancers without overhead commitment, as well as increased flexibility for demand and supply highs and lows.

Customers get on-demand service, which minimises wasted time, money and effort, downtime of mission-critical machines and frustration with unpredictable delivery, unapproachable hotlines and reticent responses, the demise of many service departments in incumbent organisations.

SWISSCOM CASE
Swisscom, one of Switzerland's largest mobile service operators, has used crowdservice to build a real-time on-demand field force in maintenance and repair, with stellar results. Requests and turnarounds for its 5-million-strong customer base are achieved in under an hour 80 per cent of the time. Thousands of freelance

engineers are employed, receiving requests via mobile app and providing technical services. After completion, they are rated by the customer to maintain quality levels. Three years after introducing the on-demand crowdservice, its customer churn problem reduced dramatically.

Through Mila Swiss, a crowdservice online marketplace (in which Swisscom has a majority stake), big brands can quickly match freelance services to residential consumers, to handle anything from trouble-shooting to high-powered technical support, at affordable prices.

Swisscom Friends is a special field community that has been set up by the brand, to connect customers with other customers or technically minded neighbours who are prepared to give support, ranging from answering questions online to handling minor technical telecom challenges in people's homes.

CHAPTER 18

Owning fractionally

Fractional ownership has taken on like crazy. Not that it's new (it started in France in the 1960s). It offers people the opportunity to buy a part-share in something they could otherwise not afford. It's already standard practice in the upper-income bracket for high-value assets like real estate (luxury-leisure second homes), art or yachts, where ownership, cost and time are shared according to holding.

But what is new is that increasingly it has a social rather than just commercial function, which means it's another market that distinguishers can scale.

Solving for social inclusion

With fractional ownership moving into middle- maybe even lower-income and young markets, brands across the world are making deliberate attempts to disrupt existing industries that have hitherto excluded these markets, or made it too difficult for them to get in.

Here are some examples:

Investments and shares
Of course, the stock exchange has always been about fractional ownership, that's what shares are about (as is Bitcoin).

But distinguishers have taken away the red tape and expensive broker fees and come up with digital concepts combined with ideas from the sharing economy that are leaping ahead, changing how people invest and winning them over in droves.

In the process, they are democratising markets, effectively breaking down barriers to entry and making investments more inclusive. Overlooked markets can now partially own assets they couldn't get to before.

South Africa's Capitec, which distinguished itself by being first to serve the unbanked with a low-cost, paperless, accessible value proposition, partnered with EasyEquities, pioneer of fractional access to shares, in order to get millions of more 'ordinary' (its words) South Africans invested in the financial markets. In the words of one executive, 'common folk to attain uncommon goals'.[127]

The Web platform of EasyEquities allows customers to buy and sell whole or part-shares directly, in publicly traded companies. Because its app and Capitec's are integrated, Capitec can trade at scale, speed and low cost and give its customers the benefit. On their bank's app via a mobile phone, customers can do in seconds what they never could before—buy or sell listed or part-shares at a 20 per cent discount thanks to no brokerage fees.

EasyEquities has also teamed up with FlexClub so that anyone can invest in a share or part of a share of a ride-hailing car or fleet for as little as ZAR 100 and receive dividends from income earned by this newly created asset class. And the same concept will easily be transferred to buildings.

A bit is good enough

Farming

In farming, it is fascinating that owning fractionally addresses two social issues simultaneously: the crisis of low productivity of smallholdings and consequent food shortage, and allowing people to release their funds to invest. The idea is simply: how to enable individuals to invest partially in a farm they would otherwise not have access to, while funding the many smallholder farmers who have low crop yield and are unable to grow because traditional banks ignore them.

A merging of crowdfarming and fractional ownership has shown that the age-old business model, that every farmer has to own as well as fund a farm, can be changed.

In crowdfarming, farms involved come in different sizes, shapes and forms, from orange farms in Naranjas del Carmen north of Valencia in Spain, to cheese farms in Saxony-Anhalt, in Germany.

Or in Nigeria (the biggest market in Africa), which imports billions of dollars of food annually, where 80 per cent of its farmers are smallholders but account for 40 per cent of the poor because they have no access to funds, crowdfarming platforms like Thrive Agric are growing ferociously month on month. Food shortages and poverty are improved because consumers are now able to fractionally invest in parts of a farm or units of rice or numbers of chickens and so on.[128] Armkart does the same with fish farms.[129]

Thrive Agric provides micro loans at scale and speed to millions of small farmers constrained by lack of capital. It also provides what it calls good-practice agricultural methods (environmentally sustainable), based on technology-driven services and scenarios. These include planting practices improved by soil and weather tests, as well as aggregated access to market linkages, large buyers and insurance. All of this 'helps them skip a long chain of middlemen', says Uka Eje, the CEO.[130]

Livestock

Culturally, livestock has always been regarded as the oldest form of wealth in Africa. Now, Livestock Wealth, the brainchild of entrepreneur Ntuthuko Shezi, has tapped into what he calls 'the 100 million cow potential in Africa', in which consumers can invest, not impacted by financial market volatility. His idea is to free up the hidden value in the farming business, a market underserved, overlooked and underperforming, in order to help farmers raise the funds they need so badly to make their farms viable.

The stock exchange is complicated and has barriers to entry. Shezi wanted the opposite to make his venture inclusive and easy.

Stokvels (buying clubs) or individuals buy a cow or part of a cow. It's irrelevant where investors live, or if they know anything about farming, or whether they want the whole or part of a livestock asset. In fact, investors come from all walks of life from many countries. Germans, Americans, Canadians, Irish, English and Chinese people who are now willing and able to own shares or portions of shares in yet another emerging new class of asset.

Zero-waste harvests

Put crowdfarming, fractional ownership and the move to zero waste together and what we get is two entrepreneurs who started a farm in Spain, with a dream to get people to buy only what they intend to consume. They allow customers to choose a tree or a beehive or a plant or a portion of a garden, and invest financially in it, thus making farms and the farmers who own them ecologically and financially regenerative. The harvest is then delivered to the investor's door on the due date, with full knowledge of all the planting and process protocols used.

And the farm is financially as well as eco-agriculturally sustainable.

Property

Many people confuse the fractional ownership of property with holiday 'timeshare'. Timeshare has come with problems—properties don't appreciate in value, they are hard to sell, the onus for maintenance is shared by owners, and usage tends to be low.

With fractional ownership, people who don't know each other jointly invest in a holiday home, which is looked after, and they have access to the property and share in the benefits and risks. This dramatically reduces costs and allows them to enjoy not only one property, but a pool of properties in one country or many.

The trend is sweeping across the US, Europe and Asia, becoming popular as an alternative investment option. In Dubai, for instance, SmartCrowd, the first regulated fractional real-estate digital platform, offers individuals and families micro investments at scale in residential properties. Investors earn rental income in the form of dividends proportionate to the investment, which can be as little as USD 1,400.

Waiting for a distinguisher is the fractional ownership of personal homes, where instead of consumers owning a whole home and therefore always being short of cash, they may prefer to own part of a home and have some cash left over to spend on other things. The next normal?

This would radically alter notions of ownership and behaviour and force banks to look at the total cost of owning a home, instead of splitting it into silo bits. Customers would, for example, have cash over for decoration, alterations, extensions, gardens, cars, etc., all of which they currently need to apply for separately, if they can afford it at all.

Hospitality

Lately, in hospitality resorts, vacation clubs and hotels, fractional ownership has taken off among the middle and some lower-income markets and it's said that this is the future of vacations in South America. In Brazil, demand in holiday accommodation has always exceeded supply and so the market was quick to take to fractional ownership despite having experienced the old problems of timesharing.

Mainly, the attraction is that it's a simple transaction, there are very long periods over which payments can be made, and these partially owned facilities can be interchanged for the millions of people that have responded.

The fractional approach doesn't just give multi-owners access to a home for holidays, it also gives them an appreciation of tourism property and an investment in a thriving market.

CHAPTER 19

Being local is in

Global brands know that to stay relevant they have to localise in every way, from management to materials, process to preference, construction to content.

That's old news and being done very well in the main.

But something else is afoot.

Perhaps accelerated by Covid-19, but in the making for some time now, locals increasingly are buying local, unpicking the conventional globalisation model in order to become more self-reliant.

Several layered forces are driving this agenda, like:

- GOVERNMENTS: for example, in the US, China and the UK, and in India, where Prime Minister Narendra Modi's 'vocal for local' campaign urges support for indigenous manufacturers pushing to turn their roots to rupees.

- MOVEMENTS: such as 'Buy Local' in the US, Canada and the UK, to name some, started and run bottom up, with pledges, signage, incentives and competitions nationwide, mobilising consumers to change their buying habits and increase the local share of sales.

- **BRANDS:** such as American Express are spurring this on in their own way. In its 'Small Business Saturday' campaign in the US, which it is replicating in other markets, such as 'Shop Small' in the UK and 'Boomerang Dollar' in Australia, customers are being rewarded with cash in local currency for buying local. Amex reported that the campaign had raised USD 20 billion in local spending in one day.[131]

- **CONSUMERS:** Local has just taken on new meaning and importance, going from fringe to mainstream buying: in the US (93 per cent), Africa as a whole (73 per cent), South Africa (about the same)[132], the Middle East (73 per cent), Europe with Italy, France, Spain, Germany, UK and most of Scandinavia (66 per cent).[133]

The 'buy local' trend is predominantly in food. In the US, food made within a 400-kilometre radius ('local') grew from USD 5 billion to 20 billion between 2010 and 2020.[134]

The research indicates that people want to be healthier, pretty much across the board—at the top, bottom and the expanding middle of the pyramid. With health so important, the research also shows that increasing numbers of consumers are abandoning pre-made, de-seasoned, mass-produced and factory-made food, because they regard fresh, seasonal, plant-based and locally sourced food as better for them.

And health insurers are reinforcing this belief by influencing and incentivising their customers' dietary choice to 'buy, eat and cook healthy', which means more fresh and local ingredients. Discovery Health in South Africa is actively promoting healthy eating/fresh food by partnering with local retailers like Woolworths and others, and Discovery Vitality in the UK has hooked up with Waitrose and others, as well as restaurants, to provide sizeable discounts to policyholders for items in baskets that benefit their bellies.

Add to that the recent lead move by the UK government to ban advertising and promotions on foods deemed to be unhealthy (containing too much salt, sugar or fat), which is bound to be copied.

Customers can't be fooled; they want the real deal. Tesco, the UK food chain, knows this only too well. It released a product range with farm names that gave the impression that the food items (meat and vegetables) had been made by local producers. In fact, the food had been imported. Consumers were not impressed and Tesco had to apologise and retract.

The move in preference, from factory to fresh, dovetails with the greater emphasis on traceability—consumers want to know more about what they consume, amid rising fears that food from afar eats up the planet, because of the carbon emissions related to transportation. Remember, it's not just the finished product getting to consumers that makes up miles travelled. It's also all the bits and pieces in the supply chain that have to get to and from the various producers.

Food miles, the distance food has travelled from its point of production to the consumer's basket, are generally high. In Australia, the food miles of the average basket amount to the same distance as going around Australia's coastline. Of all the heavy-duty trucks travelling in the UK, those carrying food account for 25 per cent, generating the equivalent of what 5.5 million typical cars would emit in carbon emissions yearly.[135]

The bludgeoning global foodie movement is influencing consumers to go wholefood, organic and enjoy the heritage of local recipes and cooking techniques. Moreover, chefs, foodstagrammers, food apps, food and health writers and bloggers as well as environmental groups are all affirming this. Social media in particular is awash with new ways to cook fresh and local and be healthy, and what is being said is being heralded as truth.

What people are learning (and not just millennials), is that food that is in season, fresh, unadulterated and locally sourced, actually tastes better and meets local palate and flavour preferences. This is one of the reasons why buying from farmer markets is growing faster in some countries than buying from grocery stores.[136] It's a global phenomenon, with the fastest growth in Europe in Germany, followed by France, with Eastern Europe catching up speedily.

And, by the way, food markets are now going e-commerce, supplying direct to customers, another consideration retailers must take into account in the changes they need to make. Some already have, like the Chinese grocery chain Freshippo, which offers fresh food chosen in store (like fish or meat), curated by a chef and cooked to eat then and there in a dining section, or delivered to be eaten at home.

Farming goes urban

Farming has gone urban, which has been taken up in various wondrous ways. Farmers are looking to be nearer to the consumer. And governments are providing initiatives to help keep city populations fed and healthier, with the lowest possible footprint, using a less-water-no-chemicals approach.

Derelict areas in cities, including land, warehouses and containers of various sorts, are being filled with seeds and soil to produce fresh, organic, local edibles, smartening things up and providing entrepreneurs with opportunities to ride the urban farming wave.

Urban vegetable gardens abound, from New York (on rooftops) to Beijing (on balconies), from Iceland (in vegetable lots) to South Africa (in artisanal gardens, in homes and atop buildings).

Vegetable patches are springing up in back and front yards, as urban agriculture takes centre stage in making food local.

The InterContinental hotel chain in New York has launched a number of urban farming projects, including beehives on rooftops that supply locals and hotel guests with delicious honey, used in drinks and dishes. Iceland's capital Reykjavik has renewed its verve for urban growing, renting allotments to people as well as schools and converting gardens to vegetable plots. In South Africa, from inner cities with decaying buildings to suburban private homes, green transformations are taking place, providing produce to growing numbers of farmer hubs and markets, as well as direct to people's homes.

In China, where it is estimated that 350 million people will be living in cities in the next decade, sourcing food locally is all the rage. Balcony farming projects are booming, involving parents and children. Over a thousand agriparks are run by local urban farmers who are incentivised by the government to improve the environmental and social fabric of cities. New technology, like sensors linked to automatic irrigation systems, combined with human effort, is bringing about this shift to localise production and consumption.

Innovations include vertical indoor farms in containers and warehouses, in France, Singapore and the US. US distinguisher Local Roots has created hydroponic farms that are popping up everywhere. They reckon that 30 million people in the US live in desert areas but could have fresh local produce at their doorstep with this system. In 12-metre-long shipping containers, called TerraFarms, high-quality produce is grown using LED lighting at certain wavelengths and sensors to monitor moisture.

Instead of bringing food to places from farms, they are bringing the farms directly to places for the picking.

Modular portal farms, managed from the cloud, are now found in schools, shopping centres, restaurants, supermarkets and hospitals across Germany, Denmark, France and Switzerland. Infarm, which started in Berlin, is probably the best-known example. The founders of Infarm say that traditional methods of farming have not only damaged the planet, but that overused soil dulls the taste of plants, and that long travel times reduce the nutrients by as much as 45 per cent. The company is working with retailers on its data-led soil-free decentralised farming method across Europe and aims to be in 10,000 supermarkets by 2022 to feed people with better, locally grown, fresh, lower cost, organic food with its speedy seed-to-feed approach.

In India, farmland in neighbouring communities is being rented to city households via Farmizen, a mobile app, on a monthly subscription basis. Consumers do their own biofarming on 56-square-metre plots allocated to them, and have access to service backup when they return to the city. The Farmizen technology gets and gives inputs to farmers on more than 50 different local varieties of vegetables, to get ever-improving crop yield in both quality and quantity.

Small but potent Helsieni encourages households to use their coffee grounds, tons of which (9 billion kilos are produced every year) would otherwise go into landfills or incinerators, in order to grow mushrooms. Being high in protein and carbon neutral, mushrooms are a nutritious alternative to meat. And they love coffee grounds. The brand is inspiring the Finnish population, who consume more coffee per capita than any other nation in the world, to grow mushrooms at home with their plentiful leftovers and is selling DIY growth kits and training people in their hyper-localisation drive.

The local brand takeover

In direct contrast to the past, when the hype was around Western global brands, customers are now feeling a greater affinity to local brands.

What some experts are saying is that the commonalities we found among cultures, which linked them globally, are diminishing and diverging, in favour of a trend towards celebrating and preserving cultural diversity.[137]

We are not saying that some global consumer brands aren't doing a superb job of increasing share by associating their brand with a local or regional flavour or concern. Like KitKat did, famously, in Japan, with their 'Kitto Katsu' ('You will win') packaging (the wrapper was designed with a blank space where a Good Luck message could be written and was a popular gift at schools during exams). Or like Nike did with its 'Nothing beats a Londoner' ad in the UK, showing ordinary London kids and their sport in local neighbourhoods. Smirnoff did the same with its inclusive brand equity programme in Europe. And Nestlé started a go-to-customer campaign in Brazil, Até Você a Bordo (Nestlé Takes You Onboard), with the first floating supermarket travelling down the Amazon River, selling food and chocolates, etc. to remote households, reaching 800,000 people a month across 18 municipalities.

We're also not saying that global B2B companies aren't making a great effort to make buyers feel they are dealing with a domestic company.

Take South Africa's ALC, a producer of container liners, which operates around the world, catering to manufacturers who need protective packaging for their goods moved in bulk (ranging from lubricating grease to food flavouring), by ship, rail or truck.

Even though the packaging is made in South Africa, ALC ensures as its number one priority that each country has excess stock in local warehouses so as to maintain a constant flow of delivery. This removes the risk of demand-planning delay, which is always a costly factor for importers. With precision, long site forecasting, ALC aggregates orders from customers all over the globe, building volumes in order to counter the cost of holding the extra stock. Also, servicing is done by locals on demand and payments are made in the local currency.

All of this said, the trend towards local must be taken seriously.

As support for local business grows, the emphasis on individual and collective social identity and heritage is making brand origin more and more important in buying decisions. People are aligning with 'homemade'. Strengthened by the Covid-19 lockdowns, trade in local goods, especially in categories like apparel and consumer goods, has fast reached a tipping point overtaking international imports.

When buying locally, consumers feel they are doing better for the environment and the community. This is true of millennials, in particular, who do 'impact investing', which means supporting brands that are planet-, community- and society-friendly.

Some of the sentiments globally include:
- environment and community (UK, Italy, France, Spain, Germany, Sweden);
- patriotism, national pride (Middle East, Norway, Latin America);
- in keeping with tradition (Thailand, Vietnam);
- want to support locals (France, Malaysia, Australia, North America, Ireland);
- increase employment (the UK, India, US).

In addition, locals seem to be better equipped to handle needs regionally and locally at speed and scale than global brands, the source of supply being closer and supply chains shorter.

Worthwhile noting is:

- By 2050 half the world's consumers will be in emerging markets.
- In the growing middle-class segment in these emerging markets, global brands are losing out to local ones.
- Seventy five per cent of the top three brands in China, Indonesia, India and Brazil are now local.[138]
- Local brands make up 69 per cent of all brand choices in Asia and are growing faster than global brands in China, Philippines, Taiwan, Vietnam and Thailand.
- Since 2010, the top three consumer brands have lost more than 5 per cent of their share in all those markets.[139]
- In fast-moving consumer goods (FMCG), local brands have gained share every year for the past five years, now nearing two-thirds of all sales globally.[140]
- Local-brand supply chains are more agile than global brands, and move faster.

- Whereas some global brands localise their brands, locals are more adept at customising for the domestic market at a micro level, gaining instant insights and feedback on the ground.

Another interesting fact is that whereas previously consumers trusted global brands over locally made products, this sentiment seems to be reversing. This is largely due to the use of social media by the smaller local suppliers to build real-time reputation and relationships. Local brands rely more on local word-of-mouth and word-of-mouse, and positive reviews are growing rapidly, deflecting buying behaviour towards homegrown.

Even before the lockdowns, trust in goods that are locally sourced and produced by small nimble nationals, instead of mass production, particularly in FMCG, was growing, and it is more than likely to continue. Local retailers will have to deal with this trend, backing local sourcing and finding ways to bring local into online and offline propositions, lest they lose major categories and customers.

In China, preference and trust for local brands has grown from 42 to 66 per cent in the last five years.[141, 142] A market second in numbers to the US, locals are becoming more credible rivals due to ever-improving contemporary design, trading up and the fact that, unlike previously, local consumers have begun to believe that they get better-quality after-sales service as well as lower prices from them.

Counter-culturing global

A more global experience of the world, consumers have never had. Especially in digital services and platforms. Everyone uses Google, Facebook, Amazon, Apple iTunes/TV/App Store, YouTube, TikTok, Twitter, Zoom, Fortnite, etc.

But we have to acknowledge that there is a parallel counter-trend that is equally powerful—going local.

This has to do with local brands giving an identity, meaning, a sense of belonging and stature that global brands do not. It's also a counter-move away from gentrification and the global high street where everything is everywhere and looks the same. Customers are seeking new curated experiences, spontaneous discovery and services that reflect the flavour of the people, place and proprietor.

Small is the new big thing they want more of.

No longer is local fringe, it's the new mass market.

Craft

The craft economy is snowballing, with 70 million US households contributing to the craft economy each year. In 2020, more than 2.5 million sellers, many of whom are women, sold goods through Etsy, the go-to platform for shoppers looking for craft goods, up from 2.1 million active sellers in the previous year. The fact that there is a real person who has made an item, someone the customer can see or contact and hold accountable for the handmade or vintage product, is a value-driver. The skills come from people who are passionate about what they make, often using time-old methods.

Here are some craft food examples:

- The fastest-growing segment in dairy is yoghurt, bought in a glass jar with clean-label branding (i.e. no branding) from local cafés, which sell it at a premium.
- Around the world, the craft spirits market is growing annually at 33 per cent,[143] with the US at the front end. Gin is in the lead globally. New, small and local distilleries are driving this growth (for instance, in the UK there are 20 per cent new distilleries a year),[144] as well as customer demand, prepared to pay a premium.
- Beer remains the world's most popular alcoholic beverage.[145] Production of craft beer is growing three times faster than traditional beer worldwide. In Ireland, while the general pub trade is suffering, brewpubs, with their own crafted beer,

are flourishing (at least they were, pre Covid-19). They sell without labels, at a premium.

- Bread forms a major part of the daily diet, which is why it went from being made by small bakeries to mass production. But today, the sale of handcrafted bread, made with traditional methods by skilled food artisans, is outgrowing traditional brands. It has boosted in-store and on-the-go bakeries, now offering gluten-free, vegan and organic products and winning over customers.
- The massive growth in specialist coffee chains, such as Starbucks, is now being outperformed by local, boutique operators, which have superior barista skills, meeting demand from an ever more discerning customer.
- From Argentina to Austria, Brazil to Belgium and Colombia to Cyprus, street food is exploding, now growing faster than the total fast-food market.[146] Customers are not just seeking fast food, but new culinary experiences and connections to a local cuisine.

What is interesting is that we used to put a label on a product, often global, to show quality and consistency. Now that doesn't seem to have the same pulling power. What now attracts customers is something made by hand. Made locally.

In Ireland, food retailer Dunnes Stores, which aggregates these local producers into its stores, is giving Tesco, the multinational chain, a hard time. By integrating the experience of visiting the local butcher, cheese- and fishmonger, breadmaker and veg farmer into their staple range, it is attracting customers across segments, winning over the global and generic Tesco brands. When customers go to Dunnes they say they feel they are getting a genuine local experience.

Micro heroes
People are identifying more and more with local, often unsung, heroes. Since Covid-19 the universe is exploding with them.

Who will ever forget people across the world standing up and cheering frontline workers in the streets and from their balconies during the lockdowns?

One way or another we have moved from Hollywood celebrities and heroes crowned by the establishment to celebrating people in informal roles contributing to the community. Kudos and respect are increasing for people who do good that other people can see, feel and relate to.

Groups are now finding their own protagonists (whether sexual, ethnic, religious or disabled), writing their own history and discovering new figureheads in local culture, past and present.

If you're not part of that community, you will never have heard of its particular micro hero (and probably never will). But these people are important to distinguishers, because they use them as micro influencers.

Even in the case of global movements, such as #MeToo and Black Lives Matter, although the causes may have been universal, it was the local figureheads with whom people identified and connected.

Local content

Google Maps is successful globally because it's an expert at local. It's not the fact that it is global that matters, it's the fact that it really knows its local stuff. And by the way, this is where Apple Maps was failing. It had poor imaging and inaccurate or incomplete information.

K-pop is way more popular in South Korea than American music, and the same is true for J-pop in Japan. Despite Spotify being the go-to app for music because it has the most comprehensive international collection, it is growing successfully in Asia because of its focus on building a hyperlocal music library.

With its young population, music streaming through mobile is booming in Africa. But the swing is to local content. In some countries like Nigeria, with 520 languages spoken in different regions, services and the music they deliver have to be curated for micro-localised listener taste, with apps featuring local artists first, so users can find them immediately.

New to the market but growing fast is MusicTime, by MTN, the service provider that has incorporated air-time billing into music streaming, meaning data is pre-packaged with the music. It's currently sprawling in South Africa, Ghana, Nigeria, Zambia, Cameroon and eSwatini, with an eye—or should we say ear—to the rest of the continent.

Netflix is keeping its edge because it is building skill in local storytelling and a portfolio of content that is rooted in local culture, outside of Hollywood. 'We believe that great stories should be able to come from anywhere on the planet,' says the company's chief product officer, Greg Peters.[147]

Many homemade successes are becoming global, but retaining their authenticity, playing to audiences that are looking for what's genuinely local even if it's not from their own country. As Netflix says, 'the more authentically local the show is, the better it travels'.[148]

Local tourism

Covid-19 has recalibrated the global tourism industry. Domestic tourism is on the rise and is likely to continue to do so in line with the tendency to go local.

Because so much local tourism has been pitched at foreign customers, locals will need to re-imagine how their fellow citizens will want to travel and tour. These new tourists don't want more of the same. They are seeking what's hyper-genuine.

And those coming from other countries want to immerse themselves, engage and participate in the culture and meet locals. They don't want generic off-the-shelf experiences but something specific to a village, region or country. They want to live, travel, eat, celebrate, shop and visit like locals, in their language and traditions. And growing numbers think they have a better chance of achieving this on their own, and are therefore going on solo adventures.

With people working more from home it is likely that short sharp holidays closer to home will replace long extended breaks. Or by working remotely in choice destinations, employees may choose places for an extended period, so as to combine work and holidays.

Alternatively, tourists, particularly the young, are likely to go for local, micro-gap holiday experiences in local destinations that offer specific points of interest, from craft to wildlife, kayaking to jazz. Airbnb, which wants its brand to help people feel at home and local wherever they stay, has launched 'Go Near' in American cities, and is partnering with countries like the UK to create advocates for local experience-based travel.

The revival of the local economy

What the pandemic taught us is that self-sufficiency, both individual and collective, is essential for sustainability. And that goes for countries as well. Countries found that they were over-reliant on imports, forcing them to compete for anything from medical equipment to bikes.

This tossed out the old economic wisdom on trade, which was that the best place for things to be made (all other things being equal) was in the country that could do it most competitively. Now countries and its inhabitants are rethinking economic agendas to re-imagine how they can make sure they have what they need, or have access to it. In areas identified as staples during emergencies, they will have to have local suppliers.

The post Covid-19 recession is possibly the first service-driven recession. And in rebuilding the economies of the world, a good deal of the focus will therefore go into local services, like stores, restaurants, domestic tourism and local arts and culture, giving further local impetus.

Countries also want to accumulate social capital. By this we mean the networks of relationships that enable people who live and work together in a society to function optimally. It's what glues them together. This can only happen if local businesses contribute and flourish to a larger extent.

A strong local economy has been shown to have higher social capital and those communities that work better together have less crime, less dumping, more respect for social norms (as was the case during Covid-19, when social distancing and other health measures were critical for its containment), better health and prosperity.[149]

Devolution, which is the decentralisation of government administration, happening in the US, China, Mexico, Brazil, the UK and Scandinavia for some time, promises to give more autonomy to local communities in responding quicker to local needs, thus giving precedence to social capital and local economies.

For global brands going local, or locals going global, the question is how do they add value in a wave that is far stronger than they have encountered until now?

The answer demands more local authenticity from both producers and consumers, brands and people.

And turns this into a distinguisher opportunity.

CHAPTER 20

Going frugal is so cool

The notion of frugality is no longer confined to emerging countries, where affordability and constrained resources are a problem for so-called bottom of the pyramid (BOP) consumers. Industrialised countries that were buying frugal products made in and for emerging economies, in a phenomenon known as reverse innovation, now want it for themselves, in order to fuel the kind of future and growth they want to see happen in their own economies.

They want sustainability, simplicity (as opposed to many and complex features, or junk design DNA) and they want frugal, which means using technology at scale to minimise wastage and maximise what's abundant, in order to make consumers, communities, cities, countries, citizens and the cosmos better off.

They want to eliminate the R&D-heavy investments that take money and time, typical of mature automobile and pharmaceutical enterprises, which have not necessarily created inventions that have changed the world.

Instead, they want to rely on intuitive innovation that musters creative power using a different frugal set of principles.

Good enough isn't good enough

The point about frugal innovation is that it's not about making do with something inferior and cheap.

Or, as some people think, about being 'good enough'. Neither products nor services, or the user experience, are compromised in a distinguisher's world.

Actually, it's about '*better*' at lower cost.

It's not necessarily making something entirely new. It may just be using ingenuity to re-imagine how something can be made better with limited means, what the Indians call in Hindi *Jugaad*, Brazilians call *jeitinho*, in Chinese it's *zizhu chuangxin* and in Kenya *jua kali*.

Vishal Rao, an Indian oncologist who made the Aum Voice Prosthesis, a speaking device for throat cancer patients who had lost their voice box, and sold it for one dollar, is a classic example. The device restores the ability to speak and to breathe *better*. The alternatives that were being offered cost a huge amount that no one could afford, and had to be replaced every six months, which no one could afford!

Rao's act was one of supreme patriotism, but it also showed that taking out complexity and cost can be done creatively.

Frugal innovation has come a long way, from being an idea for poor people with low purchasing power to something much smarter that creates a win-win for any and all, majorly impacting how increasing hordes of people produce and consume today.

In the main, it is about:

- catering for many;
- to make them inclusive;
- giving them a user-friendly, simple but not simplistic outcome;
- being eco-correct or eco-regenerative—good for the planet;
- being of high-quality, durable, lasting impact, that is better/ cheaper in the long term;

- using fewer resources—material, social (including labour, energy and time), environmental and financial;
- using ingenuity rather than long and expensive R&D;
- being developed quickly because there is no time to waste;
- using technology at scale to get all the disproportionately positive returns that make it affordable.

This kind of frugal innovation is becoming mainstream and ubiquitous, in a future unfolding before our very eyes.

It's anything but old-fashioned.

Elon Musk, modern high-tech thinker and distinguisher, is supposedly a frugal engineering genius, with many of his innovations taken directly from the movement's recipe book. Like his recycled rocket, which SpaceX launched. Or his lithium-ion batteries, which are changing the way we produce and use energy, shrinking electricity bills by 25 per cent, and which might even allow people to go off the grid completely.[150] Or the Hyperloop, a high-speed travel pod. Richard Branson's Virgin Hyperloop has tested a prototype based on Musk's vision—making an historical debut in the US in 2020—destined for Dubai so as to connect all Gulf cities within an hour.

With zero direct emissions, the Hyperloop will be high-volume low-density, in that it will transport people at higher frequency, much faster, using fewer fossil fuels and energy, the very opposite of planes and trains of the past.

Much more for many

It started off mainly in India as a move to cater to resource-constrained local masses in need. The famous case of the Jaipur foot, a prosthetic limb delivered at a fraction of the cost for thousands of needy people in rural areas, is now legend.

But it was no one-off shot.

The Indian medical landscape is littered with examples of frugal innovation, including devices for various diseases that work as well if not better than conventional products but at low cost, customised for the Indian market, changing at scale and speed the way people's health is cared for.

Aravind Eye Clinic has captured the imagination of many academics and practitioners globally for its innovative frugal approach, delivering low-cost excellence at industrial scale (evidently, they used the McDonald's fast-food chain model of how to train people to do tasks well and fast to get high standardised throughput). From the clinic's nearly 3,000 eye camps throughout the country, it screens over 2.8 million people a year, of which 280,000-odd have surgery. Fees from those who can afford it subsidise the poor.

That was before digital transformation changed how to achieve high-value, micro-customised, low-cost services at scale.

Today India is fast becoming *the* centre for medical tourism, with international patients flooding in at a rate making targets higher than those for IT. Why would consumers go to India in tidal volume instead of being treated at home, which is what traditional behaviour would have dictated?

Challenging existing cost structures and how healthcare is delivered for the average person in most mature countries, India has hacked and cracked the tourist market for health using a high-value low-cost formula. And now it is estimated to have 20 per cent of the medical tourism market globally.

Some deliberate decisions were taken to get there:

- The government has made a concerted effort to make the legal procedure, including getting tourist visas, an easy process.
- The medical conditions and quality of professionals and manufacturing services are at world standards.
- The costs are a fraction compared to those of, say, the US or the UK.
- Service quality is universally high, which means waiting lists are kept low.

- Hospitals are equipped with advanced technologies.
- Bottlenecks are removed to get things done smart and fast.

Smart cities are frugal

Smart cities are everywhere. While each has their own version of the concept, they are universal in that they are frugal. They merge the physical and digital world, using data-generated insights, AI, blockchain, Internet of Things (IoT), drones and sensors interconnected with computers and mobile phones to make cities work better for all customer-stakeholders.

Digital-enabled but people-centred, they are geared to use fewer resources.

Smart cities are smart because they make citizens smarter, able to make better decisions quicker. That's because through mobile devices they get instant relevant information anywhere anytime, thanks to billions of computers, mobiles and sensors that collect and analyse interconnected data and relay it back to citizens in real time.

As Africa becomes more urbanised, it can choose to run its cities by upgrading legacy technology and infrastructure, with all the problems, or leapfrog directly into frugal, as did Casablanca, the largest city in Morocco. With state-of-the-art technology to interconnect people, processes and public and commercial spaces, it raised standards of living and improved the economy so that its 6 million inhabitants (with more flocking in daily) could prosper without killing the planet.

The city brings frugal principles together with technology to eliminate the negatives associated with urbanisation in a place that was designed for much fewer people, and in so doing it can retain and attract talent who want to study, live and work there, and generate more employment in a regenerative cycle of give and take.

SINGAPORE CASE

Singapore's award-winning transformation, to create sustainable self-regenerative liveability and prosperity, digitally links individuals, communities and the commercial, cultural and public sector. Its vision is to have a digital economy, digital government and digital society, which means citizens empowered and enthused to use the technology.

This includes smart connected traffic and transport integrated into one system with hands-free entry and exit and one payment system, urban drone-delivery innovations, air taxis, smart health and security, smart and connected municipal and government services free of red tape, as well as smart homes, with everything intelligent and everything connected to everything. And it was first to test a 'no ground staff' airport terminal, fully automated but packed with art and greenery to keep stress levels down, ostensibly designed and built for travellers as opposed to planes.

Efforts on the ecological front have dramatically reduced CO_2 emissions, pollution and congestion (even the trees that have been planted absorb carbon), energy and water consumption and waste, and increased service responses, air quality, public green spaces, telehealth and education, employment, tourism and so much more.

Singapore's national digital-identity cloud facial-verification pioneering innovation, SingPass, effectively displacing IDs and passwords, means citizens can now transact seamlessly and securely within the public and private sector, saving on time, money, effort and paperwork.

Facial verification, unlike facial recognition, requires the explicit consent of the user. It basically is about authentication, which means it confirms that the person is actually there, such as when opening a bank account or writing a university exam.

Four million citizens can now access over 500 digital services offered by more than 180 government agencies. Activities such as completing a tax return or applying for a marriage certificate can be completed by logging in using simple facial biometric scanning.

Commercial enterprises—large and small—and banks can integrate into and leverage the ever-scaling system at speed, without the cost of building their own systems.

Virtualising medicine

Technology, together with mobile usage, is speeding up health equity and inclusiveness through frugal principles, providing top-value virtual medicine to the many at low cost.

For example, in Mexico, one million people a month are given help by MedicallHome whose paramedics use phones linked to computers and collective intelligence to diagnose patients at a cost of five dollars. A third of the time problems can be resolved successfully, saving on costly doctors' bills and the longer-term costs of not catching a disease early. Those patients who need a doctor are referred to its 6,000 accredited doctor pool and 3,000 clinics in 233 cities with discounts negotiated, based on numbers seen and treated.[151]

While this may seem like a trade-off to a profession that has been high-touch, increasingly this model and many variations of it are being adopted, particularly since Covid-19, in emerging and industrialised countries. And those in the know say there is no turning back.[152]

In the US, this new frugal way of delivering and accepting healthcare is expected to have a 50 per cent uptake by 2030, and it will get even more sophisticated as technology develops, using Big Data analytics and interactive robotics to make remote medicine mainstream.[153]

In Singapore, leading in telehealth in Southeast Asia, 64 per cent of all healthcare professionals already have some form of connected technology to diagnose and care for patients. And in countries such as Vietnam, Philippines, Indonesia, South Korea and China, telemedicine is fast being adopted as the new now norm in order to get high-performance medicine to many, fast and at low cost.

The next small thing

People wanting to live comfortably, but small, without debt or worry, in an environment they enjoy, with everything they need and nothing they don't need, is a smart frugal trend to be reckoned with. Growing feverishly worldwide, this stylish but affordable and equitable way to live has enamoured people in big numbers, and the trend is increasing.

In the US, numbers who say yes in surveys of this trend are around 60 per cent.[154] And it's not restricted to people who can't afford to have a home any other way, or for the homeless, or emergency centres. Minimalist millennials, economically sound, are going small because it's true to their values and trendy.

IKEA CASE

This is thanks in no small way (no pun intended) to distinguishers who are driving this new behaviour by providing furniture and accessories that fit, such as IKEA, which is becoming increasingly known as the small-space saver. Like clothing, cars and other durables using the frugal formula, IKEA's furniture is made to be flexible— in its case foldable, stackable, rollable, climbable, and whatever else is needed to build a functional but small living space.

Will IKEA move on to build tiny homes? Recently, they commissioned two Danish architects to design and build a tiny home that people would want, with all of the above attributes, but also modular, versatile, smart and handsome, using as little material as possible, at low cost. And they did just that. Built a tiny house for just over USD 9,000.

IKEA and its partners are using open-source architecture rather than mass production, where everything is set by rigorous standards that have to be the same. Here the notion is based on the idea of a platform that can change, morph and adapt according to the needs of the owner. The tiny-space structures can be used for flexible living or as an extra studio or backyard cottage.

Called 'Building Blocks', it is reminiscent of LEGO bricks, based on the same modular flexible principles and small (and smart) enough not to get embroiled in building regulations. Materials and machines used to make these tiny homes can be easily and affordably sourced anywhere so the structure can be replicated worldwide, once the design is downloaded. And it can be easily scaled for schools, camps or any other structures that need to be built fast and frugally. Flat-packed like furniture.

Drones are small, but are they frugal?

The future of delivery is drones.

Covid spurred this on.

Using automatic drone aircraft, iFood Brazil's virtual restaurant meals will be delivered faster, hotter and fresher at low cost, to more customers, lessening the overall environmental impact. And restaurants will be able to get to customers further away.

This new way of last-mile delivery is destined to become commonplace, and is frugal because it provides a lighter, faster, cleaner, safer, cheaper and higher quality way to connect people to food.

The hybrid model mirrors what brands like Uber Eats in America do, using drones and last-mile ground transportation. Drones take two minutes to fly and drop off the food at a hub. Its drivers pick it up and take it to the customer's doorstep or to dropzones.

Amazon has zeroed in on drone delivery. The investment will probably be profitable, but it will also be made with frugal intent. It will eliminate traffic, heavy-duty vehicles, fossil-fuel emissions, courier traffic, and even reduce the number and cost of roads and drivers (who could be retrained to become drone operators), and be potentially safer, making one-day shipping the standard for its many millions of paying Prime members.

Experts say drones are also perfect for the middle mile, remote areas that are difficult to get to and often steeped in poverty and disease. Like mobile phones, droneports are a frugal alternative to traditional infrastructure and a driver of inclusivity. They will enable drones to reach many of the poor in remote areas of Africa, Latin America and Asia where there may not even be roads, distances are great and consumers are in need of basic and vital goods.

Zipline, which started its journey into medical drone delivery in Rwanda and Ghana, parachuting emergency supplies like vaccines and blood into remote areas, has expanded its footprint into the US. It has demonstrated how frugal can be fast and cost-effective in medical healthcare (most recently for Covid-19 related drugs) and how to get take-up from an industry that is traditionally slow to take on innovation.

Making less abundant

Though frugal and abundant seem to be counterintuitive, they are not when technology is involved. And that's what's different about low-cost high-volume environments wherever customers are on the pyramid as long as people are tech-savvy and have smartphones or devices.

Combine lots of people with many smartphones, potentially generating large quantities of data, and suddenly even in low-income areas we have abundant resources that can produce huge opportunities and social impact at diminished cost.

M-KOPA CASE

From this principle, M-KOPA was born in Kenya. It ticks all the contemporary frugal boxes.

The trigger was that 70 per cent of the Kenyan population (who have mobile phones) live off the grid, in other words with no access to electricity. Notably, 1.06 billion people in the world (15 per cent of humanity) have no grid power yet.[155]

Such was the case in Kenya until the pay-as-you-go mobile phone platform gave people in low-income settings, who previously had to use expensive and toxic kerosene, affordable solar-powered lighting.

This new empowered citizen force is 900,000 strong in Kenya, Nigeria, Tanzania and Uganda, with 500 homes a day being added.[156] The fully connected IoT solar home system with a set of high-quality solar-powered appliances like TVs and fridges, etc. could stand the test anywhere in the world, say the experts. And M-KOPA remotely controls and monitors equipment to predict and prevent outages.

The cost per month for kerosene is displaced by payments to M-KOPA and the savings are considerable over the lifetime of the system. M-KOPA also funds the systems with micro loans repaid in micro payments by smartphone[157] (the word 'Kopa' means 'to borrow'), in what the brand calls affordable asset-financing.

Whoever has solar has power now for essential devices like lights and radios, and connectivity through smartphones, so they can go online to work, play, learn or start a business, upgrading living standards and earning potential. Half the users are more productive since switching to the new energy source, either at home (for example, generating income from hosting movie screenings) or getting a new job.

Millions of tonnes of carbon dioxide and black carbon are avoided and power is reduced by 20 per cent. Electronic waste is eliminated by recycling non-repairable electronic components and repurposing returned components for very low-income homes.[158]

LOCAL ROOTS CASE

If frugal means using less to be abundant, then US-original high-tech Local Roots is a forerunner. In its vertical containers it grows as much food as otherwise would be grown on 2 hectares of land. Plus, it uses 97 per cent less water, and zero pesticides or herbicides, to produce good green leafy and nutritious food in four weeks end to end, a third of the time it would take with conventional farming.

Being solar-powered, Local Roots produces market-standard food at scale with a fraction of the resources used in the past.

Each container produces 9,000 to 30,000 kilos of food per cycle, with each crop using its own algorithm to ensure optimum productivity (no two pieces of soil are the same).

So good is the system, they say, that this could mean that from now on we can expect astronauts or space tourists to have fresh produce on their long journeys to far-off planets.[159]

CHAPTER 21

Printing the future

Three-dimensional (3D) printing promises to become transformative for consumers and for every industry and profession that deals with or requires material goods.

With 3D printing (also called additive manufacturing), replicas (either in whole or in part) can be made cost-effectively fast, as needed—anything from heart valves to helmets for bikers, cutlery to cars, satellites to skin tissue bioprinted for organ transplantation.

In early versions of 3D printing, plastic was the prevailing material, used as an emulsion to consecutively add layer on layer (the additive aspect) in order to construct objects in three dimensions from a digital file (our layperson explanation). But no one wants to see more plastic being produced. Now, ingredients include ceramics, metal alloys, glass, paper, photopolymerised silicon, resin, carbon fibre, living cells and food. And there will be more materials to come.

At first, simple structures were made, using one ingredient. Then with the unstoppable advances of material science, the printers were making more complex items with a multiple mix of substances, and the race goes on to find materials yet unknown, new machines not yet conceived of, products functioning fully, end to end, with all the bits inside (like engines, circuits and batteries), and ever more sophisticated robots to make the print-ers that make the printers!

Investment—financial and emotional—is at a high as countries, an array of funded and private institutions, hubs and startups make a play for new markets. Albeit a moving landscape, here are some of the key country investors with a few of their targeted application areas: US (defence, aerospace); UK (construction, automobile, aerospace); South Korea (electronics, medical devices); Germany (automobiles); France (medical supplies,[160] outdoor advertising[161]); China (fashion, housing, education—all 150,000-odd elementary schools are to have 3D printers); UAE/Dubai (dental, hearing aids, medicine, prosthetic limbs, construction—Dubai says 25 per cent of all houses built by 2025 will be from 3D printers); Italy (jewellery); and Japan (construction, electronics, aircraft, furniture, art and crafts).

Manufacturing's makeover

Manufacturing needs more than a makeover.

3D printing is not about new product development and product substitution. The 3D printer is a product, but the con-cept of additive manufacturing is a much bigger issue with wider ramifications that affect production and consumption behaviour and the remaking of manufacturing as we have known it.

Niche and mass manufacturing will converge into mass customisation at speed and scale, because machines are able to be adapted quickly, easily and cheaply, without the previous high costs and time to retool.

And there will be hyper-personalisation, thanks to advances in generative software, which allow multiple permutations and variations to suit an individual—for example, making a biking helmet to fit the exact shape of a person's head.

Another fascinating thing about this massive change has to do with where the manufacturing is done, by whom.

Printing can in fact be done anywhere—in manufacturing plants, printing factories, farms, garages or at point of use at work or at home. Designs or digital blueprints can be created in one location and downloaded so that production can be done in another.

Production can be in the hands of producers or consumers. It can be done at industry level by, for example, manufacturers, retailers or fleet owners, by people working in SMEs, or by professionals providing services, such as dental laboratory technicians, organ donor banks, pharmacists, and school teachers.

Printers can be placed in any shared space, a bit like coffee machines, softdrink dispensers or today's copier corners; in communal buildings, office blocks, apartments, hotels, hospitals, schools and even cars.

Fusing producer and consumer

For homes, consumers can buy an affordable 3D personal printer and have it on their desktop and make stuff themselves to suit their needs in real time. Imagine never having to call out or go shopping for a spare part or printer cartridge, because it can be whipped up at home.

It's DIY gone 3D additive.

The reason costs go down with 3D printing is because instead of cutting away from raw ingredients and leaving varying amounts of waste, which is what old tools and techniques did, a 3D printer adds material when—and only if—it is needed, so there is no waste and the process becomes more affordable for more people.

What we are witnessing is the democratisation of production. Next normal? Now anyone can make goods, without huge upfront costs and overheads, namely:

- small startups;
- small and medium-sized enterprises;

- consumers as makers;
- professional users, hospitals, schools, the aftermarket.

But don't economic formulas have to change when the supplier and the buyer are the same person?

Here's a view of what the distinguisher 3D printing factory might look like.

TABLE 21.1: *New Factory: Major Resource—3D Printer*

Labour	Industrial manufacturers, new makers and 3D farms (independents not owned or controlled), users (decentralised)
Material	New and multiple mixed materials (using less and what is available)
Machine	3D printers (anywhere and everywhere)
Fuel	Data-driven generative blueprints, software and the cloud
Workforce motivator	On-demand, fast, affordable, convenient, no waste, flexible, customisable, adaptable
Marketing tools	User cases, word of mouth, social media
Reward for brand	Scale speed at low cost

Fabrication at a point of need will mean users will be talking virtually with brands and their engineers and designers, requesting on-demand online instruction and ideas as they make things themselves. This will radically alter the way brands communicate and engage with customers, and how customers behave.

And fabrication at point of use will mean that the need for storage and fulfilment, distribution or delivery will disappear, changing the face of supply chains and logistics.

An object already made or bought can be adapted or enhanced by additive manufacturing to make it truly relevant or unique. Leading this idea is IKEA's ThisAbles, which caters for the disabled market to make its furniture more user-friendly. It provides customers with a digital blueprint of additions that they can download free to make 3D objects as add-ons to furniture to make life more workable, like large handles, or bigger knobs or buttons to lift a bed, or cords for lights, with instructions on YouTube on how to install them.

What we have here is not just integrating 3D printing into the old manufacturing process. It's about turning manufacturing right on its head, requiring a radically different kind of goods factory, different behaviour from suppliers and users, and new economics.

Non-experts will be able to do expert things. They are the makings of a decentralised workforce, blurring production and consumption.

Dinner is printed

In 2019, while on the International Space Station, Russian cosmonauts fed meat cells into a 3D printer to create their dinner.

3D printing is reshaping food production and eating habits, and will continue to do so. It may even solve some of the planet's food shortage problems.

Though still at an early stage in this field, when they do take off, food-related innovations will abound fast.

Individuals can program blueprints to make food with a printer in their kitchen. They can even go further and be makers of food to suit their unique nutritional needs, biometric and even genomic profiles (including allergies), and taste preferences, with preparation done on demand. Although it sounds counterintuitive to the uninitiated, 3D can produce healthier food options, it seems.

How about some cell-cultured sushi? The latest in high-tech restaurants in Tokyo, Sushi Singularity, gives customers health-test kits from which a biosample can be obtained so that a personalised meal can be printed just for them. Other restaurant concepts include making the cutlery and crockery for each bespoke meal and making it edible, tasty, hyper palate-personalised, fast, with zero waste.

3D drives frugal innovation

If using less is the way forward, 3D additives are the vanguard.

And if the adoption of smartphones is anything to go by, emerging economies will undoubtedly leap at this technology and turn it into a frugal competitive advantage.

Here are some reasons why 3D printing fits the new frugal world:[162]

- It's fast, getting faster;
- It uses fewer materials;
- It uses less energy/electricity;
- It produces perfect replicas;
- 3D goods are lighter;
- 3D goods are stronger;
- 3D goods are more affordable—with savings of from 50 to 90 per cent;
- The software is generative, making variation, adaptation and customisation easy;
- The machines are flexible—they can make one thing one day and another the next;
- It decreases inventory;
- It reduces need for storage and delivery;
- It reduces waste—only what is needed is made;
- More people can get access to goods;
- More people can start a product-making business without high overheads.

Like everything else, over time 3D printers will evolve and their associated costs will diminish.

On that topic, it's time to mention a Togolese entrepreneur and a now-famous case of bridging the gap between 3D technology and frugal economics.

Afate Gnikou developed a 3D printer from electronic waste he collected from dumps in his capital city, Lomé. He literally combined and repurposed unusual materials and mostly made do with what was available locally (two important aspects of frugal innovation), like old mainframe computers, printers and scanners. From information gleaned from multiple sources, he put together a fully made-in-Africa frugal 3D printer, for USD 100.

WoeLab (meaning 'do it') makerspace in Lomé, the first incubator and e-fabrication laboratory in a country where 60 per cent of the population live in poverty, has made several more 3D printers from waste. Its purpose is to uplift the country, its economy and its citizens by making these and many other printers to come available in schools, cafés and other communal venues that feature in its economic and social culture.

With 3D printing, prototyping is quick and cheap for individual, industrial and professional users. Objects can be made at a fraction of the price, because once the digital blueprint file is set up, the costs of production follow close-to-zero cost economics.

3D printing has the power to build and redistribute wealth. Mostly, the capital required is low with investment needed in skills, software and materials. This should give entrepreneurs the jumpstart they need at scale.

Too important to ignore

3D printing is also pulling industries and institutions into the frugal era. For example:

- Trucks made by additive manufacturing have up to 25 per cent fewer parts, are lighter and therefore less costly to move around, as well as being more fuel efficient, which drives down logistics expenses.
- Tools made for military defence are lighter, stronger and made faster, and are therefore not only more efficient and easier to carry and use, but their transport is less costly. Soldiers are trained to use machines with structures made from the printer when and where needed as an expedition unfolds.
- Medical equipment is being made with 3D printers in field clinics during emergencies, earthquakes or floods, to enable the most rapid response, where otherwise it would take two to three months to go through due process to obtain items.
- NASA already uses 3D printing during space travel to lighten the load (a huge cost) of crafts and cargo, and has plans to enable on-demand printing for astronauts in outer space habitats like the Moon or Mars. Everything left over is turned to feedstock for the printer so it can be re-used.

Construction

Construction is being altered in mind-boggling ways by 3D printing, in terms of both production and consumption. Houses are going up at drop-dead speed at a fraction of the cost and time. China, France and the Netherlands have reported houses being constructed within days, and in Spain bungalows have been built within eight hours. In New York, design moulds for a 42-story residential and commercial building, which would normally take up to nine months to make, took on average 10 hours.[163]

Not only can urban buildings be built faster, they are stronger though lighter, flexible, energy-saving and climate-adaptive.

Construction materials can be sourced locally. In Italy, straw and rice husks have been used. In Spain, the local arm of Cemex, the celebrated Mexican construction materials manufacturer that became famous because it went from selling cement to enabling lower-income consumers in slums to build houses, has taken its expertise in cement and mixed it with that of other players to produce 3D-printed, low-cost, energy-saving homes in Spain and Morocco (the first in Africa) from cement compounds.

3D-printed housing is widely regarded as a possible answer to stylish but energy-efficient social housing in the future. As well as solving housing needs for some of the worst slums and other poor areas of the world, it is challenging the traditional linear model, which cannot cope with the volume of constructions needed for people in low-cost housing, which run globally into billions.

In Mexico, a neighbourhood of 3D-printed houses customised with different shapes and sizes and geared for safe and healthy living, for a community of 50 farmers and weavers, is scheduled to be built soon, within a 24-hour period, saving materials, costs and time.[164]

Added to all of this is that 3D printing is able to make things that humans can't (like quickly adaptable shapes and structures); active façades where biochemical processes embedded in the building material monitor temperature and bend the material to provide heat or shade as needed; wiring and piping that are in the matrix of the actual structure. These developments are saving enormous costs, and first movers are looking at opening up a zillion opportunities for new design and construction.

Surgery

In surgical practice, notoriously slow to change, 3D printing is gaining in momentum and success over 2D or 3D imaging. Innovation continues daily to provide medicine in general, and surgery specifically, with new and better understanding and tools that enable faster, affordable, elevated standards of care.

3D printing is especially taking off with medical device manufacturers, who are sharing information and open-source designs online. This is significantly reducing the time to develop these high-impact devices, and reducing their prices, giving both doctors and patients greatly improved outcomes.

For prosthetics, 3D is a major breakthrough, particularly for people who have lost limbs in embattled areas. It is significant for children who need prostheses because, as they grow, the sizes of the artificial limbs have to change and they are costly to replace. The design freedom that 3D printing offers, produces affordable (to make, buy and maintain), custom-made parts in days, rather than months.

In many low-income countries people don't have access to artificial limbs or can't afford them, and if the quality is poor or the shapes are standardised, which they often are, wearing the prostheses can be painful and cause complications. Computer modelling software combined with 3D printers can now produce a bespoke limb that is made to fit exactly.

Surgical tools, patient-specific implants made to measure, as well as life-size anatomical models of patients constructed from scanned personal data are now possible as visual aids for pre-operative planning, prototyping for simulation, and improved clinical experience during surgery. And reduced lead times and massive reductions in costs make the promise of doctors being able to offer affordable, personalised, precision medicine a reality.

In dentistry, which has been ahead in taking up digital technology, 3D printing and scanning are speeding up services, making them more accurate and patient-friendly. Gone will be uncomfortable clay moulds and dental drills. From a scan, dentists will be able to model and make repairs, crowns, implants and caps, etc. without expensive resources or laboratories, contracting the cost and time, with more comfort for patients.

This can only be a (welcome) win-win.

Arts and Culture

In the world of arts and culture, artists can upload their sketches and photographs straight from a computer to a 3D printer to create works. Museums can recreate cultural sites, like Tutankhamun's tomb in Egypt, allowing tourists to experience them without harming the original locations.

Google Arts & Culture is an initiative that, together with partners, is producing 3D-printed, small-scale versions of cultural heritage sites to bring to consumers around the world.

Artifacts can be reproduced at low cost with a high degree of detail and precision. Because of their historical significance and monetary value, artifacts are usually displayed behind glass. But now people can touch them, which is especially important for the sight-impaired.

Museums like the Smithsonian in Washington have given consumers open access to download, print and share more than three million two- and three-dimensional images and objects from its various museums, research centres, libraries and archives.

One thing is sure. While none of us knows exactly how far 3D printing can go, we do know that it will be at the heart of new distinguisher propositions.

The floodgates are open.

PART THREE

Speed up—Make things happen faster

Once an enterprise or industry is shaken up and a new value proposition has been formulated and taken shape, distinguishers make the right moves to speed things up.

In addition to delivering value at low cost, speed is what gives them the ongoing leading market edge.

They have a playbook.

Distinguishers build a compelling view and story of what needs to be told and sold inside the organisation and in the marketplace.

They know how to make the right moves and navigate the journey, finding points of light to work with, resisting negativity.

They learn fast and build agile organisations, interconnected within and with those with whom they collaborate. Dedicated to doing whatever it takes to get the job done—produce high value, at low cost, at speed and scale. This is the overriding priority.

CHAPTER 22

The art of the start

To speed up means to make the right moves to get to backers, inside the enterprise as well as outside—potential investors, co-founders, beta champion customers, technology partners, etc.

No one can avoid this.

If the change is coming from the top inside it's easier, but still a good deal of effort goes into getting others engaged and supportive 360 degrees, be it ExCo, the board, shareholders, investors, peers or employees.

As Jeff Bezos famously said: 'Be prepared to be misunderstood often.' He was. (Sandra was initially asked by her publisher to remove Amazon from her 1997 book *Customer Capitalism*, 'since there was no real evidence that people would buy books or anything online, or that it would ever make any money'!)

What Bezos meant is, don't try it unless you can withstand the fact that not everyone will agree or like you or what you have to say. You will have to endure a lot of criticism and cynicism and many messy moments.

But that's OK, say the distinguishers, because it's in the playbook.

Legacy brands are usually hurting before they make any radical change. Not great timing. It's better to change when reputation and resources are intact.

But either way, a move from mature to distinguisher brand

can work, as we've seen from major turnarounds and reinventions over the decades (e.g. IBM, LEGO, Unilever, Philips, Microsoft), if the correct moves are made.

For newcomers, the principle of doing things at speed is different because they have no baggage. However, their challenges are just as pressing and the principles we will discuss apply equally to those starting afresh.

Find a crisis if there isn't one

A critical success factor in the speed-up phase is to articulate a crisis. Unless a crisis is stated and communicated in a compelling way, it's hard to get anything started and anyone truly onboard.

People change in moments of crisis, as we've seen from the pandemic. They step up. And they speed up.

They behave differently, they hear louder, they are more receptive, they react quicker.

Nothing focuses people like a crisis. And nothing aligns them better. Diversity works when people become fixed on the task ahead.

Whether they are corporates or newcomers, distinguishers can see, sense and smell a crisis. Or if there isn't one, they invent one.

The crisis trilogy

There are basically three types of crises. Any transformation, or a plan to start one, begins with a strong statement to the powers that be indicating one or more of them:

CRISIS OF THREAT: Signs of weakness, margin loss, flatlining or declining growth, diminishing market.
Message: Look at the facts: if we don't change, we could be in serious trouble.

Data showing: Customer retention down, customer dissatisfaction ratings low, market share loss (or larger share of deteriorating pie), sales down, revenue or profit down, new competitors, low on innovation.

CRISIS OF OPPORTUNITY: New trends, new opportunities in a shifting market, changed technology landscape, major gaps or white spaces unfilled.
Message: If we change, this could be gained. If we don't, we will miss out.
Data showing: Growing markets, emerging trends, lazy assets (wasted untapped capacity), inefficiency or duplication in value chain, lucrative customer pain-points or gaps detected, changing behaviour or behaviour that could be changed, unmet needs surfacing, innovation emerging fast, hyper-personalisation needed.

CRISIS OF CONSCIOUSNESS: New trends and activism, shifting values and market behaviour, socially transformative moves or important problems in country, excluded parts of market, city, community, cause or cosmos.
Message: This is the problem and consequent damage/harm. We must fix what's terribly wrong or bad.
Data showing: Exclusion, inequality, damage, something/some people in need, unsustainability, social problem, waste, dangerous products or ingredients, movement pressure, depletion of assets/resources, unethical, unfair and unobjective conduct.

LEGO CASE

LEGO has probably had close to most of the world's share of building construction bricks, apart from some imitators. But toys have been losing out for years to a bigger market as consumers have interacted increasingly with tablets, smartphones, video-game consoles, etc., with all the consequent threats. The brand was getting an increasing share of a shrinking pie.

LEGO's opportunity was to find ways to engage kids (and

adults) by blending physical and digital elements, capitalising on the exploding world of technology—interactivity and intelligence both on- and offline—and create superb experiences that were also safe for kids.

Integral to this is LEGO's socially oriented purpose, to inspire generations of children to interact with each other, and help participate in their wellbeing through creativity and play, as opposed to just selling bricks.

Now the LEGO website draws in over 100 million customers annually, and its play apps like LEGO Life have more than nine million users, with enormous jumps in content uploading.[165]

Combined with stores, that is enough to boggle both an adult and kid's mind.

The company has made efforts to use alternative plant-based materials to combat plastic pollution and throwaway waste habits.

3D printing could be a threat or opportunity to LEGO, depending on how it plays the game.

The 3D-printing and art community has already begun to create bricks that can fit with LEGO bricks, so that people can make their own super-personalised and super-sized creations.

If embraced, this could open up opportunities in new areas that could mean new jobs, enterprises and franchising, as well as inclusiveness, and innovation in new sustainable plastic alternative materials.

The future belongs to those who see it differently

Making the powers that be understand that the future should and will be radically different, requires some potent high-level messaging.

Watch out for the small guy
The small guy with a big idea that is likely to become the next new is the real danger today.

Making the audience feel that pinch, and that the risk is that anyone can become a major force and source of competition and grab customers, is a critical component of successful distinguisher messaging at the outset.

It's pretty much accepted that startups are now the future of innovation. And let's remember that half of the Fortune 500 startups rose during an economic contraction period, as did many unicorns during the last big recession (2007–2008).[166]

Before this, it was incredibly unusual for a startup to dislodge a large player, let alone an industry, because the barriers to entry were too high. No more.

Startups can get funds with relative ease today. Increasing numbers are launched every year and the figures are growing fast. America has the most, followed by India, the UK and Canada, with many more countries hot on their heels.

More and more startups are clustering in cities that are attracting and catering to these new economic athletes, mimicking the Silicon Valley model with a critical mixture of talent, universities, support organisations, startups, facilities and lifestyle. Already this has created wealth on par with the GDP of a G7 economy.[167]

In addition, more startups are growing more quickly (10 per cent per week is a figure offered) and greater numbers are taking less time to scale and succeed at IPOs.[168]

Governments worldwide are playing an important role in giving access to funds to these startups with incentives and venture capital. The confluence of expertise and funding in incubators and accelerators is unprecedented, feeding entry numbers and success rates.

And governments are expected to support small businesses and startups post Covid-19, as they did with banks, airlines and large businesses.

Even banks, and certainly neo banks, know that although nothing is guaranteed, no failure is as bad as not seeing the next big thing.

Grab customers, not market share

We say grab customers because grabbing market share is not what's relevant.

Distinguishers are displacers in whole or in part. They dislodge others from their market pedestals.

In any revitalisation or fresh startup, the battle is not for market share and product category, it's a battle for share of customers.

This insight helps to engage people and get them aligned to a new vision. It also helps recruit the right-minded people, in order to speed things up.

Uber displaced taxis and car sales. Airbnb has somewhat displaced the hotel industry. Crowdfunders are doing a good job of displacing bank loans and investments.

SodaStream countering gigantic quantities of bottled water and softdrinks is not about the share of the drinks or water in the bottle. Its job is to get consumers to change their behaviour and make their own fizzy or flavoured water at home, effectively trying to extinguish water sold in throwaway bottles.

M-KOPA is not about a better kerosene product, less toxic, cheaper, that lasts longer. It's about how to displace kerosene and create a solar alternative for poor people in Kenya, and Africa as a whole, in order to genuinely and positively change their lives.

The brave bit is when it may mean displacing one's own product or service. It's the fear of cannibalisation, not lack of budget or resources, that prevents incumbents from doing that.

But no matter how strong their brand is, the consequence is often the same: others do it for them.

Technology alone can't do it

By now there have been too many success stories that should have woken up even the most hesitant to accept the fact that either they displace or they will be displaced.

There probably isn't an enterprise left that isn't spending something on technology. Technology budgets are easy to get and raise. But that doesn't help without a change in mind and model.

Many enterprises think technology will do the job for them or change customer behaviour.

Nothing wakes people up quite as rudely (and fast) as an agreement that not a cent should be spent on technology unless it's a vehicle for producing new, definable, measurable, customer value.

In fact, it's a great alignment tool across the various parts of an organisation.

Going further, what we know is that the use of technology can only magnify what exists. So, technology will amplify what's good to make it better, and equally it will exaggerate what's bad.

It can enlarge the gap between the distinguisher and the extinguisher.[169]

The startup that deploys technology in the old way is as lost as the old guys using new technology for the wrong things.

Inclusiveness is increasing competition and expanding markets

Added to this is the move to inclusiveness, which is making competition for customers anywhere on the pyramid more rife and moving business owners and consumers from the bottom rungs into a new middle class.

Inclusiveness also means that minorities and previously excluded people, like women or the 'pink dollar', become more powerful within economies. Social enterprises are taking on a bigger commercial role, while the informal frugal economy in Africa, India and South America is becoming formal and a formidable force.

Enterprises, NGOs, governments and others, as partners, donors, funders, venture capitalists or simply facilitators, are actively bringing more people into the pool with modern ideas and moves, and making it easier for them to get started and stay in the game.

We can't rely on old barriers to entry

Old barriers to entry are crumbling.

We are discovering this as new technologies and applications emerge, bringing not just advancement for some, but equalisation for many.

TECHNOLOGY DEMOCRATISATION

Technology and access to it is pulling down traditional forms of competitive protection.

This growing democratisation of not only funding but technology and XaaS (anything as a service) means anyone can start up and get big quickly without having the capital for expensive infrastructure.

Let's put it this way: large businesses with big infrastructure and budgets can't keep the small guys out, especially the ones with next and better ideas.

Startups and small businesses have access to the cloud and open source with sophisticated software, intelligence, insights and computing power that were previously proprietary. SaaS and IaaS, etc. provide startups with access to almost unlimited processing capacity, so they can immediately use artificial intelligence and machine-learning to build value-producing capability.

Supercomputing is not just for the few and powerful anymore.

Platforms like Shopify are making small businesses as customer-savvy as big ones. Aggregators pool individual operators so that they can be as competitive as the larger firms. Startups don't even have to carry the cost of a permanent workforce. The gig economy is overflowing with temporary resources and the crowd is on tap, virtually or physically.

And let's remember that when peer-to-peer technology replaces centralised systems, the cost to access the Internet and energy will become zero.[170]

LEAPFROGGING

Emerging markets are leapfrogging.

M-KOPA, now one of the largest IoT companies on the African continent, and the largest Microsoft user, was born in the cloud. This enables it to analyse billions of datapoints a month, monitoring power usage, linking that to payment systems, remotely controlling equipment, monitoring performance, troubleshooting and predicting maintenance to prevent outages in real time.

Its sales agents, spread out across East Africa in the field, are able to collect real-time data and location reports from their teams with smartphones, reducing data compilation from a six- to eight-hour job to one that takes less than a minute.[171] This makes it extremely competitive and poised for speedy scale.

Leapfrogging in emerging markets means these countries no longer have to wait for the great innovations, as we saw when Virgin's Hyperloop chose India as one of its major launch pads. The implication is that new brands from emerging countries can easily be transferred into richer countries, becoming serious contenders.

INTELLECTUAL PROPERTY (IP)

Then there's the change in intellectual property (IP) and whether it can create or protect market power.

It's true, patents, trademarks, copyright and trade secrets provide some barriers to avoid competitors stealing or copying. But they are also not going to win customers at scale or speed.

In fact, making what is proprietary open is often what accelerates take-up and adoption. Volvo invented the modern seatbelt and shared its patent in order to make sure it got take-up. Every car manufacturer and end-user adopted it super quick. It also solidified its positioning on safety.

We see the same today in medical devices and 3D printing. And Tesla is freely sharing its electric vehicle technology patents, in order to speed up the market for electric cars. It benefits Tesla because it helps developers create the infrastructure it needs to accommodate and accelerate adoption.

Unilever publishes its research, for example, on the impact on trachoma of hand- and face-washing so it can be shared to speed up adoption rates.

The fact is that distinguishers know how to pull together all the bits (which may or may not be protected) into outcomes and change behaviour, to build new markets.

That's the IP that matters.

What Discovery Insure has mastered is how to get people to drive safely. What Fitbit can do is make people move and exercise more. SodaStream knows how to stop people buying carbonated water in a plastic bottle in stores and make it themselves at home. It's how Unilever gets kids to wash their hands that puts them ahead, NatWest gets people and enterprises to realise financial goals quicker, and Airbnb makes people feel at home wherever they are.

What Discovery Vitality knows is how to get people eating well and staying fit to be healthier. Now they are taking that know-how to banking, at scale, speed and low cost.

That's their IP and barrier to competitive entry.

Even in pharmaceuticals, the future of patents and trade secrets is uncertain. AI and data have become more important in drug discovery and life sciences, making it more difficult to protect product inventions. The real advantage is in knowing how that product acts and reacts with patients in combination with other things—what works for whom, why, and what doesn't.

And then scale that knowledge for other patients, to create a never-ending IP advantage.

And in the on-demand streaming age where customers don't own but access, what does copyright actually mean? Spotify may pay music producers a legal fee, but Spotify's the brand that effectively controls demand and supply and owns the market.

REGULATION

Regulation used to be a protective mechanism for large businesses. But these days regulators are increasingly intent on driving competition, as we see, for example, with open banking, Germany's revised decision re Uber and the Hyperloop foray into transportation.

The point is that, provided it's good for consumers, demand will increasingly dictate regulation.

When the banks in Nairobi finally took notice of M-PESA, it had grown so popular that the establishment couldn't convince the government to stop it. Airbnb and Uber are all testament to the emerging model in which the regulation follows the innovation. In the rise of dronology we are watching it before our eyes, Amazon having got approval for it in the US and iFood in Brazil. Many others no doubt will soon follow.

Short-termism holds up innovation

Finally, there seems to be a movement away from short-termism. The quarterly result phobia is over.

Nothing groundbreaking can be built, launched and scaled with the old return on investment (ROI) model, which stipulated that you make incremental changes and earn funds back quickly.

LEGO says that becoming digitally native is a 10-year journey.

The Discovery global epic to become a world behavioural expert (not just another bank) spans two decades.

And it's not over yet.

Distinguishers show they can deliver transformational change over the longer term but deliver in short spurts. They are continuously building credibility and equity. And they are continuously investing.

Amazon keeps putting money back in, much to the dismay of people who want profit now. Bezos keeps telling them not to invest in his model if they don't get it.

He and Amazon continue to put money where his/its mouth is and the brand continues to spend more on innovation than any other in the world, more than Microsoft, Apple or Alphabet.

And it continues to outmanoeuvre them.

CHAPTER 23

Finding positive energy

Zuckerberg tells this story about Facebook's early funding challenges. An investor asked him, 'Tell me who else has built a global social network and done it successfully?', to which Zuckerberg
replied, 'That's the point, no one has.'

And that *is* the point.

But sadly, this response still happens too often.

And when new ideas get knocked and kicked back it's often
because it's the most senior in legacy enterprises who hold the
purse-strings, or old-school investors or funders who need
reassurance that the ideas will work.

Before they have happened.

Working with 'points of light'

Many extinguishers and their consultants think that the changes we are talking about are about reprioritising budgets and
timelines. They make and manage spreadsheets and believe that
execution is happening when ambitions and milestones are in
place and are being tracked.

But nothing of substance actually changes.

If there is one critical success factor distinguishers have learnt about starting something completely new, it's that it requires pulling the right people with them. Efforts can be accelerated or slowed down by the energy of the people who are involved initially.

Scaling fast means working with positive energy. Who are the people who will speed things up and who will hold things up is the first question to be answered.

Positive energy is the fuel that gets things going, keeps attracting the right people and funding, travels the journey when things get messy, and keeps the pace going and growing.

Points of light are people who come from the innovator population but have special attributes.

- Like innovators, they like the challenge that doing something different brings.
- They rely on and trust their intuition.
- But they also want the data if it exists.
- They are informed as well as inspiring.
- They don't do innovation just because they enjoy change or some new wizard technology (which innovators tend to do), but because they are truly dedicated to something new that is *better*.
- They always have a vision even and especially if it's contrary to what they are currently doing.
- They can tolerate contradictions and ambiguity. This is important if they are in an existing organisation, because for a good deal of the time they will have to live in two worlds—the old and the one for which they are fighting—and they will have to perform while they transform.
- What they have to do, they learn how to do continuously, as opposed to extinguishers who have to know how to do something before they start.
- They know how to learn with emergence, i.e. when and while it's happening, not what's already happened. As one executive put it, 'They learn from the future as it's happening, instead of from past experience.'
- They believe the opportunity is absolutely there. They just

have to get others to see it.
- They are not afraid to have the hard conversations and are consistent in their message.
- They have a vested interest in the whole, which they fiercely pursue, unlike extinguisher types who are preoccupied with preserving their own turf.
- They think open source and work open source. They are not proprietary by nature.
- They influence people because they have a purpose to which others aspire or they are able to get them to do so.
- They never forget to keep repeating this purpose to themselves and the enterprise, whenever and wherever they get a chance.
- They make sure they are on important meeting agendas, which is critical to success.

It's hard to define 'points of light', but you know them when you see them in action. It's a rare combination of fluid and solid, resilient but restless, agile by nature, but also with an ability to work within the rhythm of the enterprise culture.

Distinguishers surround themselves with smart and diverse points of light, unafraid to be challenged.

They don't only come from the top of an enterprise; they sit everywhere and anywhere and come from diverse backgrounds. They need to be found and used, in order to move at speed and scale, navigating the old while embracing the new.

It's quite a list. See Definition: points of light, for a summary, page 232.

How many do you know?

Seeing risk differently

How quickly people, inside or out, take up a new idea is somewhat related to their training and personality, but more so to how they interpret risk and the models they use to determine it.

Distinguishers want to stand out and to stand out means taking risks. The naysayers want to minimise risk, but often ironically risk more when they say no. An old cliché, perhaps, but so true.

Enterprises and industries programme behaviour because of policies around risk. And this can inhibit innovation and change or a new initiative taking off. Attitudes and protocols that protected banking and insurance in the past, for example, have in many ways been responsible for making them vulnerable to fintechs, crowdfunding and startups.

Too many layers, too many lawyers, too much control, too many committees, too much paperwork, too much protocol, taking too much time to make decisions, all in the name of better risk management, have often excluded good customers who should have been included, such as startups, gig and lower-income consumers. And included customers it should not have, as we saw from the 2008 financial crisis, in which customers were financially overextended.

In the same way, the risk model that traditional insurance companies have used has made them a target for outsiders. The risk mentality inherently puts them and their consumers in direct conflict, keeping them from risk, instead of their customers.

Isn't this ironic, given that insurance companies are in the business of protecting people? And with that model, of course when things did go wrong (which is why customers buy insurance in the first place), they endeavoured to minimise claims, to inflate their bottom line.

Enter Lemonade, which saw this as a crisis and did the opposite. It changed the model, and instead of driving a lowest-claim bottom-line model, it took a straight fee. Instead of having salespeople and brokers pushing for commission, it dealt directly with customers, cycling the savings back into a common pot. Rather than relying on averages, history and a standard one-size-fits-all application sheets to screen customers, which says nothing about individuals, it used behavioural data. Because of this approach it makes better decisions about which clients to take on, and its loss ratios are lower.

People think distinguishers are bigger risk-takers. This is wrong. Whether in an enterprise or on their own as a startup entrepreneur, they are much better at managing risk because they are better at seeing where the problems are and they are better at addressing them more proactively.

Let's put it this way: if you ask extinguishers to parachute out of a plane, they will assess the risk and probably avoid it by refusing. Rather safe than sorry will be the attitude. A distinguisher will find out what the risks are, where they are, how they can be overcome, and will practise and train to counter them and become a success at parachuting.

Attitude to risk can wreck any plan to revitalise or launch a new brand or industry. Interestingly, Amazon evidently decided to do a good deal of its drone-testing outside of the US, because the approval process there was risk-averse, reticent, tedious and long, unduly holding up progress.

Attitudes to risk are a red light. And they can be useful as a guide for newcomer recruitment and for corporates to understand who to involve early on in an organisation overhaul.

Resist the resistors

Books are still being written on how to deal with resistors and resistance. But what we know is this: it takes up massive amounts of time, is exhausting, and while often par for the course, has to be managed not magnified, otherwise it can seriously hold up any attempt to get things started or gather steam.

Trying to get consensus when speeding up can kill any high-level initiative, because people take on new ideas at different rates. Most people know this but tend to ignore it in their desire to avoid conflict and 'get the team on board'. They confuse collaboration with consensus. They think that if they get everyone's point of view they have collaborated. They end up with collective ignorance instead of collective intelligence.

TABLE 23.1: *Extinguisher and Distinguisher Attitudes to Risk*

Extinguishers	Distinguishers
minimise the enterprise's risk	minimise the customer's risk
fear the risk of doing	fear the risk of not doing
believe that history determines risk	believe that the future determines risk
use average profiles as risk indicators	use behaviour of individual customer as a risk indicator
avoid risk	find ways to mitigate risk
say, 'A lot can go wrong—let's not do it'	say, 'A lot can go right—let's do it'
frame problems as blocks and barriers	reframe problems as opportunities

Collaboration is good when there is direction, but great, bold ideas usually come from, or are picked up by, one or two points of light.

Many distinguishers agree that success at getting quick alignment in the direction to take means identifying the great idea and then managing the process of getting enough people mobilised around it to get enough momentum, rather than trying to get everyone to agree.

Distinguishers and energy points are forward-thinking, they are opportunity-spotters and once they see something that's possible, they seldom let go.

It's how to bring others along that presents the challenge and frustration, because that's what can speed things up or bring them to a halt.

Typical remarks from resistors are:

- We've tried it before and it failed.
- We have no burning platform.
- Our products or margins will suffer.
- This is risky.
- How much will it make?
- We have no resources to spare.
- How does it fit with our objectives?
- We don't have the capabilities.
- The timing is wrong.
- It doesn't fit with how we currently work.
- We're waiting for the industry to take off.
- Give me something concrete to see.

And of course, the good old, 'Who's already done it successfully?'

Negative energy may be vocal and out in the open, but it may not be, and in either cases it can cause doubt and distraction and the depletion of time and energy for those who want to get on with an idea.

It's a hard lesson to learn, but it's critical to aim for positive energy, especially initially, and bring others in, who take longer to buy into an idea, as the process develops.

It takes discipline.

And a thick skin not to let negativity fester.

Definition: 'Points of light'

'Points of light' are people who:		
Mine the big idea and go with it no matter where it comes from, and don't let their ego get in the way of the end result	Y	N
Are transparent and truth-tellers	Y	N
Are listeners but decision-makers	Y	N
Don't blame and point fingers at others, they take responsibility	Y	N
Know and learn how to influence 360 degrees	Y	N
Don't necessarily have the knowledge but learn quickly	Y	N
Don't give up when they are frustrated, they persevere	Y	N
Regard failure as a lesson learned, without taking it personally or a reflection of their own ability	Y	N
Don't have to hear they are smart, rather what effort has been put in	Y	N
Are not looking for agreement on details, rather for alignment on direction and if decisions and action are contributing to that direction	Y	N
Get excited and inspired when they see others succeed, unlike others who feel threatened or jealous	Y	N
Are there to do a job, not keep a job and are therefore unafraid to do whatever it takes	Y	N

HOW DOES HE OR SHE RATE?

CHAPTER 24

High-impact storytelling

Getting people onboard, interested and excited through story-telling is an important part of speeding up.

So, having a compelling story to tell and sell is fundamental.

Says Bezos: 'You can have the best technology, you can have the best business model, but if the storytelling isn't amazing, it won't matter.'[172]

Needless to say, a story develops over time, starting with communicating the high-level concept through to the more detailed account of what needs to be done and how.

Stories are different from business plans. This is another obvious statement, but it is often missed, which can hold up and hinder a bold plan.

The brain is wired for stories

Research shows that when a good story is told the same part of the brain lights up for the sender and the receiver.[173]

People think in stories stemming from childhood and it is the most powerful form of influence. It presents a picture that no business plan or set of numbers can. People become absorbed in stories, not in endless slides and bullet points.

As Steve Jobs so poignantly put it, 'People who know what they're talking about don't need PowerPoint.'[174]

Stories are narratives, and if well told and credible can present an exciting picture that people can identify with and respond to positively and quickly. Whereas traditional business plans instruct (and mostly are budgets), stories inspire people to want to be involved, because they believe in the better future that is being presented.

Whatever picture a story paints, it always makes assumptions, which is what some people object to. But hey, so do business plans!

Stories about a future yet to unfold take people on a journey. That's what distinguishers want, to captivate colleagues and customers alike so they can pull the vision along.

Crafting the story

After the formulation of the idea, a story has to be crafted. Nothing can start or grow without a story. It doesn't matter how simple or sophisticated a transformational idea is, it needs a strong story if others are to be enticed by it and become involved.

Distinguishers who succeed in pulling in people and funds create a story they feel passionate about, which goes beyond the obvious.

Here's one from Rover's CEO: 'Rover is not just about offering an alternative to kennels for overnight dog boarding. That's something we do, but that's not our vision. We believe at Rover that there's no development in the history of humankind that has contributed more to our happiness than the domestication of dogs.'[175] Only 40 per cent of people in America have dogs. Rover hopes to get that rate up.

Telling and selling the story

Stories have to be told but also sold. Passion goes part of the way, but the ability to actually sell the idea to the relevant audience is paramount.

At a high level, storytelling means saying what is going to be done differently and why, and who is going to gain. In Uber's case it was the consumer, but also taxi drivers who needed work and a better deal. And what was added was that Uber was also good for cities and the cosmos as car-sharing would reduce congestion and CO_2 emissions.

It began with a simple idea for consumers: 'Click a button and get a ride.' And it started in Paris on a cold snowy evening when Travis Kalanick and Garrett Camp couldn't find a cab. That's how the Uber founders began to tell their story about a future yet to happen where anyone could get a ride at any time, from someone who was around and had spare space.

Not-for-profit Portbase talks about connecting parties to build a strong and smart integrated global logistics chain in order to improve the competitive position of the Netherlands. That's the story that got to people and built the message that got strong speedy engagement and buy-in, moving the strategy forward.

Metaphors matter, hooks help

Metaphors are powerful tools because people latch on to them and they act as a binding mechanism in telling and selling stories. In Uber's case, Kalanick used running water. 'Transportation should be like running water and we want to make that happen absolutely everywhere, for everyone,' he said in public and private forums.[176]

Unilever has told many stories as its handwashing initiatives have progressed. One of the most memorable in India was, 'Always wash your hands before you eat', which was literally burnt into roti bread.

In a bold move to get more kids to wash hands, a behaviour change it believes should start at a young age, Unilever is now changing the way children recite the alphabet. Instead of 'h' standing for hat, house or horse, the company aim is that it should stand for handwashing. They are making this hook universal through schools, governments and education advisors and institutions, hoping to create a handwashing movement and get worldwide traction to accelerate a permanent behaviour change at grassroots level.

Now that's a story worth repeating!

They will also rely on professional storytellers as a backup. Lifebuoy will partner, for instance, with a range of partners like Sesame Street to create educational storytelling for children, teachers and families across Asia and Africa.

Messaging stems from stories

A lot can be learnt from brands that tell their stories well.

When Uber went to India it faced competition, from a driver force that had to be weaned off daily pay and customers who were suspicious. The brand told stories of real drivers and real riders, which changed the perception, and by 2020 Uber had 50 per cent of the market and was expanding to 200 Indian cities.[177]

Airbnb isn't a hotel chain and it's more than just a simple app that connects hosts and guests. Its story is that Airbnb is a community of people who believe in openness and are accepted and acceptable everywhere.

Belonging is a worldwide value, and is a message that speaks to the core of what Airbnb stands for, says Brian Chesky. 'We are committed to helping people belong no matter where they are in the world.'[178]

Socialising stories

Stories are also about what people say about you when you're not in the room.

Stories need to have viral potential and be translatable into messages that resonate and can be verified.

Most Airbnb messaging consists of stories told by hosts and guests to reinforce this purpose, humanise it and give it authenticity and currency. Airbnb also uses local stories to bring the brand into the social sphere, including informing on harmful stereotyping in Africa and marriage equality in Australia and elsewhere.[179]

Living the story

As an example, at Zoom, all meetings were (and still are) run on Zoom. When customers requested a visit, CEO Eric Yuan insisted on a Zoom call with them first and a face-to-face visit afterwards, only if needed.

When money was being raised, he made sure that all investors had downloaded the Zoom app. Zooming, rather than travelling, is so much part of his and the firm's DNA, that when he took a flight to Zoom's IPO, it was one of the few times he had done this in years.

Sometimes action speaks louder than words.

It's more than a tale

High-impact stories that get traction and momentum should contain:

- **A single message**. This should matter and be replicable, easy to communicate and scale. It contains the essence of what the intended or reviving brand stands for that makes it modern, meaningful and memorable—and, sometimes, culturally transferable/universal.

  Nike performed best in industry, beating digital sales estimates during the pandemic because its 'Playingfortheworld' inspired people through the power of sport to stay fit and healthy at home. It told a story in all its customers' communications, without trying hard to sell anything.

  It delivered a message of solidarity using its platform and mobile app with well-known athletic heroes and master trainers exercising and giving customised live streamed workouts. Everyone (young and old) was brought together with video footage of routines done in kitchens, bathrooms, bedrooms and basements, as a way to bring together people of all sorts and countries from around the world who believed in fitness and health.

- **A good reason for change**. There needs to be a reason to do the transformation, backed by numbers if possible. In the Unilever handwashing story, it was that one child dies every 23 seconds in the world from poor hygiene[180] and that 41 per cent of these deaths could be prevented with better handwashing behaviour.[181]

    For Rover it was that 43 per cent of people with dogs don't travel because they don't want to leave their pet in a kennel or ask family or friends for a favour.[182]

- **A stated purpose**. This needs to be compelling and should contrast the old with the new. Lifebuoy was the soap chosen to drive the handwashing awareness campaign, partly because it was a longstanding market leader in soap, but also because its stated purpose was to prevent illness and saves lives through cleanliness and better hygiene practice, thus making people feel safe achieved through handwashing. The concept was totally in sync with Unilever's Sustainable Living Plan. And couldn't have been more on the button during Covid. Slack emphasised the unexpected benefits for enterprises in its purpose because employees didn't have to travel, and now had remote-working collaboration tools that were productive and saved time and energy, bringing together all the bits that email couldn't.

- **A narrative that taps into one or more triggers**. It should be logical, emotive, and/or social. People are more inspired when it has all three. An example is Uber's story. It was logical (reason to do it, convenient, saves time, money and effort); emotive (taxi drivers need a better deal); and social (force for good, cities will have less congestion and pollution).

- **A clear market space** to be occupied, which becomes the accepted strategic framework and incorporates all the possibilities and outcomes not yet imagined. Think mobility (Uber), empowered through fitness (Nike), safe driving (Discovery Insure), global trade performance (Portbase).

Consistency is the thread that holds together the spread of an innovation. The Nike story is inspirational in that regard. Though its styles differ constantly, it's been saying the same thing over the years—that it wants to empower people mentally and physically, irrespective of hardship, age or culture.

This has led to continuous opportunities to create meaningful events, content and loads of personal stories about people becoming their best self, not about buying sneakers or why Nike sneakers are better than others. Who can forget its fabulous timeless line—'Just do it!'?

In Uber's case, even through trouble with employees, press, competitors and various regulators the brand continued to tell the story. As one executive said, 'If you're not telling your story, then people fill that box with whatever gets clicks.'[183]

Most successful distinguishers would agree with this. Says Stewart Butterfield, CEO of Slack, 'If there's one piece of advice I could go back to give myself, it is to concentrate on that storytelling part, on the convincing people. If you can't do that it doesn't matter how good the product is, it doesn't matter how good the idea was for the market, or what happens in the external factors, you don't have the people believing.'[184]

CHAPTER 25

Hacking work

One of the things learnt from the pandemic is how to work fast.

Remote work was suddenly rife and customers and enterprises of all sizes had to work differently. As Slack put it, it pushed them to become agile with Agile!

The brand went from being able to add a few company users within a system, to dramatically adding elevated numbers, doing in 72 hours what would have taken 15 months previously.

Things that seemed impossible to do a few months before turned out to be manageable because it was clear there was no choice, according to the CEO.

The usual concerns and reasons for not doing something fell away:

- only the most important work was prioritised;
- meetings were shorter;
- decisions were made faster;
- learning from mistakes was rapid and quickly rectified.

Slack was not an isolated case.

During the pandemic, many governments, enterprises and people cracked into action and found they could do things at speeds never before imagined:

- In record time, India and Pakistan repurposed their trains to become hospital wards for patients. Each cabin was converted into an isolation ward for one patient, with space provided for medicine and equipment.
- A Mercedes Formula One team and University College London collaboration re-engineered a positive airway pressure breathing aid in less than 100 hours from the start of the project.
- Asimov Robotics, a startup in India, quickly developed robots that were placed in streets and buildings to dish out hand sanitisers and masks, and in hospitals to help hand out medicines and food.
- In Brazil, community workers were trained at scale and speed to provide care and information to families and back to doctors, collect data and refer problems to nurses and doctors.
- In South Africa, several hundred people with an idle 3D printer formed a group to speedily produce masks for emergency workers.
- In China, to keep up with retail demand, Freshippo hired thousands of out-of-work restaurant and shop staff and simplified its procedures so that within two hours of training they could begin working in the ultra-high-tech grocery store.
- Within two to three weeks of the pandemic, South African Discovery Insure executives working from home repurposed the entire system (complex as it was), from rewarding people for driving better over distances, to rewarding them for driving less—staying home whenever possible.
- Within six months, Unilever went from producing around 700,000 sanitisers a month to 100 million, up to then unheard of.
- Uber was quick to introduce Uber Medics, rolled out into over 20 countries including Spain, India, France, Germany and the UK, after a request was made by the Spanish health authorities to offer free and discounted rides to healthworkers. The drivers were guaranteed full fees.[185]

Responding and adapting became more important than sticking to plans. All the red tape that was previously good practice was thrown away.

And new ways of working made agile more important and the undoubted new normal practice, in order to win customers at scale and speed.

Find the faster model

Distinguishers, whether in startups or mature companies, had already done away with the old command-and-control model before Covid-19, although the pandemic sped things up.

Napoleon's method of communication up and down a hierarchy was being displaced with a contemporary approach in which communication works sideways and new principles were being used to drive speedy delivery.

For those who start afresh it's easy to build a team using new ways of working, but if the change is to come from within an existing mature organisation it's just more difficult.

Here are three options we've encountered for starting the new model from inside. Each comes with pros and cons. Either of these can be made to work:

1. The internal project venture
Points of light are assembled to form a team to set up a project, either full time or as part of an existing job. Someone takes the lead, usually with an Exco sponsor, funded from the annual transformation budget (OpEx not CapEx). They will have a remit to do things differently, but in truth usually have to use the existing people, culture, systems and infrastructure. Consultants are often brought in to help with content and process and get people to think anew.

PROS:
- Can be set up quickly as part of an existing management programme, with resources like subject experts accessible in principle (if they cooperate, are available and on the right wavelength).
- Easy to get ExCo and board support—but they are in control with the existing governance structure and the operating rhythm remains unchanged.

CONS:
- Team has to abide by the current organisation's procedures, so there is a risk of falling back and doing more of the same.
- May suffer 'the death by a thousand paper cuts'. Anything is possible but it's a fight against the big machine and this can be highly discouraging.
- Rewards systems and performance reviews are based on old criteria, focused on individuals not teams, and tend to be competitive not collaborative.
- The project is funded out of a budget which means any budget cuts will likely affect the team's ability to execute the plan.
- Easy to start but also easy to kill.
- The consultant culture may dominate and because they usually charge fees for time, this can hold things up.

2. The free-standing venture

This is the polar opposite of the internal project team in that its aim is to create something completely separate (perhaps even a new brand) outside of the organisation, and buy time to make it work. It's funded separately, with a dedicated CapEx and OpEx outside of the annual departmental budget, and is managed like an investment (rather than a transformation project). New people, not necessarily accessed internally, need to be found to take on new ventures. May use consultants on freelance basis to join for a while to assist to do new tasks.

PROS:
- Provides autonomy to set up a separate, dedicated workforce, using new blood, some of which may come from inside (often jobs are advertised internally) with new ways of working and rewarding, ring-fenced, protected from routines, rules and existing culture.
- Predictable funding model, particularly if set up like a VC investment with tranches of funding released against clearly defined milestones. This can also help to speed up delivery of the venture as it will get funding only when targets are met.

CONS:
- Everything is built from scratch. This takes more time and money to get set up.
- More difficult to access internal resources as ventures are now seen to compete with existing models.
- Although there may be major support from the funding board with a separate budget, it is often not in harmony with funds and feelings of ExCo.
- Tends to become competitive and attracts envy, since the new venture is seen as fun, sexy and privileged.
- No access to the existing customer base can slow things down.

3. The cross venture: In between 1 and 2

Neither in nor out, it's either a team or division that sits in the organisation, but on the fringe, with a mandate and separate budget (OpEx and CapEx) to do something differently. It is most likely separated physically, in a different office or even city. It is usually run by a distinguisher maverick (not a person the culture knows or is used to) with a reasonable degree of autonomy, surrounded by points of light this person recruits or choose to join the team because they want to be part of the new purpose and action. Not everything has to be built from scratch, so it's easier and quicker. Although the venture is linked to the organisation, it is able to deliberately choose what fits and what doesn't. Because it's not an outsider, it's not seen as a competitor, so it doesn't get as much resentment and resistance. Consultants are used to both think and do new things.

PROS:
- Can get going really quickly.
- Can decide what to access and what to buy outside, does not have to use only what exists.
- Can use existing customer base for research, data-modelling, beta-testing, etc.
- Has a brand image to pull in resources and support.
- Flow of funds are available if goals are met.

CONS:
- Existing culture seeps in; constant persistent effort is needed to build a new culture and new ways of working.
- Part of the organisation is old waterfall, command and control, and part is agile, so lots of time is spent or wasted explaining why things are done differently and educating as to why this is necessary.
- Needs very strong sponsorship to get and keep it going.

The model may start in one form and end up in another as the organisation tries to transition its existing way of working into the new one, bringing more people along. With NatWest, what started as a free-standing enterprise later became a cross venture for the new value proposition and delivery. The team that had sat outside the existing organisation was moved back into the core of the business, and then people were migrated into the new model, which by that stage had been tried, tested and proven successful. This sped up the time it took to move from an old to a new model. They took it out, made it right and brought it back in.

The new model becomes the heart of the transforming legacy enterprise.

Why work is more complex

With any of the three models, new ways of working must become dominant if new consumption and production behaviours are to gather speed sustainably.

And it's just more complex today.

True distinguisher behaviour means devoting time and tasks to producing customer outcomes that cross over products, silos, brands and industries. This requires interdependencies far greater than just making and selling new versions of single, discrete products or services.

Data needs to be collected, analysed and deployed from multiple sources by multiple teams. Technology needs to fuel and integrate customer experience delivery. Servicing needs to be instant. People with different skills sets, from different places, sometimes even different enterprises, need to be brought together seamlessly and quickly.

Extinguisher companies, typified by product silos, are managed by multiple kings and queens, each aiming to build and keep their own independence from the others. But for a distinguisher enterprise, there can be only one kingdom: one kingdom with a collection (it could be hundreds) of high-performing teams with clear purpose and relevant skills.

And in order to cut down on time and effort and produce better customer results, requires collaborators.

In fact, the entire ecosystem is one interconnected kingdom though it's constantly evolving, requiring hyper-collaboration, even if one lead brand is orchestrating it.

Instead of having silos, each with its own agenda and accountability targets, new ways of work dictate that people come together irrespective of the silo, brand or industry they belong to, in order to produce the value that will set the enterprise apart.

Customers don't care about departments or who reports to whom, they care only that they get a complete customer experience with as little friction as possible.

From the get-go, these new complexities have to be managed to deliver at scale and speed:

- Every part of the network, physical and digital, must converge and work needs to be organised to make this possible.
- Because technology and data are integral to producing out-comes, each working group needs to be powered and empowered by tech so that they can join things up.
- Each group needs to be multidisciplinary, so different skills sets need to be brought together. For example, in any marketing group there could be data scientists, behavioural experts, system architects, software engineers, communication experts, content and community managers and designers, alongside traditional marketers.
- Because things are happening faster, everything needs to be more flexible.

Managing this complexity at scale and speed requires people, processes and technology to be brought together to carry out the tasks that will make the envisioned future a reality, increasingly over time zones and space.

In distinguisher enterprises, a lot of time and effort is spent by management to understand this complexity and its interdependencies, and break them down into a set of manageable issues and challenges that don't cause conflict and time delays. NatWest refers to this as moving from 'the complex to the complicated. Complexity is dealt with by the leadership team, breaking it down to smaller complicated issues that can then be delegated and dealt with.'

For example, one of the NatWest challenges was how to deal with customer data needed by many different teams—marketing, customer service, fraud, credit risk, onboarding, etc. In the past, everyone would have had their own database. Now, the data needed to be part of an integrated system that would be everywhere, accessible in different ways to everyone, so that it would be valuable to each section simultaneously.

The leadership team had to figure out how to achieve the complexity of the combination of centralisation and decentralisation. Then the experts were called in to actually build it so that complicated tasks could be achieved: for example, how to identify and manage a unique customer through the entire experience, or build a platform that could be developed simultaneously by many teams without versioning issues or conflicting code.

The 12-month plan is dead

Twenty or even ten years ago an enterprise could predict where it would be in a year's time and build a plan accordingly. Today it can't because things are moving and changing direction too quickly.

Ironically, extinguishers still feel safe with long-term large projects with specific objectives. Distinguishers don't. They go for missions, which are statements of what needs to be accomplished in continuous incremental deliverables.

It used to be that this long-term planning came from the top. Now, the mission comes from the top but the plan on how to get there comes from self-organised and autonomous working teams, in short re-iterative bits.

Missions for a particular period lead to a set of goals that are broken down into quarterly cycles and even shorter sprints. How it's done is left to the team's discretion.

The team is organised around tasks, producing customer outcomes (or its part of that). Everything they need to get it done must be within their control, end to end.

Instead of having a plan to deal with a complexity, or a complex organisational structure to navigate through, small teams have simple plans.

Amazon, famously, is decentralised into 'The Two-Pizza Team', i.e. 'a team small enough to feed on two large pizzas', who deliver key customer outcomes like 'drone-based delivery' or 'a new Echo experience'. What they do, in what order, is completely up to them.

Distinguisher enterprises build a backlog of all the customer experiences they need to create to deliver the customer outcome, and they prioritise them. The self-organising teams then deliver those experiences as quickly and robustly as possible.

First comes the backlog of things to do for customers, then comes the budget and timeline, which can change weekly or biweekly depending on feedback, and changing conditions and technology.

Factory mentality was linear. Technology today means that multiple services, i.e. micro services, can be worked on simultaneously. For example, one Amazon team may be working on 'speeding up the checkout process' and another may be working on 'delivery timing options', and because one is not dependent on the other, both can be done simultaneously to speed things up.

All work emanates from the big idea that is going to get the enterprise to change its model and modus operandi from products and services to new ways of doing things for and with customers.

Jeff Bezos expects and encourages audacious ideas. Once they get the go-ahead, he pushes to get them delivered fast. Focus is on delivering superior customer outcomes, which are well defined. There is no compromise accepted on this.

Distinguisher decisions are data-driven. At Amazon, a decision can be reversed if the data indicates it should be, even if it was initially made by a senior manager. It stops the debate that takes up time.

Extinguishers are more at home with rigid plans, because these provide the structure and order that they need to feel in control.

Distinguishers have long let go of control and find comfort in being adaptable.

Plans can be changed, prioritised and re-prioritised almost in real time. NatWest, for instance, changes its plan every second week, to correct, adjust and update.

The set missions are fixed, but how the brand gets there changes regularly.

Squads and sprints are speedy

The Amazon two-pizza team is the equivalent of a squad (or scrum). Think of the squad as a mini startup. It's self-organising and multidisciplinary, although it can ask for resources or help with problem-solving. A facilitator is allocated to make this way of working easy, identify blockers immediately and help the team constantly improve its processes to win customers.

The squad can release what it is producing on a continuous basis, as it's happening, saving time to market. Any micro service, feature or part of an app that normally takes months to deliver now gets delivered within shorter sprints.

Each squad has a mission everyone knows and cares about. Each member has an active part in choosing which task to work on, which increases engagement and motivation and optimises performance in short periods of time. Tasks are time-boxed. Delivery happens daily.

Everything on this backlog is about delivering the mission. Someone owns the backlog and is responsible for prioritisation, bringing together customer value, business value and technology, and executing instead of waiting for the organisational layers to make decisions.

The squad works in sprints, usually for a week or two, to complete a set amount of work. Each sprint has a set process, a weekly schedule, every day there's a daily stand-up on the delivery for the day. Barriers are discussed daily, escalated and removed, to get the work done faster.

Sprint reviews present work to date, with feedback, and ideas are exchanged to improve things. Ongoing customer feedback is part of the process, with instant changes made.

Squads are held accountable, with a retrospective on the health and progress of the squad and what can be improved. Work and achievement get celebrated weekly. To speed things up, squads are small by nature, but can be scaled up by putting several of them together to form bigger delivery units, sometimes called tribes. These tribes are responsible for joining up the pieces to form the new way of doing things, and to help squads thrive.

The tribes are like incubators for the squads. They look at interdependencies between the squads to avoid blockages that slow things down.

Spotify is well known for organising multiple squads into these tribes. It reports productivity improvements (getting the organisation to deliver better, quicker) of 87 per cent as a consequence.[186]

Spotify also forms guilds, which contain people with specific disciplines from squads so that they can share experiences and learn from each other. If anyone is struggling with a problem, they can share it and find a solution. The guilds are informal, voluntary, organic communities of practitioners. Anyone who is interested can join.

Spotify scales tribes into alliances, co-ordinating all the efforts in the organisation to ensure a unified and complete customer experience. This is how they facilitate complexity, i.e. making it easier and quicker to get the job done.

For distinguishers, agile is not a structure—it's a way of working.

For extinguishers, structure is the way of working.

Which means that when extinguishers change what they want to do, they have to restructure. When distinguishers are changing what they do they don't need to change structure. They adapt, change, stand up and stand down high-performing teams, avoiding lengthy, complicated, time-consuming and costly procedures.

The structures can remain in place while the transformation gathers speed.

Speed up by learning

The agile approach to measuring how quickly things have been done by a squad is by tracking progress of its backlog. Squads are assessed by their velocity and performance and discussions are used to learn how to do things faster.

At the retrospectives, which happen at least every two weeks, squads ask themselves:

- What did I/we learn in this sprint?
- How could I/we have done it faster?
- What can I/we do differently in the next sprint?

Learning is not about how to follow the process better, it's about how to get the job done quicker.

Quality assurance used to be about following a process as a goal in and of itself, to fill out paperwork or to tick certain boxes. Agile says no, the result wanted for customers comes first. Then figure out through learning and constantly changing how to get there faster. To reach the goal, releasing a new customer feature on time, for example, takes precedence over getting it documented.

Distinguishers like Spotify don't wait to do an annual employee survey followed by months of analysis and then a plan to address productivity issues. It builds health checks on a sprint-to-sprint basis, measuring productivity factors in order to continuously build capability to learn and improve tactics and tempo.

This happens at a micro level, where it matters the most because that is where the work gets done, and everyone continuously learns on the job. However, it also happens on a macro level, with tribes, guilds and alliances. Spotify's ExCo does regular retros, which is unusual, because most ExCos talk only about what they do, not how they do it. On the agenda is a standing point: How can we as an ExCo work and make decisions faster?

At the heart of distinguisher culture is moving at speed through learning. They will put an allocated amount of time and budget on 'test and learn'. At NatWest, 10 per cent of both OpEx and CapEx is ring-fenced for experimental innovation. Learning from failures is regarded as an investment in future growth and cost reduction.

When extinguishers fail, it's a sign that things have gone

wrong and that they are underdelivering and underperforming. It stalls things, slows or shuts things down.

When distinguishers fail, they have learnt (hence, the importance of failing fast, because that means they learn fast).

It speeds things up because they get good quickly at what they need to be good at.

Using new tools

There are new tools increasingly available to help make new ways of working more productive and speedier, mainly because information can be accessed and shared in real time.

This is exactly what collaboration tools like Slack, Google Suite and Zoom do.

It's not just having the tools, though, that enables new ways of working to be better and faster. It's how they are used.

When extinguishers deploy new tools, it's to tell the organisation what to do. Information is pushed from the top down, or collected from the bottom up to better govern and control. Communication is one way and not interactive. They think that speed is how quickly the enterprise can do what it has been told to do. A lot of time is spent making sure that content doesn't get shared, but is hidden in silos. Because that's how they control their kingdoms and protect themselves.

When distinguishers use new tools, they are not telling people what to do. The priority is to find and use tools that help teams achieve their mission as quickly as possible.

They want tools that allow people inside and outside the delivering ecosystem to co-create and collaborate in real time and virtually at speed.

The more tools and people that are integrated, the quicker work can get done.

The quicker work can get done, the more competitive barriers to entry go up.

TABLE 25.1: *Extinguishers vs Distinguishers—Ways of Working*

Extinguishers SPEED = HOW QUICKLY PLANS ARE EXECUTED	Distinguishers SPEED = HOW QUICKLY VALUE IS DELIVERED TO CUSTOMERS
Long-term plans	Missions defined—set clear customer outcomes required
Plans fixed	Plans prioritised and re-prioritised
Plan comes from top—people told what to do	Teams self-organised and autonomous
Follow due process	Get what needs to be done fast
Long-term projects 'big bang launch when everything is ready and perfect'	Short-term incremental deliveries
Highest paid opinion decides	Data directs decisions
Plans fixed time to execute	Backlogs constantly re-iterated
Work within red tape	Blockages can be removed
Agree and get consensus on details	Align to get direction right
Linear sequential services dependent on each other to proceed	Micro services simultaneous
Time is managed	Energy is maximised
Work within siloed constraints	Work across space and time
Control and protect information	Share information and learnings
Hide failures	Learn from failure
Individuals/silos receive budget-based bonuses	Cross teams' achievements celebrated and rewarded
Detailed, long-term planning and budgets	Budget and timeline changes reviews and retros weekly/biweekly
Functions	Multidisciplinary squads
Annual calendar	Sprint cycles
Structure dictates way of working	Structure irrelevant for ways of working

PART FOUR

Scale up–Get and stay ahead

Distinguishers have every intention of scaling from the outset.

They have a roadmap. They know what market space they want to open, occupy and own.

They scale customers' outcomes in these market spaces, because that's their stock in trade.

They drive demand using the viral model, with customers as channel and scalesforce, their lead proponents. And with constant virtuous cycles of demand from customers and supply from their ecosystem, attracting more customers and so more partners and participation, they keep on growing.

The first cohorts are enticed in to get the proposition right, then market take-up brings in the early mass market, with numbers multiplying as influence and market power gain momentum through various ongoing scaling techniques.

Using increasing digital components, distinguishers elevate customer outcomes and bring in revenue, while simultaneously pushing down cost, which culminates in disproportionate gains.

That's how they get and stay ahead.

CHAPTER 26

Making outcomes matter

It's customer outcomes that distinguishers scale.

Extinguishers scale by producing and selling more discrete products or services.

Distinguishers scale by producing better outcomes for customers, with positive impacts for multiple customer-stakeholders.

It's what they know better than anyone else how to do. It's therefore their true IP (intellectual property).

Lots of enterprises use the expression 'outcomes'. But few really understand what it means. Banking extinguishers often talk about customer outcomes, but what they mean is how many people have opened an account or taken out a loan.

Sales are not outcomes. Outcomes don't happen to organisations, they happen only to customers. And when they happen, customers are likely to stay and bring others with them.

A big part of getting outcomes to matter in a fresh or changing organisation is getting the language right. This may seem a trifle but it's not, because some of the worst failures occur when words that mean different things to different people get thrown around, leading to confusion, delay and false starts.

One way to wake up an organisation and align people quickly and sustainably is to get them to understand that any proposition, plan or process that isn't there to achieve these customer outcomes is waste.

Language aligns

Discrete products and services are a means (input), like any other, such as technology, apps and trucks.

It's the end (the customer outcome) that really matters and holds currency for the distinguisher.

Distinguishers displace products and services with new ways of doing things. Few music producers make and sell albums (the input) anymore. Most have been extinguished by brands like Spotify, who use and link productions from whoever and wherever so that customers can get better listening enjoyment (the outcome).

A focus on the product, the soap rather than handwashing, the albums rather than the listening experience, can mean scaling the wrong things (the inputs instead of the outcomes), and lead to an extinguishing syndrome—lack of differentiation, increased price competition and diminishing returns.

Fortnite's job is to get people gaming online across the world as teams and tribes collaboratively (the end/outcome), rather than as individuals, not selling video games or skins (the means/input).

When a brand and its ecosystem become the expert at delivering the outcome, it has become true and accountable to what it wants to achieve—its purpose (why it is in business).

Otherwise, the purpose is nothing but a slogan. It might sound great but in reality, it achieves nothing.

Imagine the aha moment when the Airbnb team realised that its brand was about travelling guests feeling they belonged anywhere (the outcome)—a home away from home—rather being just an accommodation platform (the input). This realisation provided the purpose internally as well as the customer outcome needed externally.

Birthed in Cape Town in 2014 to drive precision agriculture through state-of-the-art technology, Aerobotics has catapulted into the US, Europe, Australia and Latin America at breathtaking speed. Getting beyond just making and selling drones, sensors and satellites, it's become *the* expert at managing and enhancing tree and citrus fruit crops (the outcome). Knowing how to do this better than anyone else is how it attracts customers and scale.

And that's the way distinguishers give and get lifetime customer value.

And take and keep the lead.

Moving on, outcomes are then:
- the results and impacts for customers and customer-stakeholders;
- obtained from a combination of products and services embedded with intelligence, often from multiple sources delivered by the lead brand and its ecosystem, with the customer relationship owned by the brand;
- trackable (directionally), measurable (quantified and/or felt) and affirmable (can be incentivised, rewarded, shared and recognised).

Products are:
- the means, not the end result; and
- inputs to outcomes.

Customer experiences are:
- the activities customers go through (*do*) to get the desired outcome.

Brands can only talk about outcomes if customers get the 'complete experience', rather than bits of it. So an airline can provide a good airline experience, for instance, but everything that happens before and after the actual flight in the form of outcomes (or non-outcomes) is part of what creates the 'complete experience'. If that fails, everyone suffers.

What is commonly misunderstood about the customer experience is that people think it refers to only the journey the customers go through to buy a unit product or service. Consequently, a lot of money is spent on so-called 'customer journey management' in a single category, which is really just product journey mapping (i.e., the plane trip, buying and using a drone or sensor).

This perpetuates the old product approach, which is all too easy to copy.

In the Aerobotics case it's not about the better product journey to own a drone, sensor or satellite. The brand provides the full complete experience. This starts from planning—when and how farmers plant the trees; placement, rotation, fertilising, irrigation, monitoring for health problems and pests and rectifying disease—to predicting yield and harvesting. It engages with all the activities farmers go through to get an enhanced crop-management outcome, so as to reduce risk and grow crop yields. All the while it uses intelligent tools from insights gathered from data, powered by AI and machine learning. Its very specific purpose is to minimise resources while optimising results for each individual farm. That way it brings back into the conduit individual experiences to build the collective experience that makes Aerobotics the expert.

Part of the complete experience may of course be embedded in the product. The Philips Sonicare e-toothbrushes, with pressure and 3D mouth-mapping sensors, give personalised guidance and tips to improve brushing habits through its app, on customers' smartphones. The objective is to merge the smart product with the customer's activities to get a better oral hygiene outcome. It nudges customers to brush their teeth, gives tactical feedback during brushing, which tells the customers when to move onto the next part of the mouth, warns when the pressure is too high, makes sure that the customer is brushing at the right time and switches off automatically or lowers the pressure to suit that customer's oral profile.[187]

Find the correlates that matter

To scale markets, customer outcomes have to be articulated, translated into goals, tracked, measured and celebrated, shared and recognised both by customers and the brand, so that the new ways of doing things get traction, needed for scale.

Distinguishers therefore make it their business to understand in great depth the correlates that get to a customer outcome. Airbnb knows exactly what goes into a good lodging experience that leads to good reviews, anything from the quality and colour of the bedlinen to the layout of the room, the amenities required, and the impact of price, i.e. how much a host can charge. They know how to guide people to local delights, make them feel they belong and how to connect hosts and guests to get the best relationship.

And it's this capability that creates the demand that keeps growing.

NatWest's new journey is about helping people, families and businesses to achieve their financial goals faster. Prerequisites to this range from being able to buy a house sooner in life, pay off a mortgage earlier, reach a savings goal quicker or go into retirement early, if that's what the customers want. A startup or a mature enterprise should be able to accelerate growth sooner than average, and a startup should be able to take off quicker.

Unilever knows exactly what the most critical health-impact moments are for washing hands, in a new mom or child's day, to reduce disease and early mortality: before eating, after a toilet visit, or before while bathing. It also knows what methods work to get commitment and habits to stick, ranging from soap sensors to sticker diaries. It measures the impact of these methods on mission-critical handwashing moments, to gauge the impact on diarrhoea and other diseases like eye infections, and the brand has learnt to quantify the impact that handwashing interventions have on diseases. For example, in India these have led to 25 per cent fewer incidents of diarrhoea, a 15 per cent drop in respiratory infections and 46 per cent fewer eye infections.[188] They also know that a combination of hand- and face-washing techniques can reduce trachoma (blindness) and through its efforts, it has reduced this by 30 per cent in Kenya, Zambia and Ethiopia.[189]

Some 60 per cent of road accidents are caused by risky driving, which is what Discovery Insure wants to stop. It knows all the variables that lead to poor driving and has made it its business to get a better driving outcome for each of its customers by helping them set and achieve goals, rather than just selling them car insurance.

It also knows what causes accidents, like drinking and driving, driving late at night, driving at high speed, using cellphones while driving, etc. Its data-points can correlate the effects on driving of weather or road conditions like potholes, time of day, routes and the customer/car combination, so that the brand can alert and incentivise people not to disrupt their goals. For example, it provides special discounts to use Uber on weekend nights, to dissuade customers from driving at this time.

Set and track goals

Once the causations and correlates are known, goals can be set by customers themselves or co-created with the brand, in order to achieve the desired outcome.

They may be very tangible and quantifiable, as in Fitbit's case, whose customers go through a daily experience to reach goals like blood pressure and weight levels to get to a connected health outcome.

Nike does the same. With the aim of maintaining customers' physical and mental wellbeing, it offers virtual workouts through its Nike Training Club on YouTube, encouraging sport at home with professional athletes who give workout classes with customers, setting specific goals and measuring progress.

Sometimes goals may be less easy to measure. For instance, Spotify customer goals could be 'to keep discovering new music', 'to be more mindful about choosing what I enjoy', 'be brave enough to share my listening history'.

Either way, if goals are set, tracked and measured, behaviour is more likely to change and become infectious, spreading to larger groups of people.

Data is used by enterprises to track goals. Here are some examples:

DISCOVERY INSURE CASE

Each road trip done by a customer is analysed to see which of the correlates could be improved upon. Every drive counts, which is why every drive is monitored and tracked against set goals. With its intricate design of telematics and AI-powered data analytics, the brand monitors driver behaviour in real time to determine progress, and it knows that this motivates both individuals and truck drivers to change their driving behaviour. To counter fears of surveillance, guarantees are made to consumers that the data received will not impact their premiums adversely.

Every customer has a driving DNA related to important variables, like acceleration, braking, cornering, speed, etc. The brand tracks where each car is and can react to deviations in the data or driving behaviour, such as if someone else is driving the car, or it's involved in an accident, in which case it can proactively react with alerts and emergency assistance.

NATWEST CASE

NatWest knows that the sooner a person starts saving in life, the better that person's saving habits will be throughout life and the quicker her or his goals will be reached. And how much money that saves customers over time. This means getting them to open a savings account earlier, by giving them a higher rate for smaller regular amounts, not just for large amounts, which is what most traditional banks still do.

What it also knows is that people who set goals and achieve them, tend to keep saving more and thus they get to a desired outcome quicker. Instead of just opening a savings account, customers are asked to set a goal, such as saving for a holiday or children's university fees, and to state how much needs to be saved by when, and to keep setting new goals. NatWest then tracks how they are doing and nudges them when they falter, celebrating achievements often, breaking goals down into achievable bite-size milestones.

Energy and spend go into getting the NatWest customer outcome and this is recognised and embedded in internal performance metrics. Instead of KPIs being only about how many new accounts were opened, they are about what customers achieved, like 'How many customers started a savings account early?', 'How many customers achieved their financial goals quicker?', 'How many customers paid their mortgage more quickly than they anticipated/the average?', 'How many customers repaid their credit cards more quickly?'

The customer's win dictates the company's win.

NOOM CASE

Instead of just giving people recipes and menus to control their weight, Noom, the weight-loss app, uses AI, evidence-based guidelines of physiology, psychology and cognitive behavioural therapy. Self-dubbed the Weight Watchers' disruptor, Noom has quadrupled its turnover for the last three years, with more than 50 million users now and a growing base every year.

Founded by Google engineer Artem Petakov, it has found a way to create healthier eating habits in a durable way. It changes the weight-loss industry model from putting people on a diet to fundamentally changing their behaviour to permanently adopt new ways of eating by educating them about what's good for them. It acknowledges that every person's behavioural psychology and physiology is different.

Knowing that nearly 80 per cent of people who lose weight regain it after five years, the brand wants to ensure an eating outcome that lasts, by understanding what factors lead to the maintaining or breaking of eating habits for each individual person and their reaction to each type of food.[190]

This behavioural change to eating has led to outcomes that are sustainable, says the brand, with 60 per cent of users able to maintain their weight loss one year after being on Noom.[191]

After establishing details of their eating and family history, Noom, which localises foodbases and recommendations, reprogrammes people and through a system of education holds them to a plan, using small goals, so that they can lose weight regularly as well as keep it off for good.

Asset-light, the model combines AI and virtual coaches paired to customers, interacting with users via an app that also tracks users' weight, food, exercise, blood pressure and blood sugar. It then correlates these variables with its 3.7 million food-item databases, to see where the problems are, if any.

At the heart of the programme is weight-result tracking (some smart scales can connect automatically). Weight graph trends provide instant feedback, and easy-to-use interfaces allow consumers to log in meals and keep track of their intake.

Noom doesn't believe people have the inclination or time to come to meetings. So it has built powerful and supportive virtual communities so that people can discuss problems with each other and share their struggles and successes. Like other distinguisher brands, it has found that tracking and sharing is critical to making changed behaviour stick. Those users who record and track what they eat, and how far they are from their goal, lose more than those who don't. And Noom ensures that they get plenty of positive reinforcement through badges, feedback and affirmation.

Reward outcomes, not purchases

Which brings us to rewards.

A mistake that extinguishers make is rewarding customers for buying more from them, or staying on with them, so-called loyalty programmes. Sometimes these are embedded into margins, which pushes prices up, but that aside, mostly it's just a no-win because everyone does it and it doesn't do much to build and scale new markets.

What does build and scale new markets is investing in rewards to encourage people to adopt and stay with new behaviours to reach better outcomes, translated into goals for themselves.

When new outcomes are delivered, such as better fitness (Fitbit), or safer driving (Discovery Insure) and quicker financial goals (NatWest), customers stay longer, which is one of the oft-missed levers to keep the customer base scaling.

It's also a way of ensuring that the right thing is being scaled.

Most insurance brands sell health insurance better, quicker and cheaper, in order to compete. They base premiums on age and health status. Discovery Vitality has done it differently. It has a complete wellness system, which taps into consumer data, tracking fitness levels through health assessments and wearables like Nike, Fitbit and others, as well as nutrition, recording what customers buy and eat, incentivising them through discounts to buy healthier foods from partner food stores, Uber Eats and others.

And the same formula is used in all of its additive businesses, like Discovery Insure and Discovery Bank.

But what it is known and loved for by its customers is its reward system. Rewards are based on achieving goals that put individuals into status categories: gold, silver, bronze, diamond, etc. The reward stack varies according to this status, from dynamic interest rates and lower premiums, to flight and gym discounts (at 300 physical fitness facilities), special prices available from 50 high-calibre partners, to e-money or cash linked to improved fitness, nutrition, driving or financial goals once they are set and met. And recently it has added a 'shared-value rewards currency', which customers can spend at partner stores, such as Nike, iStore (Apple SA) and many others.

Customers who are active in the programme are not only healthier, says Discovery Vitality, but also better with their finances. Customers who drive well are less risky, so they get a lower premium on their life cover. And success is recognised inside the organisation. In the first year of its life, over 70 per cent of the new behavioural bank's customer base was already on a high reward level.[192]

Its feedback on rewards is the following. Rewards must be:

- convertible (customers have options);
- cross company (a multi-user customer should be able to use rewards in any business, for example, driving better with Discovery Insure means getting e-money from Discovery Bank);
- simple (if they are too complicated this puts off customers);
- sizeable and significant (they should be large enough to motivate);
- made in a reasonable amount of time (not over too long a period);
- earned even at a lower level of achievement (bite-sized milestones);
- competitive (so that people can see where they rank);
- linked where possible to behaviour change wanted (be outcome-based).

Philips embeds rewards in its Sonicare for Kids toothbrush. Gamified rewards get kids to brush their teeth correctly. The app's digital pet, Sparkly, encourages kids to look after their teeth, monitoring when they have bacteria in their mouth and showing that after the brushing cycle the bacteria 'monsters' have gone.

Virtual badges are given for brushing twice a day and rewards are given by parents, in the form of a cinema trip or a toy. By linking the habit to the reward with virtual badges, money or events that parents pay for, kids are incentivised to change their toothbrushing behaviour and achieve better oral hygiene outcomes, which propels the business model forward.

FITBIT CASE
Data-capture technology, continuously evolving, empowers decision-making to get outcomes because it's sensing what's

happening and monitoring results and impacts. With live sources of data, it gives instant feedback to customers to enhance and optimise their performance.

Many of these apps come with virtual assistant support, which helps people react and change their behaviour to reach whatever objectives they've set for themselves.

Leading in this field is Fitbit, recently bought by Google, clearly because of its interest in the wearables sector. Fitbit started in 2007, selling sensors in small wearable devices to track a person's physical activity. Today, one in five adults in the US are using a fitness tracker,[193] the majority in urban and suburban areas (40 per cent of the population), with global projections for 2022 of 900 million users.

But the fitness tracker is a means to an end, a health and fitness outcome that Fitbit enables now through various services.

Research is still building up on the subject, but what Fitbit can say is that people who track themselves are more likely to change their behaviour than those who don't. What Fitbit does is empower people through data. It discovered that people who count their steps each day will walk more than people who don't. And people who measure how much water they drink will drink more than those who don't. Once they track themselves with a specific goal in mind, they self-regulate their behaviour. And with new habits follow better results, which rewards and motivates people to keep going.

Fitbit has deliberately made its brand into a social experience. It understands the power of a strong network. As a result, it encourages the community on its app, offering customers ways to connect with others for support and inspiration. In the first year, it connected users to contacts and its strategy paid off. It saw a 98 per cent increase in customers who connected to one friend, and overall users averaged more than six friends.

The data reveals the correlation between having support from friends and family and customers being more physically active: users with one or more friends on the platform take 700 more steps per day on average than users without friends.[194]

So it allows customers to track, share and compare data with others like themselves to see how they are doing comparatively. That is how they learn best practice from the crowd and improve fitness performance.

The app has feed updates to help customers monitor themselves and be motivated to move more through data. Friends jointly watch the charts for results.

It has also added gamification, so that people can do things together, such as go for a virtual walk, or challenge contacts, setting each other specific goals to accomplish. Fitbit says another correlation is that consumers who are more socially connected with their friends regularly are more likely to have higher activity rates.

Customers can also attend virtual workouts led by talented trainers, and workouts with other people globally, get to know them and become friends—and join one of over 20 fitness, nutrition, wellness and weight-loss communities.

The tracker sends customers push notifications to help them monitor their movement throughout the day. And the brand rewards people when goals are reached. Points are allocated based on things like steps, active minutes and sleep, which users can convert into discount rewards with a growing network of partners like Adidas and Blue Apron, etc.

Often, just the fact that the customer can see the change is the reward and is then self-regulating.

The Fitbit app also allows its users to share inspirational moments with others from their daily routine, including exercise summaries, badges, trophies and photos and more, to receive encouragement and celebrate progress, which keeps momentum going.

Fitness tracking is becoming increasingly prevalent in insurance packages and employee wellness programmes, with companies that offer wearables experiencing less employee churn and overall better employee satisfaction scores.[195] Fitbit Health Solutions is dead set on improving health outcomes for employees and driving positive returns for employers, by empowering employees to become more active in their health decision-making so they can think, work and live better.

A premium service includes a total eat-drink-sleep-move wellness programme, personalised workouts and guided meditations combined with advanced insights (like reports on heart rate and so on which can be shared with health professionals), sleep tools, etc.

Recently, a product range for kids and their parents was launched, promoting children to increase their physical activities and fitness.

What we can learn from Fitbit and other cases are these critical success factors in delivering outcomes at scale:

- Know the correlates that deliver an outcome, using advanced technology.
- Track activity and results per customer and intervene to ensure success.
- Use the technology to learn and build intelligence that can be leveraged to draw in larger numbers of customers.
- Get customers to self-anchor, i.e. create a future vision of a preferred state that mirrors the desired outcome.
- Break this down to daily or weekly bite-size, achievable goals.
- Track and measure success against these goals.
- Use nudges if necessary.
- Connect customers with like-minded others to compare, share what they've learned and adjust their behaviour.
- Add a competitive element.
- Find ways to reward and celebrate achievement with them.
- Connect their results to the enterprise KPIs.

CHAPTER 27

Defining the roadmap

What's the similarity between Fortnite and Airbnb? On the face of it, nothing, except that both brands go beyond the obvious (games and accommodation), by providing socially connected outcomes for their customers.

But there is a difference. The outcomes are consumed and produced in different market spaces.[196]

The market space is always expressed from the customer's point of view and represents the strategic space/territory/playground the distinguisher wants to open, occupy and own and produce outcomes for.

It should never be confused with an embellished statement of the product.

PHILIPS—A CASE IN POINT

In India, where one in five people are set to be over 50 years old by 2050, Philips' healthcare arm is delivering health services into patients' homes, with teams of nurses, paramedics and respiratory therapists monitored remotely by doctors.[197]

THE PRODUCT VIEW = Respiratory home healthcare (but it's a description of what Philips delivers—the *input*)

THE MARKET SPACE = Enhanced respiratory wellness (is a description of the desired result or the *customer outcome*)

If outcomes are the 'what' that needs to be scaled, market spaces are the 'where' (the competitive area) in which the brand chooses to excel and the strategic frame in which scaling takes place.

So, for Aerobotics, from selling drones and sensors that were all too susceptible to competitive pressure, the 'what' became building capability to provide superior crop management outcomes in the 'where', namely the farm productivity space.

So:

Extinguishers make and move improved discrete products and services to get more market share of a category.

Distinguishers use and combine products and services (their own or others), including intelligence, in order to deliver the customer outcome, to get enlarged share of customer spend in their chosen market space.

Market spaces defined

Getting an organisation from a product statement to a market space definition of its business is a defining moment.

It's a very quick way to align people and give the process traction, direction and focus.

How large the market space is to be is a strategic choice depending on many factors, but it boils down to the distinguisher's interpretation of the market, where it's going or could go, and pure ambition, i.e., how much of the space the brand wants to occupy and take.

It turns out there is no correlation between the size of an enterprise and that of a market space. A small company or a startup may go for a large ambitious market space to kick off with, and a large mature company may choose a smaller space, because it's closer to what it knows and understands, and its comfort zone.

It's entirely dependent on how the distinguisher sees the world and the brand's place in it.

Here are some pointers about size. The larger the market space:

- The further from the so-called core business;

- The larger the revenue opportunity;

- The more competition is blocked;

- The larger the ecosystem required;

- The more wealth potential for all.

The market space (aggregation of outcomes) informs missions to be accomplished by teams, products and services, decisions on people, partnering, acquisitions, marketing, processes and technology, etc., as well as would-be or could-be competitors.

It comes first in any distinguisher's plan.

It's defining in that it guides how far an enterprise goes and when it stretches itself too wide.

Anything done outside of the space is waste.

Anything not done or not done well, leaves gaps, which invites competition in.

Let's look at some examples of market spaces, from the cases already discussed (see Table 27.1).

Market spaces evolve over time

As we see from so many distinguisher examples, market spaces evolve over time as the brand becomes bolder in delivering a bigger and broader set of outcomes.

TABLE 27.1: *Product Category vs Market Space*

Brand	Product (MEANS)	Market space in which outcomes are delivered (END)
Nespresso	Coffee, cafés	Home coffee-making
Netflix	TV broadcasting, DVDs, DVD rentals, cinemas	On-demand movie entertainment
Unilever	Soap bars	Personal hygiene management
Discovery Insure	Car insurance	Great safe driving
Uber	Taxis, buses, trains, car ownership, trucks, delivery	People and goods mobility
Neighbor	Cupboards, sheds, attics	Space optimisation
M-KOPA	Kerosene lamps	Solar-connected homes
Zoom	Meeting venues	Remote communication and collaboration
Slack	Workplace messaging app	Virtual productivity
Fitbit	Wearables	Connected health
SodaStream	Water, soda in plastic bottles	Home-crafted beveraging
Spotify	CDs, mp3s, units of music	Enhanced listening time
NatWest	Current accounts, savings accounts, personal loans, credit cards, mortgages, investments	Financial goal attainment
Aerobotics	Drones and sensors	Farm productivity

The brand will morph, but a useful construct to start with is:

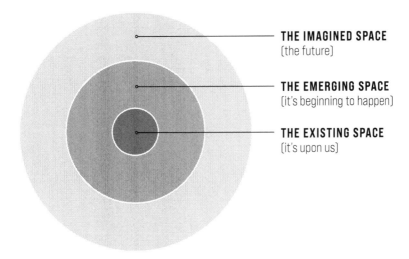

THE IMAGINED SPACE
(the future)

THE EMERGING SPACE
(it's beginning to happen)

THE EXISTING SPACE
(it's upon us)

FIGURE 27.1: *Existing Emerging Imagined Market Space*

If there is a morphing of market space, timing differs depending on the circumstance.

Market spaces define competition

If Slack is defined only as a tool or piece of software that displaces email, other team-software tools are the competition.

However, if Slack is to become the engine for 'virtual productivity', it could be taking on remote tools as well as substituting physical venues like offices and conference centres (which would include hotels, plus travel). Or it could complement every conference by having a remote built-in option in each room. Or it could expand into learning (for practitioner communities supporting learning on the job), or facilitate the inclusion of other creative people (connecting freelance gig workers instantly) and other collaborative design tools (connecting and integrating with them).

Looking at the market space reveals true competition. Fortnite and LEGO start to brush competitive sides in certain age categories, because although their products are distinctive (and orthodox thinking would place them in very different categories, i.e. toys vs games), they are both competing for kids' spare time and both claiming that their consumers gain important skills from their brands.

Add another level of complexity to this argument, and Fitbit—which now has wearables for kids to increase their physical activity—is also vying for kids to spend more spare time with it, moving around.

And if social entertainment is Fortnite's game, not just gaming, it's no wonder that it has also encroached on live concerts, albums by well-known artists and content from movie directors. During the pandemic it hosted a live rap concert that attracted almost 30 million live viewers.

Which is why Netflix admits that it loses more customer time to Fortnite than to HBO Go, its entertainment competitor, as customers seek alternative ways to spend their spare time, including participating in amateur videos, as TikTok's one billion users do.

On the surface, it looks as if Spotify's major competitor is anyone offering music. But since its space is 'enhanced listening time', more of its investment is going into podcasts. Music and music companies, and their resultant royalties, could therefore end up with a diluted share of its growing new revenue pot. And with 70 per cent of Spotify's revenue going to royalties, this is significant.[198]

Following this strategic thread, Spotify is also breaking into news, and educational and entertainment for adults as well as kids, getting more share of ear. Next, probably, will be audiobooks or anything that can be listened to while doing something else.

Market spaces define the playground

Market space is something of a strategic roadmap that comes to life when put into a visual, which we've done below for four cases. As one executive once put it, 'One market space visual is worth more than a 100-page strategy document.'

LEGO CASE

LEGO, the world's best-known toymaker, is no toymaker. Toys are products and LEGO is about so much more.

The word 'LEGO' comes from the Danish words *'leg godt'*, to 'play well'. Building blocks have always been a great way for kids and adults to play together.

Looking at the brand over the years, from its first transformation in the 1990s, it moved from making interlocking bricks for construction toys, to become a distinguisher in the 'learning through play' market space. This merged education and entertainment to bring about a new generation of LEGO offerings to make the case to teachers, parents, kids and adults that play is an integral part of the learning process, and that LEGO, with its unbelievable structural possibilities, was the best brand to achieve this.

From there, LEGO moved into the emerging market space that it itself invented in 'skill development through play'. The value proposition was manifested in an array of construction offerings, supposedly enhancing kids' brain- and skills-building through creative problem-solving, social skills, spatial, engineering and maths-learning, motor skills, self-confidence, scientific awareness

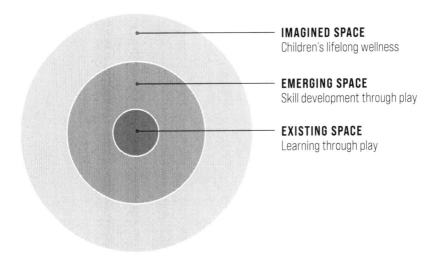

IMAGINED SPACE
Children's lifelong wellness

EMERGING SPACE
Skill development through play

EXISTING SPACE
Learning through play

FIGURE 27.2: *Market Spaces LEGO case*

(cause and effect), task accomplishment, collaboration and leadership (co-operative play), creativity and imagination, etc.[199]

Moving into this imagined space, LEGO would have to go further, becoming the expert in children's lifelong wellbeing, rather than building bricks (which 3D printing can produce). This would entail understanding the role of play in general and LEGO-play specifically, in achieving physical, mental, emotional and even spiritual wellbeing at various stages in a child's life. In other words, LEGO would find new ways of play that tangibly convinced stakeholders that kids would be better off with LEGO than without it.

A challenge indeed.

Market spaces inform what ecosystem is needed

UBER CASE
Uber's strategic roadmap could look like this:
- The first space was 'personal mobility', namely the movement of people.
- This then produced a new industry and morphed into the movement or 'mobility of people and goods'.
- Next, Uber is headed for a still imagined space, which is the orchestration of the total operating system for mass transportation, which it calls 'city mobility'. That Uber ambition is to own the strategic piece or market space, namely 'city mobility', which involves anything that moves in the smart cities of the future.

That means working with urban planners and local municipalities to grow cities to minimise congestion, emissions, hold-ups and accidents, and maximise accessibility, speed and safety. Its millions of trips a day covering several hundred cities can provide insights into the building of city infrastructure. Already it is sharing ride-pattern data with cities like Boston so that the city's road-maintenance planning can be improved.

The point here is that as the brand scales, it actively goes from modal (car) to multimodal (cars, etc.) to an intermodal ecosystem across public and private sectors of everything.

And, of course, this cannot discount playing a role in electric mobility, which is why Uber is moving with this at a rapid pace. Already it has discovered that drivers of electric vehicles in Europe and Africa tend to be rated higher and are more engaged on the Uber platform.[200] Its role in electric vehicle adoption, diffusion and scaling and the alternative generation of electricity, will become central to retaining its lead position in city mobility.

As we see from this example and others, the market space becomes a guide to building the needed ecosystem to scale.

And the larger the space, the greater the ecosystem and the more value it produces, while also setting up barriers to entry.

Scaling the market space entails not only finding partners but also working with what could otherwise have been competitors. For example, as it progresses into and scales city mobility, Uber will at some point have to find a way to incorporate Virgin's Hyperloop, the new way of transportation which is about moving people and goods in travel pods through tunnels at 1,600 kilometres an hour, and is expected to take travellers from airports to city centres in minutes.

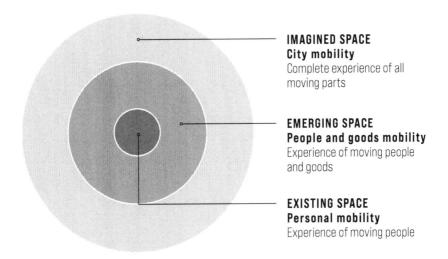

FIGURE 27.3: *Market Spaces Uber case*

And, ultimately, Uber must become the all-encompassing digital mobility gateway for all transport systems, including other ride-hailing services.

FITBIT CASE

- Fitbit started by selling activity trackers (goods).
- It then moved into the 'fitness management space' with a range of connected products, including scales and wearables capturing fitness data.
- Then it progressed into the 'self-enhancement' market space (which it helped invent) by helping customers change their behaviour and optimise their decisions, including comparing their performance with others and connecting to Fitbit tools such as heart monitors to improve their performance.
- It then redefined its market space, effectively creating an eco-system for a much more ambitious plan to connect the digital to the physical to achieve health at home and at work.

This entails, for example, asking how a person feels at certain times of the day, personalised digital interventions, health coaching, as

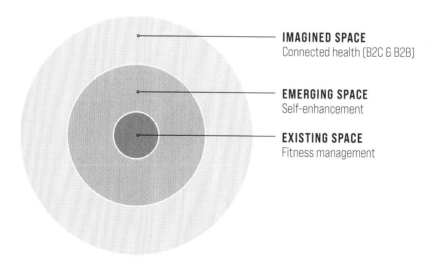

IMAGINED SPACE
Connected health (B2C & B2B)

EMERGING SPACE
Self-enhancement

EXISTING SPACE
Fitness management

FIGURE 27.4: *Market Spaces Fitbit case*

well as tracking over 100 disease- and lifestyle-related metrics. It made this data accessible to participants and providers, in the interest of elevating and scaling the brand and its offering.

Market spaces dictate the technology required

PORTBASE DUTCH PORTS CASE
A hypothetical market space for logistics comes from Portbase, working with Dutch ports going smart.

- 'Digital port infrastructure management' is about the connection of everything coming in and out of ports, which is significantly different from the old, tedious, time-consuming, paper-trailing. Digital logistics now allow supply chains throughout the Netherlands to run more cost- and time-effectively, including into and out of the ports, an outcome which can easily be measured and scaled.

   What has already emerged through blockchain in Amsterdam and Rotterdam, is a fully integrated supply logistics platform. The outcome is intended to be end-to-end shared intelligence and delivery. The entire ecosystem, including receivers, carriers, terminals and port authorities are bound together into one collaborating transparent network.
- The imagined space elevates the proposition from an outcome of end-to-end supply to encompass 'global trade performance', from the origin of goods all the way to consumers, including the first and last mile. It would connect all Dutch imports and exports with its entire ecosystem (suppliers, shippers, containers, etc.). Everything blockchain has to offer, like letters of credit, cross-border payments, certificates of origin, proof of authenticity and ethical sourcing and supplier practice, would be the backbone of the logistics proposition.

This is clearly a win for Dutch ports and the trade economics of the country, with all its concomitant benefits, and potentially makes it a gateway to and from Europe.

The next step could be to get beyond one country and have ports working together with mainland hauliers and carriers to build a scaled international logistics trade platform, inland—from remote areas to cities—and outbound, across sea and sky to end-user destinations.

Technology-enabled, this ecosystem would bring together advanced AI (predicting everything from weather to customer demand, supply and prices), drones and other delivery and fulfilment innovations. It would enable high-speed, low-cost, low-congestion, automated warehousing, with additive manufacturing, autonomous robots and on-demand inventory production. And the management systems would be co-ordinated by blockchain to facilitate fully integrated and open collaboration and payment.

It would be an 'uber Uber', so to speak, where the intellectual property is knowing who needs what goods and who has what goods worldwide, at any given moment. And it would build the ability to respond and match in real time, and get the goods there at scale and speed as well as low cost, by obliterating duplication and wasted resources, with a win for all parties, suppliers, carriers and end users.

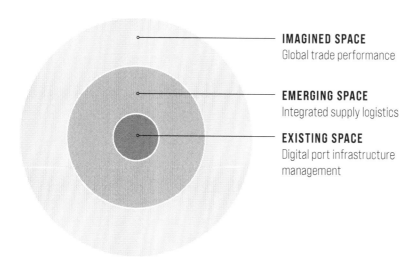

IMAGINED SPACE
Global trade performance

EMERGING SPACE
Integrated supply logistics

EXISTING SPACE
Digital port infrastructure management

FIGURE 27.5: *Market Spaces Portbase Dutch ports case*

CHAPTER 28

Using the viral model

For extinguishers, a win is achieving market share in line with annual budgets.

They use segmentation and traditional paid marketing levers, distribution, advertising promotion and sales peppered with 'digital marketing' and 'social media', in order to get to as many customers as they can. Each of these customers are kept unrelated, though they may share common characteristics. Together they add up to getting a market share.

To get market share in a product or service category, extinguishers aim to sell as much as possible as quickly as possible by broadcasting to customers at large, hoping to meet targets (the 'spray and pray' approach), relying on big-budget mass media upfront.

If retention falls off, market share will be re-obtained through the acquisition of new customers, which can often be expensive.

Distinguishers, however, use a viral mindset and model. If outcomes are the 'what' they need to scale, and market spaces 'where' they are staking their strategic claim, the viral model is the 'how'.

The primary concern is to deliver outcomes in a market space and do this well, in order to get customer lock-on, so that customers become part of their marketing mechanism.

They don't just want acquisition, they want adoption of new ways of doing things, i.e., sustained changed behaviour.

They know that the brand may sell initially and the acquisition rate may also be high, but if new behaviour doesn't stick because outcomes are poor, they will ultimately fail.

Customers as scalesforce

Distinguishers rely less on traditional marketing (bought media) to acquire customers at scale. Instead, they concentrate on owned and earned media to generate content, reviews and referrals, with customers as their authentic messengers.

Take Noom. When it was about to shoot its first national TV ad, the founders were unhappy with the actors sent by the production company because they didn't look like they had had a real weight struggle. So, instead of proceeding, executives sent emails to their users asking for a one-minute video of themselves by midnight that day, discussing the brand and what it had done for them. Two hundred replies were received in time and three were chosen to tell their stories.

With resounding success.

Distinguishers know how to:

- Change audiences from being passive listeners to active content-makers and distributors;
- Get them to share the content to get disproportionately positive peer-to-peer spread;
- Make this an ongoing and an integral part of their scaling strategy.

The Internet is what makes what was one step, word of mouth, now a viral phenomenon, possible at scale with high velocity and speed, irrespective of whether the offering is digital or physical.

Being interactive by nature, the Internet has fundamentally transformed media from being controlled and paid by brands

with one-way broadcasting methods, into one virally interconnected space, in which customers become the scalesforce, helping
to grow and amplify the market.

By combining devices with customers, distinguishers have
a new scaling distribution and sales channel, a way to get a few
customers to engage with and entice large numbers quickly.

It is through using customers as a channel, with all the engaging, connecting and content-sharing they do with others, that
makes a brand viral.

Nielsen's 1-9-90 cascading rule is interesting in this context:
content, its research reveals, is usually created by only 1 per cent
of users and distributed by 9 per cent to the remaining 90 per
cent of content-receivers.[201]

So vital is it that the superspreaders (the 1 per cent) are super
super happy.

Extinguishers are notoriously bad at customer stickiness
because they concentrate on the numbers they get by selling
goods that just tick that box.

Distinguishers make sure customers love the experience
because then they lock on and become the viral resource, both
for B2B and B2C. They act as advocate, adviser, influencer, social
proofer, reviewer, referrer, promoter, sharer, user case or recruiter.

Getting share of positive voice

Let's be clear, word of mouth has always been important.
According to Nielsen's research, 92 per cent of consumers believe
recommendations if they come from their own network.[202]

This coincides with what the big brands we've discussed have
experienced. For instance:

- It is Rover's pet-owners who have largely grown its market
  and taken it to mass scale, 90 per cent of them recommending
  the service to others.[203]

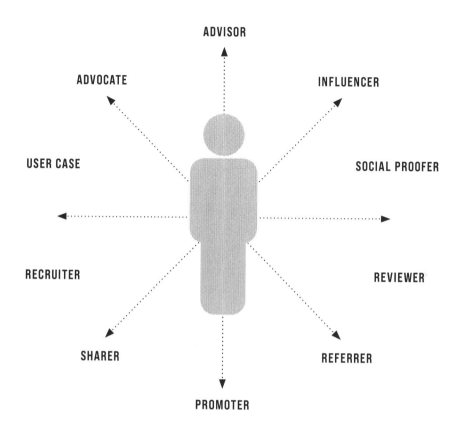

FIGURE 28.1: *Customers as Scalesforce*

- 95 per cent of Uber's customers heard about the brand from other customers.[204]
- The enormous organic traffic Slack enjoys is 90 per cent driven by word-of-mouth consumers.[205]
- In Unilever's behaviour change to get kids and moms to wash their hands with soap at critical times, 90 per cent of its participators speak or 'chat' to friends, family and neighbours about their experience and the brand reports that this has increased its positive impact.[206]

Paradoxically, while social media is digital and impartial, it enables conversations to take place between brands and its customers, adding a human dimension and flow to engagement that wasn't there before.

It has also given customers a voice.

In the old model, brands bought and controlled what was said about them. Share of voice simply amounted to the percentage of brand budget it spent, compared to the total spend in that category.

The distinguisher needs a share of positive voice in order to be viral. But by this we mean that they want the dominant piece of whatever is being said and written of interest in the chosen market space.

But they can't pay their way to it, it must be earned through social credit. Because customers want and trust what's real and true, as opposed to what's bought and broadcast.

If the brand content is not relevant and doesn't stand out because it's not interesting enough, or if the brand is not delivering the promise, no one will care about it or talk about it. It will fizzle out.

The content can be self-generated from inside the organisation as long as it's not about hard-sell, but about what helps the customers make an informed decision. Close to 90 per cent of global travellers make decisions based on online reviews.[207] Which is why Airbnb's content is carefully curated to contain a collection of stories and experiences from its hosts and guests, about how they have managed to connect and make people enjoy authentic local hospitality.

When new behaviours have to be scaled instead of just selling stuff, the viral model works through constant influence and referral.

FIRST the brand will seek to create awareness among innovators and early adopters to get take-up, consciously using customers to build the brand's credibility and desirability, learning, re-iterating and innovating to be able to keep amplifying positive effects.

THEN it will use the viral model and customers as the major channel and scalesforce, in order to get in the next cohort of early mass consumers—people who watch and listen to other people before they jump the chasm—to multiply the market further.

FINALLY, it will keep scaling to hold on to the existing market, gaining new users, plus it will get increased usage and revenue per customer, and leverage from customers that have locked-on to pull others in.

FIGURE 28.2: *Market Share Model vs Viral Model*

EXTINGUISHER'S MARKET SHARE MODEL
Media as channel, traditional funnel

DISTINGUISHER'S VIRAL MODEL
Customer as channel, viral funnel

FORTNITE CASE

Let's take Fortnite to demonstrate. It didn't start with a big advertising launch to get numbers quickly. It was more concerned with bringing people in, holding on to them, getting usage up and then activating them to bring in others.

Awareness was all important, but by seeding it with the right people meant that early adopters soon heard about it and Fortnite made it easy for them to convert—the age limit was only 10 years and the app could be downloaded to any device: Xbox, PlayStation, Nintendo, Windows, Mac, iPhone and Android.

It introduced 10-week seasons to keep people coming back to gain retention. New short versions had limited-time game modes, creating a feeling of scarcity, keeping current players engaged. And with every new game they played, they brought in others. Additionally, the availability of skins, exclusive deals, promotions and dances was limited for a period to evoke a sense of urgency.

Because Fortnite wanted instant global reach, it deliberately embedded what was familiar and popular in current world culture.[208]

Each new game generated content. Fortnite moved outside typical gaming boundaries (i.e. shooting), introducing dance moves for their characters, such as those of some popular K-pop groups.

These went viral with influencers and videographers from all genres (including sports stars) who danced and posted their content on social media. This culminated in the Fortnite Dance Challenge, which amassed more than one billion views on YouTube in one year.[209] The winner's dance was embedded into the Fortnite game.

Other brands joined in, which led to more exposure and impact. For example, in one of its campaigns, Uber Eats linked discounts to how many times a Fortnite user scored a 'kill'. So large was the response that it had to reduce the length of the offer from a week to a day!

And its viralisation continues.

CHAPTER 29

Getting market take-up

Distinguishers are canny about making the right moves to get to the right people in the right sequence in order to get initial market take-up. Done well, this acts as the foundation for building rapid and sustained scaleability.

There is agreement on some fundamentals for this:

Principle 1: Get the proposition and offering right

No one could have done a better job than Jeff Bezos when he announced on the news his ambition to be the first to launch a drone delivery service. 'Amazon Prime Air' will use drones to deliver packages weighing up to five pounds (two kilos) to a customer's house, in less than half an hour.

His interview on US TV's 60 Minutes, in which he showed a video of what the service would look like, was described as a stroke of genius and caused a sensation. What had been considered as science fiction—a fleet of shipping drones taking to the sky—felt real and possible, which got everyone talking and resulted in over 16 million searches on Google.

Which was exactly what Amazon wanted.

That was seven years ago plus and a lot has been

accomplished. But Amazon isn't ready to do drone deliveries at scale yet. It has spent years testing vehicle designs and delivery mechanisms to discover how best to deliver packages in a variety of operating environments in multiple international locations. It is set to go live in 2021.

Though others are in the game, Amazon has the existing logistics system and a base of customers who want parcels ever faster. But drones to people's homes are still in the early stages of adoption not only because of the need for regulation approval, but also because the system has to work, i.e. it has to get goods to customers in 30 minutes. It has to be a good alternative for the market to take it up at scale and speed.

Principle 1 is making sure that what the market gets works, and that the promise is delivered. If the offering underwhelms, no advertising in the world will help. Some customers may try it, but the market will not take off.

We see this over and over again.

The idea of Nespresso was good, to build a world where espresso was available in people's homes. But the coffee-maker was large and chunky, hard to move and clean. Also, there was a limited range of pod options, all of which meant it had few takers. That was, until it was transformed into the small, sleek, stylish machines we see today, with a wide range of pods to please many individuals, producing an essentially consistent coffee-making and -tasting experience.

Zoom was launched into a crowded market, but no brand had actually got the product right so there was no real market take-up. No one had got people to change their behaviour, to Zoom instead of call by phone, to Zoom instead of getting into a plane or a car to go to a meeting. Eric Yuan, having come from one of these not-got-it-right incumbents, insisted that what he would do was build a better Web conferencing experience that the market could not resist—effortless and happy making (his words).

And it's exactly what happened because what people say is that they have stuck with Zoom because 'It works'.

The same with Uber. It moved with astonishing speed. It didn't just happen, it was carefully crafted, making sure the experience was superb so that it would be talked about, and when it was, people would say, 'It works, it's easy, try it'.

Overdoing it isn't the answer either. Initially, it will only slow things down. Most winners agree that to speed things up, a minimum viable (or loveable) experience is good enough, whether it's a new way of saving, collaborating remotely, using 3D printing for construction of social housing, or Zooming instead of travelling.

Good enough is good enough for starters, as long as it isn't a cop-out.

That said, distinguishers concentrate on getting any obstacles to adoption sorted early. Research by BP in France, Germany, Spain and the UK revealed that fast charging could be one of the biggest motivators to encourage the uptake of electric vehicles. And that's where it has put its efforts, investing in and testing ultra-fast public chargers in the UK and Germany, before its rollout on its several thousand forecourts.

Obviously, getting the proposition right is a journey, and an ongoing one, to keep minimising every bit of friction in the customer experience. But there isn't a distinguisher, even those wanting to work at speed, who won't test with customers and get the offering working well enough before going to market.

As Airbnb's Brian Chetsky says, it's better to find one person and get the experience right and then scale, than go to many, have it not so right, and then try to scale.

Principle 2: Find customers who can help to get the proposition right

Kickstarter was lucky. It built its business around innovators, because the nature of the projects coming in were highly creative and appealed to those types.

But this is not always the case. And when it isn't, a concerted effort has to be made to find and get to the first cohort, who are the innovators and early adopters.

However, they must also be fairly representative of the market to come. They need to be found and chosen carefully, therefore, because whatever is done for them will have to work for everyone.

We say this because getting to geeks or outliers with a great idea and getting validation from only them can be dangerous and ultimately slow down the process.

If the wrong people are chosen, the wrong things can be scaled.

At the other extreme, another typical mistake is when brands try their innovation on resistors (aka late adopters or laggards), or their largest B2B customers, instead of early adopters (i.e. people interested in trying the new). They believe that if resistors buy in, everyone else will. We've heard that a zillion times. Resistors will never drive take-up because they are not looking for change, even if it's for the better. If resistors are used to trial an innovation, nothing will happen, and definitely not quickly.

The first group of customers acts as a laboratory for development, either on a paid or unpaid basis, by agreement or choice. The objective is to get to that minimum viable (or loveable) proposition through prototyping, so that there is something to take to market to start the re-iterative learning process.

It's a fine line to walk, making sure it's good enough, not under or over the threshold. But distinguishers know how to do this and are not afraid to experiment.

The group chosen should be leaders in their industry or community and have a keen concern in the brand's proposition. They become the testimonials of early user cases.

Uber went for high-tech people in San Francisco, who were not afraid to push a button to get a cab, and then were happy when it arrived within five minutes. Legend has it, they started telling their families and friends, or were overheard at a restaurant or in the street hailing 'an Uber'.

To build the learning and scale, the first group should be

part of an affinity segment rather than a demographic, i.e., people interested in and/or doing the same thing, i.e. wanting to buy craft (Etsy) or transforming their infrastructure to cloud (Amazon) or concerned that they need to save more (NatWest), or committed to transform a city with low-cost 3D-printed housing (Cemex Morocco), or new home-owners interested in decorating or in old homes needing a makeover (IKEA), or companies looking for new ways to work better remotely (Slack), or a business entering an export market (Shopify).

Principle 3: Get and react to feedback

Asking for feedback is a way to test ideas, but it is also a way to get early-adopter first-movers on board.

It's a way to co-create a new proposition as well, which is what IKEA did when it tested its virtual reality app to see if and how people could re-imagine their homes with different furnishing and decoration (it has close to 3,000 products), through their mobile phones.

Feedback also comes from media coverage, which is important during the take-off stage in order to get an early-adopter following. But, say some executives, what is significant too are the comments made—what people are picking up and sharing. The positive things users are saying can be amplified.

Changes don't have to be major. Through constant granular feedback, small changes can make a significant impact on growth.

It's not about the quantity of feedback and data gathered, it's about getting quality responses. What distinguishers say is that at some point you know when it's right because enough of the right people are saying the same thing. 'It's like a choir singing the same thing in harmony. You can hear it,' said one executive.

This approach is distinctly different from old pilot tests that take too much time and are based on average responses. If they are not well received, they are withdrawn, which could be because the wrong people were chosen.

The object is to keep modelling an idea until it works, and because it's likely never to have been done before, try it out only with people who have sufficient imagination and interest in making it happen.

Needless to say, feedback is an ongoing process. Employees from Fortnite actively engage with the game's players on social media, constantly getting and building in new ideas to improve the offering. It's part of their DNA.

Principle 4: Build purposeful messaging

What has become increasingly evident is the importance of a stated, powerful purpose in enlisting the first-cohort customers.

Here's the interesting difference in approach:

Extinguishers look for the same demographic customer profile at which to aim their brand in a defined product or service category (e.g. a car). But initially with new ways of doing things in market spaces, firstly there is no 'category' as such yet (think Uber mobility); secondly, people wanting or first responding to *doing* something different (e.g. ride-share rather than using a car) cut across traditional market demographics like age, income, education, etc.

Distinguishers also don't want innovators or early adopters of new technologies or products. What they do want is people who identify with and are attracted to a stated purpose, and are drawn to the promise of an outcome that will change their habits and lives in some way.

This fits with what we know from research; that what consumers are likely to support and recommend today is a brand that has a purpose that reflects new needs, values and social issues, and that this is an across-the-world phenomenon, particularly among younger consumers.[210]

The Airbnb case is worth repeating. What the founders wanted was to get beyond accommodation, and make it about people who travel for pleasure or business, who want be made to feel welcome anywhere, like a local.

Its purpose was to displace large, and largely disconnected, places where people were used to staying, and get travellers connected to hosts, cities and countries feel accepted and safe.[211]

Slack wanted early adopters on board who identified with its stated purpose to revolutionise how people work to make it simpler, more pleasant and productive.

Rover initially sought to attract sitters, walkers and owners who love dogs, so as not to be just another dog-lodging platform.

The stated purpose motivates customers to change their behaviour and talk to others about their experiences. And it holds the enterprise accountable to deliver on that promise or purpose.

From the purpose comes a clever, memorable, meaningful one-liner that resonates with customers and they can repeat to others, containing a good reason to try it. For example:

- Zoom's first billboard read 'Video conferencing that doesn't suck'.
- Slack's success was partly in its powerful message that no one could forget: 'The email killer'.
- SodaStream's 'Be a sparkling water maker' was a hit on billboards strategically placed where people worked and lived and near stores chosen to stock the machine.
- M-PESA's success was because the market resonated with the aspirational simple strong line, 'Send money home'.
- Trustpilot's 'Be heard' video series was aimed at both consumers and enterprises to profile the potent power of trusted reviews.
- Rover's 'dog people' convinced people that their pet would be cared for by trusted dog-lovers, -sitters and -walkers while they were at work or travelling.
- M-KOPA solar's line, 'Power for everyone', oozed inclusiveness and impact.
- Airbnb's 'Belong anywhere' took it from room or house occupation to connecting people to communities, cities and countries.

- Noom's, 'A smarter way to lose weight', immediately differentiated it from short-term dieting and face-to-face meetings for millennials who want to engage digitally.

Principle 5: Use more content, less broadcasting ... Please!

Distinguishers make sure that they are where the customers are to maximise exposure. Advertising, whether by TV, billboard, print, radio, etc., was always placed where customers were, of course. Whole industries were built around media selection practice. But customers (especially the newer generations) don't spend as much of their time in these traditional media anymore, and they don't respond in the same way to them.

That's not to say traditional media can't be used as a tool to give exposure and create awareness. It can and does, especially at early stages, in order to make audiences aware fast. But it needs to be complemented with content-based communication, because customers do their exploration and evaluation of purchases increasingly on social media, through searches and on websites.

From being an interruption, advertising now has to add value through content, and have its own authentic pulling power. It needs to be interesting enough, relevant enough and real enough to be displayed in searches, not just up there when paid for.

What matters is not what the brand says about itself, but what is being said about it.

Startups don't have big budgets or time, so they have learnt how to scale fast and frugally. Zoom achieved mass popularity by spending its money on marketing as an exception, mainly on billboards. Eric Yuan describes the evolving approach: 'It's hard to market a brand within a short period of time. After we had our first billboard, my neighbor, she told me "I saw your billboard." I think, "wow, this is great". Then I told our marketing team "Let's have another one." Soon, a lot of other people they say, "We saw your billboard." OK, "Let's add a third one".[212]

Principle 6: Manage capacity

Although the big issue for getting take-up is how to get early-adopter followers quickly, moving fast also means having a plan for controlled demand and supply take-up, so as not to disappoint.

Some broker-type startups, like Uber, Airbnb, Neighbor and Rover, first sought out suppliers (drivers, hosts, empty spaces, pet-sitters). Airbnb went to Craigslist (which advertises homes for rent, among other things) and got users to come onto the Airbnb platform and made it extremely easy to do so. They then famously paid for hosts to get professional photos done to entice lodgers. And they met every host at the start!

Both Uber and Airbnb simultaneously looked for cities and events (sports and conferences) to identify when and where it might be difficult for people to find a taxi or accommodation easily.

From the get-go, Rover reached out to dog communities. Said the CEO, Aaron Easterly, 'We would take trips to dog parks and dog events as a way of seeding the market and getting the critical mass of sitters. Over time, we stopped having our investors go to dog parks. But that was how we started. It was really about the "feet on the street".'[213]

Others build up demand first, demonstrating that they have customers even before they have something to sell, so that they can attract supply, either because they need negotiating power, for example Spotify, or to speed up getting funding. In order to get funding, Monzo had tens of thousands of people waiting to become customers while they were still building supply.

The brand also needs to scale what's needed inside the business, including a culture and new ways of working.

It needs to be sure it can deal with take-up, because it has enough bandwidth, computing power, customer backup services and operational support.

As they are dealing with more customers, the ability to handle more traffic is all important. In a zero-margin cost model more people can't necessarily help, because it adds cost and takes time to scale.

What they have to do is ramp up systems and processes to cope with demand. When something new is done for the first time, brands don't know what the problems and bottlenecks will be. With controlled scaling, these can be identified and resolved in a way that does not damage the customer experience.

Without this controlled take-up, a brand can crash and burn.

Because of issues related to capacity, bugs and lack of customer support, HBO Go, the Netflix contender in the US, lost early customers and got a bad reputation, which halted its momentum. It was an important lesson because it's hard to get a second chance.

When Spotify and Facebook first sought out customers, they made sure it was in a controlled way, so that they could handle capacity and keep experience levels high.

They did this by invitation only. Numbers were limited, to manage capability, but additionally this created what is known as a 'scarcity bias'—when availability decreases, desire increases (only up to a point of course, before customers get irritated).

They got the customer to do the inviting for them and they were able to include only a certain number of people. 'Wanna be' customers had to seek out someone with an invitation if they wanted to participate.

Other brands initially took on customers in batches. Netflix did that early on, by creating the now often-used 'waiting list'.

Part of managing capacity is making sure that the brand can make customers who come in first ultra-happy, otherwise the viral model falls flat. Zoom's CEO is one of many who is adamant about this. The emphasis, he says, initially must be on keeping customers because they will bring in new users. That means everything needs to work and be made easy, even cancellations.

Extinguishers would just replace customers. Distinguishers can't. They are a major part of their marketing machine, positive or negative.

SLACK CASE

Slack has grown exponentially. Was there a pent-up need that the brand filled? Did emails contain such severe pain-points that people were ready and waiting to buy a new collaborative tool? Or did Butterfield and his small team just see things differently from others?

It wasn't the first collaborative team tool to enter the market. But it was the first to experience exponential growth. Why?

Slack's CEO is adamant that they are not selling software; they are selling better team productivity and a relief from stress due to information overload. Plus, they make it possible to extract value from corporate archives in a way that was never done before, because everything is integrated and easy to access remotely.

At the beginning, the management of Slack spent time finding fewer than 10 companies to try out its offering. The object was to help it iron out any issues before the market was exposed to it, as well as get awareness in the marketplace.[214]

When Slack was ready to launch it invited feedback from the crowd on its preview release, which it refused to call beta because Butterfield felt it wouldn't be taken seriously enough. Press contacts were used to invite people to be part of the test. Eight thousand people responded on the first day, and two weeks later the figure doubled.

When the Slack tool was made available to the public, the brand had already acquired half a million active daily users, and within four months this number had doubled to 1.1 million active users.[215]

Slack soon discovered that different-sized teams needed very different things. So, it worked progressively with different-sized teams to get the offering right.

Feedback was the backbone of the initial strategy. To get it right, 'We started inviting teams in batches and watched what happened. Then we made some changes, watched what happened, made some more changes.'[216]

Slack looked for ways to get that feedback any way it could, including via its app, and a command-and-help button, so it could tell what customers liked and disliked, and fix or amplify it accordingly.

Getting and acting on feedback is a part of the Slack culture. It continuously learns from users and is supported by software that detects sentiment and themes with precision from customer feedback, in order to help the brand understand what customers are saying about it. It is also a way to quantify positive feedback targets and measure progress.

Twitter was Slack's most important social media platform to create a voice that complemented its 'Email killer' message. It got massive awareness through it, as well as feedback from and communication to customers, using the channel to support users rather than building up a huge service team.

Fifty per cent of consumers, after reading a positive review about a company, will visit the website.[217] In whatever endeavours Slack used to popularise itself on social media, the aim was to create what it calls 'a curiosity gap', i.e., get people curious enough to stop what they are doing and go onto its website, where they would be exposed to relevant content to entice them in.

Slack has the highest conversion rate among freemium software products to date (30 per cent), because it systematically worked to build up its social credit.[218] It didn't use media to hard sell, but rather created interest in more collaborative ways of working to get productivity up. Through content it gave customers tricks, tools and techniques on collaboration, and how to get this working remotely.

Slack created Slack Frontiers, an annual two-day virtual conference. This, it found, was an important way to get people to share what they were doing and their challenges in pioneering workplace cutting-edge technology. It wanted to get feedback not just on its products, but on new and innovative ways of working.

It famously allowed people to talk about what they didn't like about Slack, and openly shared its product roadmap to get feedback, rather than keep it secret.

Which is what extinguishers do.

CHAPTER 30

Driving market multiplication

After initial take-up, which could be anything from 10 to 10,000 customers, the next job is to multiply the customer base by onboarding the early mass market.

The challenge, whether B2B or B2C, is to get people never exposed to the new idea or new way of doing things, to make the call. Unless they try it, the brand will not get sign-ups in large numbers.

These are the major multipliers, each of which builds markets, all of which build the viralisation. This is what distinguishers are after.

Multiplier 1: Freemiums, free trials and discounts

Trial has to come before permanent behaviour change. Distinguishers often are successful at using freemiums, free trials or monetary incentives like discounts as multipliers, because it makes it easy for people to move to trial fast.

The fact that young kids didn't have to pay for Fortnite was part of the reason for its huge uptake and wild popularity. Once in, fan users invited their friends to join, who did so quickly and in massive quantities because there were no costs. Within two weeks of its release, it had 10 million users.[219] Within 10 months, it had 125 million.[220]

The free-to-use game was monetised by a series of micro transactions through its virtual store, to allow players to differentiate themselves through cosmetic skins (costumes), and enhance their gaming experience with additions, updates and preview modes, all with limited availability.

In the Uber and hotel partnerships, to get fast awareness for their enhanced traveller experience from start to finish, first signers got a discount off their ride. Uber has used this approach throughout its scaling, particularly when it enters new markets or cities, and it has been responsible for unusually accelerated penetration.

It argues that this tactic is an expedient way to remove perceived barriers, especially if the risk seems high. M-PESA went to great pains to get users, many of whom up until then had no experience of dealing with financial institutions, let alone mobile wallets, and so were particularly sensitive to risks, to register initially at no cost. Customers who required a SIM card received one for free. The uptake was a gigantic success.

Many innovations that require a change in behaviour have failed because the cost is seen as too high without proof that it works or will deliver the value promised. The legendary case of Xerox, the first to invent the mouse that never happened, is difficult to forget. Because people had to change their work habits and pay a high price to do so without having experienced it, it was seen as just too risky!

The point is, it's not just getting people to purchase something that distinguishers care about, it's getting them to change what they do—and making it easier if money is an inhibitor. A large part of the Lifebuoy handwashing behaviour change success in countries across Asia and Africa during Covid-19 came about because national schools initially got free samples of hand sanitiser for the whole school, together with free educational resources and kits directly related to changing hand hygiene, which multiplied handwashing quickly. Added to this were free e-learning tools and cleverly curated motivational programmes aimed at kids and parents when the schools were shut.[221, 222]

It's difficult to sell change unless people get to experience what it's about. The more complex the product, the more time is required for trial.

In the old days, a trial would have been called product sampling, and it would apply to physical goods in the supermarket. Today, with more complex products, many of which are intangible and digital or have a high digital component, free trials and freemiums are everywhere.

Uber did 'the first drive is on us'. Rover gave the first dog walk free. Slack made it free for the first teams that took it on. Thereafter it charged for more people to come on with 'fair pricing' to reflect usage. Others give away something for a period of time, like Zoom, which offered a 40-minute limit for free accounts, because it discovered that 45 minutes was the ideal length for a video conference.[223]

All of them use free trials as multipliers to get a share of customers and their voice as quickly as possible.

Some brands also give access to resources and users during the free trial period, to make sure that potential customers really get to experience the brand. Noom provides a support specialist to answer questions, and chat groups so that newcomers can talk to other users on the same free trial journey.

Others, like Spotify, give customers free access, as long as they are prepared to listen to advertising. Harry's will send a starter grooming kit for a couple of dollars (and at other times for nothing) and if customers are not happy, they can return it.

This form of trial is what Amazon has perfected: it makes it as easy as possible to return goods like fashion and it even sends boxes pre-labelled for ease of return. The goods are on trial and the return is free.

Converting from free

How to convert people from the free or freemium pool of customers to subscription is of course the real challenge. People who are good at conversion get 20 to 30 per cent multiplier rates.[224]

What works with free-trial fast tracking is a series of tactics, like what are known as 'embedded aha moments'. These happen in flashes and distinguishers know or make it their business to find out what they are.

It's the movement when customers know and acknowledge that it is a better way of doing things.

In Uber's case, it's when the customer presses the button and the car arrives, when they don't have to stay in the car to pay the driver because it's done automatically via the app.

Another technique used to leverage the 'aha moment' is to capture people's name, email address, payment details and mobile number when they join, even if they get a first free buy. Then, the second paid buy is easy and they register for that. The free-to-paid conversion rate is 50 per cent higher when a brand gets credit card details, compared with when it doesn't.[225]

On the back of this technique, brands can nudge people to come back or to begin the paying process, as Uber and Zoom do.

Even if the first try is free, brands also deliberately showcase their best features to get customers converted. It's an important lesson, but not intuitively obvious to the traditionalist, who wants to save money until there is a commitment.

For example, Spotify promotes its Discovery playlist, one of its most-loved features, immediately to encourage new users to listen more and more. And once they do, they get better and better outcomes, which perpetuates the cycle.

The point here to note is that if the multiplier technique is done with integrity and intent, i.e., delivers more customer value, it's a total win all round.

Distinguishers become expert at acquiring and multiplying customers, unlike others who fail because they think customers will come to them if the offering is good enough. Zoom's Yuan says, 'Without a freemium I think you're going to lose the opportunity to let many users test your product. We make our freemium product work so well … … That's why every day there are so many users coming to our website. If they like our product, very soon they are going to pay for the subscription.'[226]

Making yes easy

As all these examples show, it's important to make it as easy as possible for people to say 'yes'.

- Slack did this by using a bottom-up approach in buyer firms. It didn't even try to convert an entire customer organisation at once, because it knew that would involve all sorts of bureaucratic decision-making that would hold things up. Instead, Slack went to interested mid-level manager teams with a pent-up desire to work differently, and it made it affordable enough so they could expense it easily. Then it systematically spread the brand organisation-wide, by training teams to train others.
- When the South African Discovery Group moved into banking, a key objective was to get its own and new customers fully onboarded, compliance-checked and transacting in under five minutes. And in the early onboarding phase it made sure that no task took more than three clicks to complete.
- Once Fortnite got users to play through its freemium model, it then offered consumers skins, items and coins, etc. to customise their characters. But they were priced low to make it easy. And the game was made easy to understand so that customers could get started quickly, before they understood the complexities and then became masters at it.

Multiplier 2: Screen equity

In the old marketing model, the levers for scaling were mental and physical presence: i.e. 'Was the brand available, does the customer know it?' 'Does the customer like it?' 'Can the customer find it?' 'Can the customer buy it?'

The marketing lever was to make the brand known and liked through advertising, and have it stocked in the store where the customer could find it and buy it. That meant advertising more and increasing the distribution footprint and points of sale.

'To be within an arm's length', was the aim for any mass-market brand, to paraphrase the famous Coca-Cola line.

As more goods and services are being bought and/or delivered through digital channels, brands still need to be present, but this now means on the screens of computers, mobile phones and other devices.

Some people go as far as to say that without screen presence there is no viralisation. It's the new high street.

When customers and screens converge, they form the new channel to market which, when combined with new ways of marketing, become a multiplier.

Google's scaling success was that people had to start with it when they entered online. That was its genius.

When enterprises pay Google for advertising, they are paying for this screen equity. If their brand doesn't show up on Google they don't exist, in the same way that a store hidden on a side street that can't be found does not exist. It's only when the brand is present on people's screens that customers are likely to buy and the brand will multiply.

There are four ways of getting screen presence:

1. The ultimate screen presence, or 'real estate', is to be an installed app on someone's smartphone. Most brands offer apps free to get this presence that they can then monetise. Nike, for example, has a suite of free apps: one for people to discover its shoes and clothing; Nike Training Club app for fitness plans and workouts; Nike Run Club, a running tracker and coaching app; and Nike SNKRS, for the dedicated

sneaker community, where people can tailor-make and order unique sneakers. Nike's apps have member passes and inboxes, allowing the brand to track customers and send them personalised communication.

2. Create an 'owned' channel, like a website or an account on Instagram, Facebook, Twitter, et al, and so appear on feeds and search engines through the brand's own content. Today, this 'organic' content is what gets a brand screen presence, via bookmarks, followers and search results. That's provided the content is relevant or recognised by Google's or Amazon's algorithms, a whole science called 'search engine optimisation'. Rover has created 'TheDogPeople.com' in order to get screen presence and become a top-rated pet blog because it provides tips and articles that get people closer to their pets, not because it tries to sell dog-sitting.

3. Earn presence, as people engage with the brand via social media platforms or talk about the brand for whatever reason and merits, and therefore appear on screens via social media.

4. Buy it through digital advertising, appearing on screens or through Public Relations (PR), in which case the brand will be seen quickly and then be amplified by digital (and traditional) channels.

Owned and earned presence is more powerful than bought, since it's more credible. And it's credible attention that matters.

People give it their attention because they engage with the brand voluntarily, as opposed to when advertising interrupts and spams them.

If well targeted to an online affinity group who would find the message relevant enough to want to engage, a mass reach campaign can be a very successful multiplier. When Rover started to recruit customers in the US, it sought out potential travellers all looking for the same thing—their next trip. Rover reached out to them with strong messaging on Facebook and Instagram: 'Passport? Suitcase? Dog-sitter? Try a 5-star Rover sitter near you!' Each ad had a 'Book Now' call to action that linked to the company website, direct to a booking function.[227]

More and more the screen is mobile (mainly, but not exclusively in B2C markets), and some startups are going 'mobile only', concentrating on apps to get customers bought in quickly, even dispensing with websites (or making websites mobile native, i.e. optimised for a mobile screen). Especially in leapfrogging markets like India, or in segments which are mobile only.

Distinguishers make sure customers have their app on their phones. Once on, they can boost user engagement and sales conversion, by talking to them, advising them, nudging them and whatever else is needed to build and retain the relationship. The brand is present and active in their daily lives.

Being there and staying there

Being there and staying there is only possible when the app is engaging because the app speaks to ease and relevance. Back to Rover. Despite being new to dog-walking, it quickly grew to be the most downloaded and best reviewed dog-walking app in the US, and consequently scaled dramatically. Pet-parents could schedule a walk for their dog within an hour on the same day or every week with a Rover-certified dog-walker of their choice, or one the customer has used before, give information on dog behaviour, and how to enter the house with Rover's free, secure lockboxes. The app also alerts the owner when the walk starts and ends and provides a GPS map of the walk, photos and notes on bathroom breaks.

Some extinguishers think it's enough to just be on an app store. But there are millions of apps on app stores and some are never used. Apps have to be downloaded, installed, used and continue to be used if market multiplication is going to happen.

But how many apps can a customer have? The truth is there is a physical limitation on the mobile phone (ranging from memory to screen space), which makes it a scarce resource. Because the space is highly valuable, the app has to be useful and the interaction constant, otherwise the customer will simply remove it.

Some interesting stats:[228]

- 80 per cent of mobile time is spent on apps.
- On average, smartphone owners use 9 apps per day and 30 apps each month (the figure for millennials and younger groups is higher).
- 62 per cent of the apps downloaded don't get used.
- 25 per cent get used only once.
- Over 70 per cent are discarded around 90 days after downloading.

The point is that whoever gets on, and keeps on, gets screen equity.

Which is why Google is counteracting by installing its own apps on its Android devices. In fact, it's why they make mobile phones and mobile operating systems—in order to be the starting point for people's lives online, now happening through their mobile phones.

With B2B the principle is the same, but these buyers are still mainly purchasing online from a web browser on a computer screen, which will no doubt change as mobile habits get increasing traction.

Installed app base

In sum, getting people to download, install and use the app is the biggest acquisition expense today, but it is also a major multiplier.

The race is on to get an 'installed app base', as many distinguishers are doing, like Fitbit, with a footprint of over 6.8 million downloads across its personal trainer apps across 155 countries.[229]

And investors today are looking at 'installed app base' to assess value when they buy or invest in a company.

This may be complemented by destination experience stores in the 'real world'. But getting onto screens is such a serious part of multiplying customer acquisition and conversion today, that producers are moving at stellar speed to a direct-to-customer model, so they can use this screen multiplier to scale faster than they could via traditional channels and chains.

Multiplier 3: Social proofing

Distinguishers use social proofing as a multiplier. They know they have to maintain authenticity to give the brand the kind of credibility that will pull in the market en masse.

Buying social proofing doesn't work anymore, it only works with peer-to-peer distributed content, which then becomes viralised as it's connected to and accessed by others.

What enterprises want today are fans who like the brand and start referring to it, to stop potential customers going through a search. With this as a multiplier, customers go straight to the brand's website, giving it all the arising benefits.

Experts and influencers

The days of paying celebrities to endorse a brand are coming to an end. Customers are increasingly gravitating to what they consider to come from true experts.

The most obvious one we all know is when experts give their stamp of approval. Fitbit gets health and tech industry experts to speak about the quality of its products on its website, for instance, which gives it enormous credibility and keeps it rated the number one fitness tracker on the market.

Influencers have a dedicated social following (sometimes very large) and, when viewed as experts within their niche are called 'winfluencers', because they are bound to win over customers. If not, they are not experts, and they are not really effective. They can't just be famous, they also have to be knowledgeable on a subject, a trusted authority.

They have an impact on social media conversations, beliefs and subsequent behaviour, and therefore are pivotal when a brand wants to change its business or social practice.

Experts help build up trust and recommendations, which serve as social proof and a multiplier. They influence because they create and distribute content. We know that content from influencers gets a share of voice, which drives more engagement than content shared directly from brands, some say eight times as much.[230] Fortnite's experience shows it can be even more. In one year (2018) 50 billion YouTube views were generated by creators, compared to the 600 million it generated through paid content.[231]

Micro influencers, people with a strong social media influence in a niche area, usually with around 2,000 followers, are more trusted than those with large followings. They are not famous but held in super-high esteem within a small community.

Customers feel more socially connected to micro influencers, because they are more like them, rather than unattainable. Consequently, their content feels more genuine and authentic. Also, because they interact with followers personally, relationships build, which makes them even more effective as a multiplier.

Research shows that 82 per cent of consumers are more likely to act on a recommendation if it comes from a micro influencer they identify with, who has credibility in that market space or category, than from a social media celebrity or (macro influencer).[232] This is significant since brands now spend nearly half of their influencer marketing budgets on micro-influencer campaigns, growing both in size and stature in investments.[233]

Google isn't associated with any single person or personality. It deliberately stays away from celebrity culture. But it has a big network of micro influencers that it calls on, for interventions ranging from launching a new phone or laptop, to Google Play, its movie, music, book, multimedia store. If they are positive they act as referrals by recommending to customers in their network.

Testimonials

Innovators and early adopters are driven by the fact that something is novel. They don't mind trying a new way of doing things even if it doesn't work out. They won't go back if it doesn't work, but they are willing to risk trying.

Contrast this with the early mass market who don't care that it's new. What they want to know is that it works and will deliver value to them. They don't take risks and they look for users (innovators and early adopters) to validate the brand and its benefit before they buy or change their behaviour.

Testimonials are a powerful use of this social proofing, B2B and B2C, which is why reviews are so important. The higher the ratings the higher the market multiplication.

Reviews are not just opinions, they are what users feel after they have experienced a product. Amazon has a best-sellers book list, for example, based on what over one million customers say, not what it says or they are paid to say, and it sells 65 per cent of all the books sold in the world that way.[234]

In B2B it's about getting customers to work with the brand initially, during prototyping and re-iteration, in order to build up case studies and user testimonials. Once this positive feedback content comes from actual users, it gives the brand credibility, which leads to the wanted multiplication.

And research confirms that a huge proportion of B2B customers trust peer non-paid recommendations more than any other type of advertising.[235]

Slack set out to intentionally do this and got a lot of consequent traction. It asks its biggest evangelists for reviews, tweets or customer videos. One of the initial CEO testimonials read, 'The biggest thing is no one thinks about Slack, it just always works', which is exactly what the market wanted to hear to give it the confidence to buy in, which it did.

A brand can be its own testimonial by showing that it has achieved certain goals, like number of new users, number of downloads, number of referrals, etc. Or it can generate its own content when it receives mentions or praise, like 'thank you' posts, as Tesla did when it won Germany's innovation award of the year, or if it gets lots of love or likes, as Slack did when it created a special Twitter account called SlackLoveTweets to retweet all of its user accolades.

Or it can ask for reviews, as Amazon does when a purchase is made.

Either way, user-generated content is a valuable, fast-working and cost-effective viral asset, which needs to be encouraged, incentivised if necessary, and most important of all used, so that it can be converted organically into winning customers at scale and speed and low cost.

Multiplier 4: Sharing equity

Most digital services have simple sharing functions that act as a multiplier. They are a fast way to build and maintain salience to get new people to find out about the brand from existing users.

Fortnite deliberately introduces moments in games that are shareable. And a replay model so that people can see great shots and ponder and wonder over them.

Spotify prides itself on high shareability. Customers can share a song, podcast or playlist very easily with other people on Facebook, Instagram, Twitter, WhatsApp, etc., which has shown to bring other users in.

People share the brand's content on social networks, and if the content is good it could be all that's needed for people to buy in. When the sharing is done peer to peer, as opposed to being amplified by marketing dollars, the brand gains credibility and customers.

To get sharing equity the brand must take the lead. Not only must content, user-generated or not, be interesting and what people care about, but it must also be what people want to share.

So, for instance, at the end of every year Spotify gives customers an end-of-year 'Wrapped Playlist', a curated list of their top 100 most-listened-to songs of that year, in a shareable social graphic. It also tells customers what their listening time is, the number of different songs they listen to and their most-listened-to artists and top genres. This content customers share with others on social media.

According to Spotify, people love to share things that tell other people about who they are, which increases its credibility as a music brand and continues to bring more and more customers into the fold.

Spotify also shows artists who their fans are, how much listening time they got and in which countries. This encourages musicians to celebrate with their fans and draws in followers who want to be part of the show.

What Spotify creates is equity out of sharing, because its content value is high enough. Not only do people want to share it, they also want to consume it.

The following begets a following.

Popularity breeds more popularity.

That's how multipliers work.

Multiplier 5: Social utility

Distinguishers actively seek to build social utility. They do this by enabling people to do things together virtually.

Some of the greatest innovations we see today are built for multi-users at the outset. The value lies in what people can achieve together. And the multiplication comes from customers inviting others to join, acting effectively as recruiters or super-spreaders.

M-PESA customers who transfer money to others need to bring them on board by downloading the app and joining the community.

When the WhatsApp app is installed and the user is trying to connect with people who don't have the app to form, say, a neighbourhood or investment group, the brand will invite that person on the customer's behalf to join, or customers can create their own groups. The point is that when social utility (group behaviour/social connectedness) is built into a distinguisher model it feeds on itself, bringing in more customers.

It took WhatsApp two years to reach 200 million active users using this multiplier, and 10 years after its inception it has 2 billion users in 180 countries.[236, 237]

It may not have got the numbers if customers had had to pay for it.

But here's the thing. Every one of the users has been acquired by another user.

WhatsApp has no advertising budget, salespeople or stores.

The alternative to leveraging social utility power is to build features into single-user products later on. Users then get others to join the brand, in order for them to be able to connect and do things together.

A few examples of this are:

- Netflix Party enables people to watch a movie together, but they have to join the brand's app.
- Fitbit's users can invite friends to support them in reaching a goal, such as weight loss or walking with them, but conditional on being on the Fitbit app.
- With NatWest, people can share costs together, like renting a flat. If one person pays the rent, they can request it from others, bringing them onto the app.

Spotify not only uses shareability, it also uses social utility to multiply its market. Multi-user functionalities allow people to co-create collaborative music playlists. So, for example, users can add, remove and re-order tracks for weddings and house parties, etc. Fifteen per cent of all its playlists are now collaborative and continue to multiply the customer base.[238]

Customers can also get access to and subscribe to other people's playlists assembled from the Spotify library, from friends, celebrities or unknown individuals who have similar listening tastes, making customers creators of social utility and super-content curators.

The followership they generate keeps attracting more and more customers, and more and more stickiness.

Perfect for distinguishers who want to scale.

Multiplier 6: Align with movements

Another multiplier is to piggyback on movements for which the brand has affinity. The distinguishers recruit new customers from its association/disassociation with a movement/anti-movement or cause that they share.

This is not bandwagon stuff, it's about seriously aligning to what the movement/anti-movement stands for and is trying to achieve. Let's try and forget when Pepsi aired an ad that borrowed imagery from a Black Lives Matter protest to sell its softdrink, which backfired and caused an uproar.

Some good examples:

- Just nine days after President Trump signed an order to close the border for refugees, Airbnb aired an advert during SuperBowl, saying 'We believe no matter who you are, where you're from, who you love or who you worship, we all belong. The world is more beautiful the more you accept it.' This message, aligning with the Dreamers movement (which focuses on giving amnesty to undocumented immigrants and advocating human rights for refugees), caused huge public approval and praise. This pulled in customers with similar or an aspiring purpose, reaffirming Airbnb's position on 'belonging anywhere' and political stance.

- Nike was active at the height of the Black Lives Matter movement protests. In a brilliant move, Nike changed its famous endline 'Just do it' to 'For once, don't do it', meaning 'Don't sit back and be silent'. Nike was able to leverage its longstanding support for black athletes and mobilise new customer sympathisers.

Distinguishers may also share an agenda with movements to change behaviour.

SodaStream tapped into the Less Plastic movement in the UK in a big way. In addition to promoting the benefit of making soda at home, it campaigned about the bigger cause of saving oceans from plastic. It also builds lots of activities around pledges for saving the planet and earth from plastic, attracting consumers already leaning in that direction.

The movement effectively uses its clout to change behaviour and the brand rides on this, converting the new and pent-up demand with its offering.

The Debt Free movement in the UK is gaining momentum, which catalysed NatWest's campaign to promote financial capability, including more savings, better management of spending by setting budgets, tracking expenditure and paying off credit card debt.

The point is, the movement motivated and scaled debt-free behaviour, which then helped to swell the brand at speed.

CHAPTER 31

Keep scaling

Scaling starts at the beginning of the process, not at the end. Everything, from shaking up insiders and investors, through shaping the proposition, to preparing to go to market, is done with the full intentionality to scale fast.

Once a base of early adopters has been entrenched, scaling is ongoing with the express aim to make brands infectious to many, and then to become the new global standard.

With the new way of doing things up and running, competitors inevitably enter, old and new.

Even the mighty Microsoft had to acknowledge that Slack's entry and exponential growth meant it needed a new version of Teams. There are thousands of ride-sharing app players worldwide, all seeking a piece of the Uber transport revolution pie.

The question then is how distinguishers continue to scale in the face of competition, keep enlarging markets, and increase stickiness, to get a bigger share of customers.

Driving virtuous cycles

Basic to scaling is building networking effects through virtuous cycles.

Extinguishers don't do this. They form linear distribution systems to get offerings from origin to customer. From silos that each deliver their products and services out into the market.

Distinguishers have two jobs in launching a new way of doing things: create a critical mass of demand and a critical mass of supply.

Firstly, supply (providers who will produce the outcome) is needed. When Uber started, it first looked for suppliers (drivers) before trying to get customers, as did Airbnb (hosts).

Virtual restaurants with chefs didn't just happen. Uber Eats has helped start 4,000 of them, exclusive to its Uber app. It analysed neighbourhoods, identified demand for types of food, and sought out appropriate restaurants it thought were a fit.

The second job is to stimulate and harness demand, which of course increasingly attracts suppliers, which extends and upgrades the offering, providing more value into the market space, getting an uptick in demand. The starting point may differ but the principle holds.

For Netflix, lots of small communities were already sharing video with each other and it decided to mobilise the hunger for on-demand entertainment and make a business out of it. The unwavering demand drove suppliers to provide their content, which brought in more customers, which lifted up both the quantity and quality of content supplied. Netflix finally had sufficient market power to command its own exclusive productions, which soon got to Oscar-winning standards, kicking in even more brand demand and supply pull.

YouTube, which follows the same virtuous cycle strategy, has managed to make its content providers famous, i.e. YouTubers, who became influencers and celebrities, attracting more users, making them even more popular, in one giant self-sustaining loop.

Suppliers can be service or product providers, developers or partners, each of whom play a critical part in the production and delivery of the outcome.

- As Zoom moves to constantly improve communication between its users, for whom having interoperable hardware suppliers has become an important factor, so manufacturers like Dell, Logitech, Polycom and others making devices and pre-assembled kits that keep improving the user's experience set up competitive barriers for Zoom, making the brand even more valuable.

- Unilever cleverly built up its own network of education, health, humanitarian and behavioural change experts. It also used its customers as service providers, whom it calls promoters. It started as a handful of women in hinterland India and grew to become 50,000 people reaching 3 million households. These suppliers, who were equipped by Unilever with business skills and micro-financing, earning income they would otherwise not have had, built demand for personal hygiene and handwashing in their own community among families and friends, driving demand, which brought in more suppliers, which built greater demand.

- With increasing numbers of small businesses subscribing to Shopify, developers with new applications like inventory management, reporting accounting and marketing keep coming on stream, so that retailers can plug into them to help manage their businesses better. Shopify's open-source and API technology enables these developers to access data and build on top of its platform. It also assists others, like consultants, to help online small businesses better design, build and even operate their sites and fulfilments. This way, Shopify's platform piles on increasing layers of value, further enticing more people in and generating more spend per customer.

Distinguishers actively nurture and equip suppliers so they can excel at a high standard, to attract demand to trigger the positive feedback loop.

In India, Amazon helps small manufacturers of local goods digitise their business so they can sell local goods to Indian consumers from the Amazon site, as well as to a worldwide market. The more manufacturers they can get doing this well, the bigger the market becomes, the more manufacturers they will additionally attract.

Airbnb made owner accommodation attractive by getting in its own photographers at the outset to make sure potential lodgers would be attracted. This way they effectively set the standard for future owners.

Etsy helped sellers to promote their goods online and off at art fairs, to drive demand, as well as acquired a company to help sellers market their goods better online. Plus, they matched sellers with pre-approved manufacturers from which to source and buy raw materials and merchandise, which drove demand up further and brought in more craft suppliers.

iFood has bought a company in order to make artificial intelligence and machine learning the engine that grows the business exponentially, evidently so far twice as fast as the global leaders. It takes its wealth of data and turns it into insights for restaurants, more than half of which are small businesses. From market intelligence on customer behaviour, among other things, it helps them adapt their menus to sales flow, adjust ingredient utilisation, map to optimise delivery area ratios and use promotions that will work well for that particular area.

iFood also allows restaurants to buy from its platform and gets discounts for them from manufacturers in the region of 20 per cent. For its scooter couriers it has provided its own payment terminal, which has drastically reduced delivery times, and it can accept normal cards as well as meal voucher cards provided by employees. And through its advanced technology counters it reduces fraudulent payments.

Additionally, it has a courier-scoring reward system offering discounts on services and products to them and their families, and so far, is the only company in Brazil to provide accident insurance.

Uber Works allows its drivers to find temporary work in the food industry, including McDonald's, PepsiCo, UPS and Walgreens, in partnership arrangements to keep its supply of gig-economy workers fully occupied in order to retain supply and thus demand. How this will evolve once drivers become Uber employees we have yet to see.

Spotify has gone so far as to create a marketplace to keep its demand-and-supply loop going. Artists can now find a designer to create visuals on Canvas to help them create eye-catching visuals. The intention is to get artists to create more engagement 'album covers' which evidently means users are 20 per cent more likely to add the song to their playlist and 145 per cent more likely to share it with others.[239]

Industrial investors can be part of this virtuous cycle if they are an integral part of the ecosystem, not just fund suppliers.

The more they join, the bigger the potential keeps growing.

Not all brands do this when seeking funders. MaaS did, so did Spotify. Spotify has major music labels as funders, who both own and earn from them.

MaaS has car manufacturers, bus operators, insurance companies and transport service providers as investors, which all have a part to play in the strategic puzzle to connect different providers in one transborder transport network. To achieve this, it has assembled partners and investors, including BP, with its vast service network, which is changing from being an oil commodity company to enabling mobility and transport in connected cities that want a low-carbon world.

Acquisitions can also bring about virtuous exponential effects. Take Taskrabbit, bought by IKEA. Taskrabbit's hundreds of thousands of taskers have done many assemblies across 45 cities in the US, UK and Canada. For IKEA, it's a reliable cost-effective way to get expert delivery and assembly services done on demand for its customers so they can shop wherever, however and whenever they like.

For Taskrabbit, it's an opportunity to grow with IKEA as it

moves into its merged digital on- and offline future, scaling over multiple countries at reduced cost.

The better it is at household errands and chores (delivery and assembly included) the more likely IKEA will gain customer patronage, and the more IKEA gains and grows, the larger Taskrabbit becomes.

Co-branding: 1 + 1 = 3 plus

Co-branding can be an effective way for brands to get reach into a partner's customer base, which would otherwise take longer to get, if they got it at all. It's a virtuous circle of sorts, because as one partner gains so does the other, and so on.

Both need to have a trusted reputation and similar messaging and common ground for co-branding to make strategic sense. LEGO and Shell famously had to break up their partnership, in which the former made Shell-branded petrol stations and cars, to be sold in the latter's global network. This was after Greenpeace ran a 1 minute 45 seconds YouTube video which depicted a LEGO-Shell drilling rig in a LEGO Arctic, with wildlife getting submersed in crude oil, which received millions of views and loads of criticism.[240]

Co-branding is ideal for the expanding market when the partner is actually filling a gap in the market space.

Many riders will listen to music while in a car, the average riding time being 30 minutes.

Uber riders can stream their Spotify music playlists in the Uber car in which they are riding. If customers link their Uber and Spotify apps, they can control their music wirelessly as they wait for a pickup. Additionally, they will be prompted by the Uber app to play from their Spotify account in the car and their playlist will be on when the car picks them up.

A co-win.

But making Spotify available in Uber fleets goes a step further. Uber is able to capture non-Uber riders who want Spotify as a value-add who may have gone to Uber rivals, and Spotify is able to massify its reach because non-Spotify customer Uberites can listen to its music.

Ramping up numbers for both with all the consequent viral effects.

Interestingly, Spotify's Chief Executive, Daniel Ek said, 'Instead of just doing car integrations, we thought "What's the next generation of transportation system"?'.[241]

Distinguisher thinking.

Spotify uses the same logic with other partners with whom it shares a market space. People listen to music in Starbucks. Shops get a Spotify premium subscription, so they can curate their own playlists that can be accessed by its customers through its mobile app. The theory is that Starbucks draws in more customers as a consequence and Spotify gets more sign-ups as well as giving artists more exposure.

The Uber and co-branding partnerships with hotels and restaurants are a scaling mechanism because they give access to new customers who may otherwise not choose them.

For customers, the advantage—apart from a complete transport and hospitality service in the relevant hotels—is that from the car they can use the Uber app to take them automatically into the hotel's app to book or check in, or order from a restaurant. Hotel customers leverage Uber customers' most-frequented top local hotspots in cities and provide guests with recommendations so that they get the best of local amenities. When out, they can set ride reminders, request vehicles to and from nearby locations and addresses will automatically be on the booking screen.

Rides can be booked by the hotel, which can provide tracking for customers and bills can be charged on one invoice.

The beginning of the end for shuttles, for which customers had to wait their turn to fit the shuttles' schedules (extinguisher thinking).

Netflix looks to co-brand with brands with whom it shares customers—its average customer is 31 years old and hates ads, the brand reckons.[242] Instead of using paid advertising, as its rivals do, or getting people to pay Netflix to use their brand willy nilly in its movies, it wants to take the authentic route and place brands in its content only if these resonate with its market, and enhance the Netflix brand as well as its partners'. And through this approach build awareness, content and salience for Netflix, in the words of the CEO, competing for viewer satisfaction (instead of just advertising revenue, which extinguisher logic would dictate).

Slack and Zoom have co-branded not only to gain access to each other's customers but to deliberately block out competition. As they forge ahead as leaders in collaboration (Slack) and remote communication (Zoom) they are together able to produce better work productivity outcomes—a competitive barrier to other players like Microsoft or Cisco.

Keeping amplification going

Distinguishers keep momentum and scaling going in various ways, often through partnerships or acquisition. Typically, however, this is to complement what they do, so they can add more value in their chosen market space, not just buy out new competitors who are trying to do what they do. As recent examples demonstrate, i.e., Salesforce/Slack, Uber/Postman, IKEA/Geomagical Labs.

Taking the brand global

Digital platforms are global in scope, allowing brands to be born global or become global, connecting with customers and suppliers in any country at speed and low cost.

Especially if the brand is built from the start to be global, as umpteen examples are today, like Facebook, Amazon, Spotify, Netflix, Airbnb, Uber, YouTube, Fortnite, Apple or Kickstarter, or built to be culturally relevant, like TikTok.

This ability to get instant global reach applies equally to small and medium-size enterprises, the crowd, developers, freelancers, etc., all of whom can plug into these platforms and scale at speed and low cost.

Many distinguishers, however, still scale in one country and then geo-expand. If the barriers to country entry are highly regulated, this is often done faster through partnering or acquisition.

If there is an existing customer base with which the brand has such a natural fit, the merging of the two is a no-brainer win-win, with immediate potential for scale at speed. For example, Netflix has partnered with numerous paid-TV companies, even in those enterprises and countries where there was previous hostility towards it. To date, this has given it access to another 300-plus million paying TV households worldwide, rapidly scaling the brand globally with still more country prospects to come.

Globalisation involves serious localisation today, as we've discussed. In fact, brands who have done it say that localisation is a major scaler. In India, for example, Netflix users are among the largest groups to download content globally and there is a growing trend to watch its content on smartphones. Netflix has galvanised its position there with its three-dollar 'mobile only' plan (an average person earns about $2,000 a year in India),[243] plus local content, both through licensing and original shows and movies, to make sure it gets the lion's share of this mobile market.[244]

Only 10 per cent of India's 1.3-billion-strong market can speak English, which prompted the American brand (which has over 12 language platforms so far) to offer an interface—from sign-up, payment, through to searches and content—in Hindi, which is spoken by half a billion Indians.[245] Others have done the same to drive scale in India, like Facebook, Google and Amazon (including via Alexa) with great success. Amazon also has sellers signing up on its platform in Hindi.

It's what a brand knows better than anyone else that enables it to globalise, even if it means doing it with partners or acquisitions to gain access.

Discovery has scaled into the US, Europe, the UK and China with 20 million customers as a result of its Vitality programme and the fact that, through it, Discovery is ahead in the world in tracking and monitoring customers' physical and nutritional wellness. Add to that the largest most scientific way to influence financial behaviour, and the opportunities to globalise and scale become endless. Access to markets through partnering and acquisition keeps mounting. The incumbents get the benefit of Discovery's immense know-how and database, with configurations built to adapt to each market and Discovery gets access to a new client base, to whom it can offer so much more than just the old-fashioned copyable product.

Noom has managed to globalise quickly to Japan, Korea, South America and Germany, growing its base by 80 per cent, by adapting languages and cuisine to suit local tastes and popular packaged food brand availability. Also, it ran several experiments to get the pricing mechanism right for each country, i.e. subscriptions, in-app purchases or a premium (paid-for) app.

It hired local coaches, which has not only removed language barriers but reduced time-zone related delays in response and notifications to suit cultures, all of which has significantly decreased time to market and increased engagement three to four times.

Making the market space additive

That market spaces are additive by nature is part of the scaling formula. Once articulated, a market space needs to be filled with products and services, whether from inside an organisation or through partnerships and acquisitions.

The more value added, the more the barrier to competition. The more additive, the more the potential to grow customers and revenue from the existing and form the new base.

As Rover sitters became more popular, customers started asking for other services from them. That got Rover into pet insurance and grooming, 24/7 support, vet consultations and security, which has achieved greater scale for the brand and more spend per customer, in the 14,000 cities in the US and in its expansion to London and Germany. And because new ideas came from the customer community, it has taken almost zero intentional effort, says the CEO.[246]

This has significantly increased the share of customer wallet, but has also brought new users on board. A quarter of the customers who have used the in-home grooming services have never used Rover before.[247] A very low percentage (20 per cent) of people who apply to be groomers are accepted and they get paid infinitely more than they would if they worked in a dog parlour, to ensure standards are kept high.

Fitbit is now one of the largest fitness social networks in the world. Not for nothing. Fitbit never stops adding products to its portfolio to fill the connected health market space to fulfil its ambitions, like continuous, wrist-based heart-rate tracking, guided breathing sessions, which research shows can reduce stress and anxiety and lower blood pressure. Through its acquisition of Twine Health's clinically proven health-coaching platform, it can now get even more additive, focusing on more serious conditions like hypertension and diabetes, which are high on the list of poor health culprits, particularly in the US.

Discovery from South Africa is an interesting case because what it did was to fill its market space with a brand-new enterprise venture. On the surface it looks like it diversified into banking, but actually its move was an important portion of its quest to occupy and own the healthy-lifestyle space, of which, it argued, financial wellness is a critical part.

Most customers lack the kind of savvy required to make well-informed money-related decisions. They may save, for example, but not necessarily know what to do with their savings, to ensure both short- and long-term security.

A move into banking to achieve a healthier set of customers required more than just digitising existing offerings. It meant

Discovery becoming a pioneering example of how to help customers use digital tools to improve their financial behaviour.

But if there was one thing Discovery had learnt over decades, it was how to change people's behaviour patterns. The brand, which refers to itself as 'the first behavioural bank', meant it could leverage its existing customer base where they have other insurance and investment products with Discovery. Which brought them at scale, speed and low cost into banking, accomplished even during lockdown.

The fact that GoBear's base doesn't have traditional credit histories left a gap created by incumbent extinguishers, which made the brand a success growth story. GoBear, having made the investment in becoming the expert not at selling products but at analysing Asian customers' financial health and risk, built a platform where these customers could be digitally operative.

This done, it has partnered with incumbent enterprises like Chubb and Allianz (travel insurance), and made acquisitions like AsiaKredit, a consumer lender, as an additive scaling device. It is now a financial supermarket, offering its installed base online insurance and digital lending loans as a service (LaaS). This allows consumers to purchase items in instalments from its mobile app, allowing the fintech powerhouse to ride a scaling wave.

Zoom is working on a series of extensions to its offering to enhance customer outcomes. Through AI it will be able to achieve real-time language translation for customers. Zoom for commuters will mean the ability to remotely hold meetings while driving, Zoom Snackpass will allow customers to order food during a meeting, Zoom's bandwidth will enable people with poor bandwidth to be able to participate, Zoom polling makes real-time surveys for participants possible, and Zoom drive-ins will enable up to a thousand attendees to be displayed on cinema screens and accessed from cars.

For social activities after work hours, there is Zooming along karaoke, displaying lyrics and songs, and built-in pub quizzes and other fun activities with workmates.

And CEO Yuan believes that, one day, 'there may even be a technology which creates a realistic handshake or allows you to smell the coffee a colleague is drinking in their office on the other side of the globe'.[248]

Zoom has also made itself into a marketplace platform where paid users can create, host and monetise events like fitness classes, concerts, stand-up shows, music lessons, travel or sport. The list of partners is growing more awesome by the day, and they can host up to a thousand attendees, promote shared events and sell tickets. Consumers can search, and either get whatever is offered free, or pay and buy a ticket, or donate to a fundraiser.

Moving into new revenue streams

Once the brand has created a new way of doing things for something specific and got that right, it's easy without being costly to stretch the concept and brand to mean new things, in order to get more customer spend or attract new customers, as these interesting examples demonstrate:

- SodaStream, having got customers from buying carbonated water as a category to the home-brewing market space, will get market multiplication by continuing to get numbers of customers switching behaviour from cans to its machines, but also by occupying more and more of that space with new products and services, such as beer, tea and alcohol, made at home with carbonated water, thereby increasing share of the new home-market activity it itself created.

- Livestock Wealth, the livestock crowdfunding platform which started with 26 cows and now has thousands in several farms throughout South Africa, is continuing to scale by building out its array of agricultural assets in the fractional investment space, for example, sugarcane, macadamia nut trees (South Africa is the world's largest producer), maize plants or a new concept called 'connected gardens', which grows organic vegetables. The future will be about anything that it can make into a new asset class, provided to consumers either as a whole or in part as an alternative to financial shares or unit trusts.

- Why stick to dogs, when 47.1 million households in the US have a cat and research shows that 68 per cent of cat-owners wouldn't feel comfortable leaving their cat alone for more than two days without care when they travel? Rover didn't, and now is the market leader with tens of thousands of cat-sitters across the US, Canada and the UK.[249]

- Drone delivery will not be limited to food. iFood can keep scaling by delivering items like medicine, drugs, organs and blood for starters, which are essentials and therefore will command high demand. Amazon is already doing this in the UK.

- iFood, having scaled in numbers of users and cities in Brazil, grew its market even further by leveraging its network to get to low-cost meals to consumers under its own private label, called Loop. At zero delivery cost it offers healthy affordable lunchtime meals so that these don't have to be prepared at home or bought outside of the workspace. It offers a very low-cost meal during idle times to keep couriers and restaurants busy and bring down its overall cost of delivery.

  It has also created a new platform called iFood shop, to deliver groceries for supermarkets, and the number of user cities and partner stores is growing exponentially at nearly half a million orders per day. That's 12 million clients a month buying their day-to-day provisions, delivered at convenient pre-arranged times, paid via the iFood app, with iFood taking care of the entire delivery process.[250]

Becoming a micro satisfier
To keep growing requires hyper-personalisation of outcomes

at scale. This sounds like a contradiction in terms, but it isn't, because it's the new mass production, which does not depend on standardisation in order to grow.

The distinguisher brand gets to more people the more it is able to micro satisfy, catering to millions of individual preferences.

It's not about personalising a product, it's about personalising the customer's experience and that's very different because it happens in real time in the customer's space, not in the factory.

These individual experiences are ever changing. Every time a Noom customer's weight changes, the system will work out an appropropriate adjustment, i.e. update what needs to be adjusted for that particular person.

NatWest tracks an individual's spending and makes suggestions based on that, not customer averages. If customers overspend on something, they are told how to compensate in real time, in order to get back to their financial goal.

Personalised experiences are unique. Fitbit is constantly innovating to get services to consumers that are user-specific. Its health and fitness platform delivers smarter and smarter insights so that individuals are empowered to make ever better decisions.

The personal trainer intelligent app offers video-based exercise routines with certified coaches, customised depending on the level of fitness required and the speed of progress. It delivers insights to help each person reach individual goals. It targets specific areas of the person's body needing attention: legs, arms, etc., recommending routines to fix those spots, and it offers music the person likes as motivation to stay on the move.

That's how Amazon got started and kept on scaling. It never ever tried to treat everyone the same. It never said, 'We have bought x number of books and we want customers (whoever they are) to buy them because we need to get rid of them.'

The brand prided itself on its ability to recommend a book based on what it knew about a particular person's interests and taste and what other types of people shared these preferences. And then find it for them. It aimed to micro satisfy.

It's one of the reasons Netflix went from small to scale and keeps on scaling. It has thousands of mini taste types or groups according to the combination of movie genres they enjoy watching. Recommendations are hyper-personalised based on these tastes and the more it is micro satisfying, the more customers use the service and have no reason to choose any opposition.

Beyond taste differences, Spotify now has a patent to extract data-points that tell them the emotional state of the customers, their accent, gender, age and the environment in which they are situated in order to micro-refine its recommendations.[251]

Mass customisation is a product concept. A unit of product or service needs to be made partially different for an individual customer.

Outcomes that micro satisfy consist of multiple products, services, touchpoints and interventions, connected by technology and powered by real-time data and feedback loops over time for a particular customer, ever satisfying, as more is learnt and known about the user.

And it is that capability, which engenders the positive share of voice, that makes a brand go and stay viral.

What makes it a scaling lever is that although the data collected is customer-specific, through technology aggregated learning and intelligence are built up, which can be deployed for other correlated customers, building the brand power and market pull.

With more listeners and better data, Spotify says it is able to give fans the kind of experience that shows that Spotify really gets them.[252] And really getting them means really keeping them.

Once a brand can do that and get behavioural change to stick, customer lock-on brings potential for more spend as well as viral scaling.

Building the new marketing machine

Scaling markets at speed means building a marketing machine that both acquires and holds on to customers.

The new marketing machine is built on technology stacks, including sophisticated data-sets and digital tracking systems on both customers and prospects. From the data obtained from existing customers, the technology learns who to target and retarget, i.e., those people for whom the brand will be most likely to deliver satisfying outcomes.

In other words, the system learns who should become and keep being a customer, with spend optimised to achieve this. For example, when acquiring customers with their freemium version, Spotify will target people who are most likely to become paying subscribers thereafter.

As well, the data-set of customers and non-customers is accumulated and correlated so as to anticipate responses. NatWest knows which individual (a customer or non-customer) is most likely to respond to what message in what channel, at what time. For instance, customer type A will respond to a 'savings goal' message (as opposed to a 'spending less' message), on Facebook (rather than on Instagram), on a Monday (not a Thursday), at noon (rather than in the evening).

And it knows what life event will trigger that saving need, e.g. going to university or getting married. This is done using third-party data that identifies others entering the life event, which builds the audience targeted.

Fortnite (Epic Games) knows which existing customers will repeatedly buy while gaming. It can then acquire customers like them who are more likely to behave in the same way (twinning). It also learns, with in-app advertising, to prompt people to buy things at the best time specifically for them.

With these data analytics, Fortnite can figure out a way to advertise in a non-invasive way that doesn't interfere with the customer experience. In fact, it can enhance it, e.g. pre-empt and offer an upgrade when it's needed the most.

Because the data-set is so sophisticated, it is also possible to build a scaling platform model that includes non-digital engagement touchpoints that get to the right people at the right place, at the right time with the right message. For example, with such rich pools of real-time data, an IKEA or Nike can build scale by spending marketing money where the return will be the highest, both to win new and keep existing customers.

This marketing machine powered by technology and data is what will get the right people into the Nike store in Paris to either buy items there, or later online, from a device. It knows which customers, existing or prospective, live in Paris and can invite them in via its app, email or social media. And through location targeting, it knows which existing customers or prospects are in Paris on a trip, so it can entice them into the store.

Distinguishers concentrate on winning customers they can keep in order to scale, because they want to keep magnifying the customer base. As opposed to extinguishers who get whoever they can to tick the budget box, and say whatever needs to be said to get them, replacing customers lost at high cost.

(Note: 96 per cent of unhappy customers don't complain, but of them 91 per cent will leave and never come back.)[253]

Distinguishers know what customers are doing from the first engagement and they monitor fall-off rates so they can learn, improve, engage, nudge and rectify when needed in real time to keep them. Also, it means that when someone comes into the marketing funnel and doesn't buy, they can be identified and dealt with differently next time round, in order to try and get them on board.

Amazon tracks the book a customer buys on Kindle to see whether he or she started it or finished it and what they thought of it, and nudges them along the way to complete, and whatever it has learnt about that customer is absorbed into the system, in order to be able to recommend the next book to them.

Because every customer counts.

CHAPTER 32

Getting disproportionate gains

Distinguishers live in a world of disproportionate gains. Or put differently, as they are evolving to become the new lead players, so is the economics.

It's about giving more value to get disproportionately more.

Extinguishers fear giving more value because it costs them.

Distinguishers fear *not* giving more value, because it costs them.

For extinguishers, the objective is to make and sell discrete units of goods at the lowest possible cost and highest possible margin.

They grow by making more stuff. Because the more that's made, the more the unit cost goes down. Goods (units of products or services) are then costed, using various formulas, with margins added (with fixed costs or a portion of them often embedded), in order to get a set required return.

Any innovation is tested for feasibility, based on whether it meets the return and horizon criteria. If not, it isn't done, and this can and often does leave a gap for others to fill.

The extinguisher's old economies of scale approach goes like this:
1. What products and services can I make and sell at a margin to make the projected budget and return in a given time horizon?
2. How do I recover my R&D and costs quickly?

3. How many units of products or services do we have to make, in order to get costs down to achieve 1 and 2?

For distinguishers, the questions are quite different. They ask:
1. What needs to be done to fill our defined market space with sufficient value, in order to scale changed customer behaviour, shifting it to new ways of doing things?
2. What will it take to attract, acquire and keep customers and become indispensable to them and the undisputed leader in this market space?
3. What will it cost?
4. How many customers do we need in order to cover the initial investment to start leveraging disproportionate returns, i.e. get to the tipping point?
5. How long will it take?
6. How do we keep innovating to repeat the 1-5 loop?

Distinguishers don't just work with a different mindset, it's a whole different economic model.

They reverse the curve

The first thing to note is that because there is a different model and mindset at work, the intent, pace and criteria for success are different.

The extinguisher has to make and sell more discrete units in a standardised way to get economies of scale. The inevitable happens, competitors come in, there is a 'dipping point' where margins go down, and as the market commoditises, there is a downward spiral (see Figure 32.1).

They counter this with incremental innovation (better existing products and services), and are invariably copied so each version has a finite cycle, limiting the life of each investment.

Returns grow upfront but then they dissipate because old

FIGURE 32.1 *Investment Model: Extinguisher Product Decreasing Returns vs Distinguisher Customer Increasing Returns*

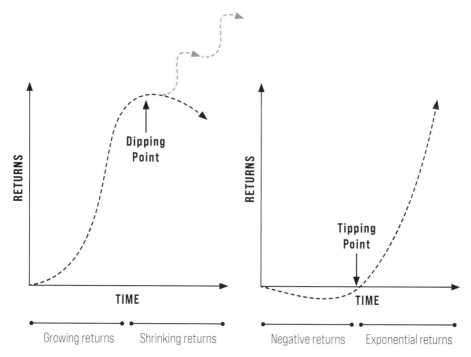

protective devices, like patents, no longer hold. Neither do large capital infrastructures to keep others out as they once did. The cycle keeps repeating itself with many iterations of the product or service life cycle, often referred to as the innovation S curve (see Figure 32.1 top right), which perpetuates a 'more of the same' mentality for investing.

Distinguisher logic is this: units of products and services, no matter how good they are, invariably lose value over time, but customers gain value over time.

So, the investment upfront is about getting more customers and holding on to them.

The focus is on whatever it takes to get adoption and buy-in, in a constant reinforcing cycle of demand and supply, for larger and larger customer numbers.

At the outset this will bring a period of negative returns, but when the distinguisher reaches the tipping point and behaviour has changed, disproportionate gains kick in (see Figure 32.1).

Whether incumbent or startup, the gains from their initial investment never come to an end, because it (the investment in customer lock-on) is constantly being leveraged.

As such it goes on the balance sheet as an asset and not an expense (sunk cost) to be recovered quickly.

Success at acquiring and converting customers at scale needs and attracts constant tranches of this investment, which becomes easier and easier to get, as investors see the potential building and get used to the new model, keeping the process going.

The exponential gains don't always abide by conventional economic logic, they often result in positive cashflows—money flowing in versus flowing out. As well as a high-market capitalisation, reflecting current and future customer equity and market power, rather than traditional profit (think Salesforce acquiring Slack for USD 27.7 billion, despite no 'profit' yet made).

The free cashflow is used to kick in steps 1-6 in order to get the increasing scale at speed that produces lower and lower cost, keeping the distinguisher competitive.

Especially with customers themselves an integral part of the scalesforce, part of the value creating process without adding costs.

They are digitally driven

The more digitally based the enterprise is, the more disproportionate gains kick in. And, needless to say, digital penetration will continue to swing up.

On the consumption side, anywhere customers (mainly but not only millennials), who are digitally savvy, are pushing for it. And on the production side, increases in computing power and storage capacity and a decrease in price (storage computation and transmission) make it increasingly possible for enterprises to adopt and use digital faster and more cost-effectively.

But a caveat: being digital (in part or in whole) doesn't guarantee anything if the old-product diminishing-returns model is still the dominant culture and motivation.

Typically, then, digital is used to become more efficient at what is already being done to further reduce costs in marketing, distribution, manufacturing, customer service and general operations.

And often, yes, these extinguishers and reports will boast an increase in productivity and profits as a consequence. But it doesn't necessarily mean they have opened up more markets or won more customers. Or that they will escape shrinking returns.

In this model, digital may grow in adoption but its role is simply a cost-cutter.

Whereas in the distinguisher enterprise, digital is used strategically to produce the platforms and/or propositions that push customer value up, delivering outcomes that have better and better appeal, experiences that get ever richer, with gains for all customer-stakeholders. The new next.

For the born-digital brands or those going more digital the economics changes.

They don't have a cost of goods or inventory (or as much of it), so they have nothing they have to cover, except the initial investment.

Once that first-wave investment is covered, scaling can be done at high speed and low cost, because the marginal cost of scaling, i.e., the next item, next customer, next configuration or next country, is low and keeps getting lower at incredible speed.

For distinguishers who are product-makers, for whom the advanced technology with higher data and digital components is driving customer value and adding engagement and enhanced services, the economics also change. Because they are able to use the new economics pushing value up and costs down.

Additionally, the funds that previously were needed for finite infrastructure or assets, which often proved an expensive investment and competitive entry barrier, can now be accessed as a service, shared with others via aggregators or the cloud, or by going from buying the hardware to 'software as a service'.

And, parts of the production process can be outsourced on demand to external providers to reduce overhead costs.

Changing the economics.

They use more resources that are abundant

Another reason for disproportionate gains is that resources that drive value are now infinite, not scarce.

The more they are used the more they grow in value.

Distinguishers know how to leverage this.

The old model was built around tangible assets and finite resources that get depleted as they are consumed. But it was these physical factories, buildings, inventories and hard items that sparkled on balance sheets, enticed investors and pleased shareholders.

As we all know today, some of the most invigorated and invigorating enterprises don't have any of these, and they certainly don't rely on them to be the value producers.

They use abundant resources, for example.

DATA

Importantly, data grows as it is being used and re-used, instead of becoming used up or depleted.

Data is infinite in the sense that there is no limit to how much a brand can have, store and therefore turn to value, provided it is converted to the customer's benefit, with consent.

The more data the brand has, the more likely it is that it can produce value.

And the more value it produces for customers, the more likely it is that they will obtain even more data from customers willingly.

With the investment to capture that data already made, the cost of acquiring more data and value goes down.

LEARNING

Learning is elastic and ongoing. The more it's used, the smarter the brand becomes.

Combinations of machine learning, artificial intelligence and algorithms enable what is learnt from data to make propositions increasingly better at lower and lower cost.

If what the brand knows how to do better than anyone else keeps improving through learning, with the investment to acquire that learning already made, costs to keep getting smarter begin to approximate zero.

Aerobotics scales by knowing more and more how to manage and enhance the crop performance of nut and citrus fruit trees and it keeps on getting smarter as it learns.

As it grows, with more data-sets on trees and citrus fruit than any other player in the world, we are told, it is able to continue to scale at low cost and speed by getting:

- **more reach**: getting to more customers and more countries—it is in 18 countries now;
- **more role**: broadening the offering by providing more to customers in its chosen market space, e.g., irrigation and water management;
- **more range**: adapting for more crop types, i.e., other kinds of trees and farming.

All at low cost and high speed.

As Aerobotics's co-founder put it: 'Once we have data from one crop in one country we can scale the learning fast and cost-effectively for multiple crops in multiple countries doing more per crop.'

Rover, by the way, saw nearly USD 4 million in its cat billings during its first test, a figure which originally took two years and much more investment for dogs.

This is what sets the enterprise ahead, making it difficult for others to catch up.

A virtuous cycle indeed.

Learning also increases the speeds at which problems are identified, such as detecting fraud or managing risk, which further saves on time, money and energy. Lemonade has groups of 'uniform insurers' who share similar risk behaviours, which are compiled by AI algorithms that gather extensive customer data and monitor loss ratios. The more data accumulated, the more the brand learns about recursive risk patterns, enabling more precise assessments in shorter times with potential to decrease costs.

EXTERNAL RESOURCES

Like the crowd, freelance workers can be brought together from anywhere whenever needed, making the workforce vast and fast, without having to carry fixed overheads.

While this has advantages, co-ordinating touchpoints to keep quality standards high, own customer relationships and capture data will be the overriding challenge. Only then can what's known about and experienced by customers be tapped, grown and shared, to build expertise at low cost.

CUSTOMERS

As a part of the marketing machine customers are now a massive, viral, marketing, low/no-cost abundant resource.

As well, for every unit of investment made to acquire or keep a customer, there is an opportunity to get infinite value if customer lock-on is achieved through referral, advocacy, testimony, influence and sheer value-add information, which elevates outcomes. Every time a customer gives another customer advice on how to use a product better, whether it's a sophisticated piece of software or a SodaStream flavour or recipe, it elevates the value proposition at low cost.

They are able to remove time, space, distance and energy constraints

Technology has removed the constraints of old resource logic because one or many customers can be handled simultaneously, and instead of this costing more, it costs less. So distinguisher scaling can be done without forfeiting value. Here are some of the benefits.

ENGAGEMENT/TIME WITH CUSTOMERS

Pre digital, engagement time spent with customers was a cost and often considered a liability because of constraints and expenses. Now, engagement can be automated and unlimited time can be given to unlimited customers at low cost. From Amazon's Alexa (now going into cars), to robots in hospitals to bank bots serving millions of customers simultaneously, working 24/7.

And bots don't sleep, go on lunch or get tired, bored or rude.

CAPACITY/SPACE

If virtual everywhere alternatives become the new normal for sufficient portions of the population, capacity is no longer a restraint. Zoom can easily scale from 1 to 1,000 attendees having a meeting. The more customers that fill a virtual space or marketplace, the less it costs, without quality being sacrificed.

INTERNET/DISTANCE

The Internet has replaced some of the needs for physical stores and for much of the face-to-face service, and where that's the case, removes constraints of distance. Digital footprint is increasingly enough to bring in infinite numbers of consumers from anywhere anytime simultaneously, each getting high-quality service at lower costs.

LABOUR/PHYSICAL AND MENTAL ENERGY

Today, labour can be substituted or enhanced by machines to overcome mental and physical energy constraints. Robots never have to take a coffee break, are always on top form, can be steadier than a surgeon's hand, and are learning to become empathetic as well. Consumers, no matter how many, each always get services anywhere anytime at peak performance.

They drive revenues up and costs down

The investment in the customer base is leveraged by distinguishers who get revenues increasingly up and costs increasingly down.

This is the exponential prize.

Revenues go up in the following way:

NUMBER OF CUSTOMERS x

- **Length of spend**—greater 'lock on' and retention means an increase in spend per customer over time, i.e. lifetime spend, with a decrease in cost to serve and cost to replace.
- **Depth of spend**—increases in the size of the core (people who buy books on Amazon increase their spend on books, people who use Uber have increased their spend on non-ownership mobility, people who use Spotify spend more money on music than they did on CDs, people using Airbnb have increased their spend on accommodation away from home. As well as increases in their share of the core, whether physical or downloadable content (virtual), paid for upfront or by subscription.
- **Breadth of spend**—get more revenue per customer through extra value adds in the chosen market space, e.g. Etsy's move to advertising on the seller's behalf, or Rover offering dog grooming.

  Or getting breadth of spend by taking customers into new market spaces. From new ways of buying and reading books,

Amazon could take people into food, fashion, white goods, electronics, entertainment, virtual destination experiences and so on, at minimum marginal cost. Or Uber's move into Uber Eats, Spotify's move into podcast listening.

- **Diversity of spend**—new revenue streams coming from partners through things like advertising, licensing, data monetisation, channel fees, kick-backs and revenue sharing.

And costs go down because of the new economies that kick in from abundant resources:

NUMBER OF CUSTOMERS x

- **Economies of skill**—the more data (information), the more they know (knowledge), the more they become the expert (intelligence), the more skilled (repeating this with intention) distinguishers get at ever lowering costs. For example, the more people Unilever teaches to wash their hands the better they get at it and the less it costs per person.
- **Economies of sweep**—the more digital platforms are used for delivering an experience, the bigger the numbers of customers that can be swept up into these virtual places at lower and lower costs and speed. The number is infinite, one or one million people can be on a platform at any given moment.
- **Economies of stretch**—the more the investment is stretched into new areas, extending both features and geographies, the cheaper it gets over time with digital. And the faster. Compare the cost and how long it would take a physical hotel to expand into new markets compared to an Airbnb. And because Unilever is using mobile technologies and digital services to stretch its impact geographically, vast and fast at low cost.
- **Economies of spread**—the more content is spread from inside the enterprises and out, i.e. from customers and influencers, the more viral the marketing is at increasingly lower costs.

Distinguishers use a different combination of these economic levers. Uber is really good at length, depth and breadth of spend which they combine with all the cost economies.

Amazon has mastered it all with its fastest-growing revenue being the diversity of spend it is getting from advertising.

But more importantly, having cracked the new economic formula, Amazon has been able to embed it into how people think and do business cases. Which informs investment decisions.

Which is where extinguishers fail.

They pass savings on to customers

Disproportionate gains come when savings are passed on to customers, because this gets stickiness, which brings in opportunities for more revenue per customer as well as new customers, with all the viral spin, including decreasing costs.

It's not just the new economics at work. Getting customers to behave differently can actually reduce costs. Through its great safe-driving rewards, Discovery Insure gains increasing numbers of customers, who stay longer, with fewer claims, make smaller claims and incur less costs to repair vehicles. This gets kicked back into the reward system, i.e., back to the customers to reinforce behaviour and stickiness.

There are variations on this theme. Brands born digital or going digital do this superbly well. An example is Lemonade's idea talked about earlier in the book, to create a customer pot with what's left over from claims and give it to the policyholder's favourite charity. NatWest is taking the costs saved from going mobile and giving it back to customers in the form of higher interest rates on savings.

For product-makers going more digital, new production techniques (automation, additive manufacturing, etc.), new materials (less waste) and distribution, delivery and service (drones, freelance workers, online engagement, etc.) create savings that they can channel back to customers, as IKEA is doing in the form of modern, stylish, fashionable, furniture at affordable prices.

Amazon has always been about taking out the cost of the middleman in order to deliver a better service to users and share whatever the savings are with customers.

The brand has spent billions over the years and continues to do so now with drones to deliver ever faster to its millions of households worldwide. The objective: to get goods to customers super quick and free of charge.

With an already installed customer and app base, brands can keep adding value at low or no cost as they expand globally. Discovery Vitality is not a digital-native organisation but has globalised by making sure it has re-usable platform components, easily configured and reconfigured to support the specific needs of each market at low cost.

Also, brands do it through partnerships and acquisitions as they move into additive areas. Adding its behavioural scoring expertise to banking partners with an established infrastructure has led to savings that has allowed GoBear to offer even lower rates to customers so that they can scale quickly.

The point is this: passing on the benefits, from wherever they come, is part of the distinguisher's game plan. They give customers the benefit of the disproportionate gains because this retains their customer base and wins them more customers. Which keeps them scaling at speed and low cost in a positive loop.

Just what a distinguisher needs … to get and keep ahead.

Endnotes

1 https://sumo.com/stories/slack-marketing
2 https://www.shrm.org/resourcesandtools/hr-topics/technology/pages/slack-zoom-ceos-discuss-remote-work.aspx
3 https://www.sportskeeda.com/esports/how-many-people-play-fortnite-2021
4 https://www.theguardian.com/food/2020/jul/14/nespresso-coffee-capsule-pods-branding-clooney-nestle-recycling-environment?CMP=share
5 Sandra Vandermerwe, 2014, *Breaking Through, 2nd edition: Implementing Disruptive Customer Centricity*, London: Palgrave Macmillan
6 https://www.geekwire.com/2018/rover-raises-giant-155m-funding-round-investors-bet-big-high-tech-pet-care-marketplace/
7 https://medium.com/@jgolden/lessons-learned-scaling-airbnb-100x-b862364fb3a7
8 https://news.crunchbase.com/news/ubers-eats-ad-push-explained/
9 https://digital.hbs.edu/platform-digit/submission/ifood-delivers-great-results-in-brazil-going-beyond-connecting-restaurants-with-customers/
10 https://www.reuters.com/article/health-coronavirus-brazil-ifood-idUSL1N2BO3D4
11 https://digital.hbs.edu/platform-digit/submission/ifood-delivers-great-results-in-brazil-going-beyond-connecting-restaurants-with-customers/
12 https://www.restaurantdive.com/news/ghost-kitchens-global-market-euromonitor/581374/
13 https://www.restaurantdive.com/news/ghost-kitchens-global-market-euromonitor/581374/
14 https://www.businessofapps.com/data/spotify-statistics
15 https://www.theverge.com/2019/4/29/18522297/spotify-100-million-users-apple-music-podcasting-free-users-advertising-voice-speakers
16 https://www.mckinsey.com/industries/healthcare-systems-and-services/our-insights/how-discovery-keeps-innovating#
17 https://www.technologyreview.com/2018/09/17/140149/ikea-designs-future-autonomous-cars-that-work-as-hotels-stores-and-meeting-rooms/
18 https://digital.hbs.edu/platform-digit/submission/all-eyes-on-shopify-a-winner-take-all/
19 https://theconversation.com/why-sales-of-bottled-water-overtaking-soft-drinks-is-nothing-to-celebrate-41695
20 http://www.connectingafrica.com/author.asp?section_id=761&doc_id=762180
21 https://www.theverge.com/2020/4/30/21242421/zoom-300-million-users-incorrect-meeting-participants-statement
22 https://www.forbes.com/sites/alexkonrad/2020/04/03/all-eyes-on-zoom-how-the-at-home-eras-breakout-tool-is-coping-with-surging-demand-and-scrutiny/

23   https://cmxhub.com/achieving-massive-marketplace-growth-how-rover-grew-3500-in-one-year-through-letting-their-community-run-with-the-dogs/

24   https://www.qualtrics.com/blog/online-review-stats/

25   https://ie.oberlo.com/blog/online-review-statistics

26   https://smallbiztrends.com/2020/06/trustpilot-location-reviews.html

27   https://www.siliconrepublic.com/enterprise/trustpilot-fake-reviews

28   https://www.smartcompany.com.au/industries/retail/luxury-fashion-industry/

29   https://www.ibm.com/downloads/cas/EXK4XKX8

30   https://www.rttnews.com/3125695/dutch-ports-manager-portbase-joins-blockchain-platform-tradelens.aspx?refresh=1

31   https://newsroom.ibm.com/2020-06-25-Sustainable-Seafood-Gets-a-Boost-from-IBM-Blockchain-Technology-for-Insight-into-the-Journey-from-Sea-to-Table

32   https://www.commonwealthfund.org/publications/issue-briefs/2017/oct/paying-prescription-drugs-around-world-why-us-outlier

33   https://www.finextra.com/newsarticle/35899/gobear-raises-17-million-for-underbanked-play

34   https://mixpanel.com/customers/lemonade-drives-growth-mixpanels-user-insights/

35   https://www.nasdaq.com/articles/3-reasons-lemonade-could-make-you-rich-in-2021-and-beyond-2021-03-16

36   https://www.businessinsider.com/gobear-acquires-digital-lender-asiakredit-2020-5?IR=T

37   https://techcrunch.com/2020/05/26/gobear-raises-17-million-to-expand-its-consumer-financial-services-for-asian-markets/

38   https://hbr.org/2015/05/customer-data-designing-for-transparency-and-trust

39   https://www.forbes.com/sites/bernardmarr/2017/08/24/disney-uses-big-data-iot-and-machine-learning-to-boost-customer-experience/#582954523387

40   https://www.businesslive.co.za/fm/fm-fox/entrepreneurs/2020-06-04-entrepreneur-zulzi-founder-vutlharhi-donald-valoyi-hits-a-home-run/

41   https://hbr.org/2015/01/the-strategic-value-of-apis

42   https://platform.ifttt.com/blog/introducing_the_team_plan

43   http://www.nytimes.com/2019/06/19/style/slack-replace-email-ipo-listing.html

44   https://slack.com/intl/en-ie/blog/news/slack-has-10-million-daily-active-users

45   https://www.businessinsider.com/banking-as-a-service-platform-providers?r=US&IR=T

46   https://www.mckinsey.com/industries/financial-services/our-insights/open-bankings-next-wave-perspectives-from-three-fintech-ceos#.

47   https://www.mckinsey.com/industries/financial-services/our-insights/open-bankings-next-wave-perspectives-from-three-fintech-ceos#.

48   https://www.forbes.com/sites/christinemoorman/2018/08/23/adobe-how-to-dominate-the-subscription-economy/#4a198a5952e8

49   https://www.businessinsider.com/banking-as-a-service-platform-providers?r=US&IR=T

50   https://www.sunrun.com/go-solar-center/solar-terms/definition/solar-as-a-service

51   https://www.prnewswire.com/news-releases/global-shared-mobility-market-to-grow-at-a-cagr-of-8-over-the-period-between-2018-and-2026-reaching-a-value-of-us-608-bn-by-2026-transparency-market-research-300998575.html

52   https://venturebeat.com/2019/05/15/adobes-path-from-200-million-to-5-billion-in-recurring-revenue/

53   https://www.latimes.com/health/la-xpm-2014-mar-21-la-he-keeping-stuff-20140322-story.html

54   https://ec.europa.eu/eurostat/web/products-eurostat-news/-/DDN-20191029-1

55   https://www.businessofapps.com/data/spotify-statistics/

56   https://circos.co/about/story/

57   Sandra Vandermerwe and Marika Taishoff, 1998, Amazon.com: *Marketing a new Electronic Go-Between Service Provider*, ECCH

58   https://www.mckinsey.com/business-functions/mckinsey-digital/our-insights/the-covid-19-recovery-will-be-digital-a-plan-for-the-first-90-days

59   https://www.businessofapps.com/data/discord-statistics/

60   https://www.bankmycell.com/blog/how-many-phones-are-in-the-world

61   https://tech.economictimes.indiatimes.com/news/mobile/mobile-apps-fight-screen-space/47351981?redirect=1

62   https://www.examiner.com.au/story/4972456/are-smartphones-dumbing-us-down-or-opening-doors-to-a-brave-new-world/

63   https://news.crunchbase.com/news/whats-driving-the-digital-banking-boom-in-latin-america/

64   https://link.springer.com/article/10.1057/s41287-017-0121-4

65   https://www.zdnet.com/article/mobile-in-sub-saharan-africa-can-worlds-fastest-growing-mobile-region-keep-it-up/

66   https://technext.ng/2020/07/06/kenya-leads-africas-mobile-money-revolution-with-m-pesa-dominating-over-98-of-its-market/

67   www.forbes.com/sites/tobyshapshak/2020/04/06/vodacom-and-safaricom-acquire-m-pesa-to-accelerate-mobile-money-services-in-africa/#37becd68a392

68   https://arxiv.org/ftp/arxiv/papers/1712/1712.05840.pdf

69   https://www.unilever.com/planet-and-society/health-and-wellbeing/handwashing-for-life/

70   https://www.cnbc.com/2019/01/24/smartphones-72percent-of-people-will-use-only-mobile-for-internet-by-2025.html

71   https://www.altfi.com/article/6256_breaking-monzo-sails-past-4m-customers-but-growth-rate-slows

72   https://themanifest.com/mobile-apps/popularity-google-maps-trends-navigation-apps-2018

73   https://pay.google.com/intl/en_in/about/

74   https://thenextweb.com/in/2020/07/29/whatsapp-pay-moves-one-step-closer-to-indian-launch/

75   https://en.wikipedia.org/wiki/Unified_Payments_Interface

76   https://iupana.com/2020/02/17/whatsapp-banking-takes-off-in-brazil/?lang=en#widget/?lang=en

77   https://www.reuters.com/article/us-facebook-brazil-whatsapp/brazil-central-bank-authorises-tests-of-facebooks-whatsapp-pay-mastercard-and-visa-say-idUSKCN24W337

78   https://www.ncbi.nlm.nih.gov/pmc/articles/PMC6618173/

79   https://www.prnewswire.com/news-releases/world-market-for-wearable-devices-set-to-reach-62-82-billion-by-2025---increasing-penetration-of-iot--related-devices-drives-market-growth-300974593.html

80   https://www.wordstream.com/blog/ws/2019/04/03/automotive-marketing

81   https://www.ibm.com/downloads/cas/EXK4XKX8

82   https://www.broadbandsearch.net/blog/mobile-desktop-internet-usage-statistics

83   https://www.forbes.com/sites/forbesinsights/2020/03/05/what-legos-retail-expansion-teaches-us-about-digital-leadership-for-any-business/?sh=39c5870b32f3

84   https://www.straitstimes.com/singapore/9-in-10-here-want-to-continue-working-from-home-survey

85   https://www.irishtimes.com/business/economy/majority-of-employees-don-t-want-to-return-to-pre-covid-working-patterns-1.4302645

86   https://hbr.org/2020/11/our-work-from-anywhere-future

87   https://www.statista.com/statistics/234488/number-of-amazon-employees/

88   https://www.theverge.com/2020/10/9/21508964/microsoft-remote-work-from-home-covid-19-coronavirus

89   https://www.shrm.org/resourcesandtools/hr-topics/technology/pages/slack-zoom-ceos-discuss-remote-work.aspx

90   https://www.usatoday.com/story/news/nation/2014/05/08/bike-commuting-popularity-grows/8846311/

91   https://www.globenewswire.com/news-release/2020/01/29/1976914/0/en/Global-Bicycle-Market-Growth-Trends-and-Forecasts-2020-2025.html

92   https://www.uci.org/news/2020/2020-cycling-boom-in-the-usa

93   https://www.un.org/development/desa/dspd/wp-content/uploads/sites/22/2020/08/sg_policy_brief_covid-19_and_education_august_2020.pdf

94   https://www.weforum.org/agenda/2020/04/coronavirus-education-global-covid19-online-digital-learning/

95   https://www.insidehighered.com/blogs/technology-and-learning/19-trillion-global-higher-ed-market

96   https://www.bloomberg.com/news/articles/2020-03-19/colleges-are-going-online-because-of-the-coronavirus

97   https://www.classcentral.com/report/coursera-2020-year-review/

98   https://www.cnbc.com/2020/06/17/threat-unleashed-by-covid-that-could-sink-high-priced-college-degrees.html

99   Ibid.

100   https://blog.coursera.org/facebook-partners-with-coursera-to-launch-social-media-marketing-professional-certificate/

101   https://www.wltx.com/article/news/education/south-carolina-homeschooling-numbers-on-the-rise-due-to-covid/101-d6ea79d5-0b91-46a6-bfef-9418ed6484e4

102   https://medium.com/@Origin_Learning/microlearning-a-top-2020-learning-trend-6d438a1e35a4

103   https://www.elearninglearning.com/2020/micro-learning/?open-article-id=13614198&article-title=micro-learning-through-social-media--education-on-the-go&blog-domain=beyondcampus.com&blog-title=beyond-campus-innovations

104   https://www.waitrose.com/content/dam/waitrose/Inspiration/About%20Us%20New/Waitrose%20and%20Partners%20Taking%20Action%20On%20Plastics%20April%202019.pdf

105   https://www.renewableenergyworld.com/2019/08/05/a-deluge-of-batteries-is-about-to-rewire-the-power-grid/#gref

106   Ibid.

107   https://www.ncbi.nlm.nih.gov/pmc/articles/PMC3734908/

108   https://www.businesswire.com/news/home/20190507005006/en/Cohealo-Surpasses-2500-Shares-of-Medical-Equipment-for-Health-System-Partners

109   Ibid.

110   https://www.autonomy.paris/en/long-reads/maas-is-blossoming-to-give-people-the-freedom-of-mobility-transitioning-to-a-new-paradigm/

111   https://www.autonomy.paris/en/long-reads/maas-is-blossoming-to-give-people-the-freedom-of-mobility-transitioning-to-a-new-paradigm/

112   https://escp.eu/news/how-frugal-innovation-will-be-best-antidote-businesses-wake-covid-19-crisis

113   https://buymeonce.com/blogs/articles-tips/buymeonce-s-8-reasons-to-be-optimistic-for-2020

114   https://time.com/5684011/patagonia/

115   https://www.nytimes.com/interactive/2019/climate/sustainable-clothing.html

116   https://www.thefashionlaw.com/global-companies-expected-to-lose-1-trillion-in-brand-value-due-to-covid-19/

117   https://youtu.be/hKUOkiKHD8U

118   https://ipropertymanagement.com/research/airbnb-statistics

119   https://www.businesswire.com/news/home/20160822005319/en/Rover.com-Releases-"Rover-Cards"-New-Dog-Walking-Technology-That-Offers-Peace-of-Mind-to-U.S.-Pet-Owners

120   https://www.omnicoreagency.com/youtube-statistics/

121   https://tapadoo.com/mobile-app-ratings-reviews/

122   https://www.kickstarter.com/projects/snapmaker/snapmaker-20-modular-3-in-1-3d-printers

123   https://gaps.com/patreon-earners/

124   https://www.testbirds.com/blog/celebrating-the-biggest-crowd-on-earth/

125   https://informationsecurity.report/news.aspx

126   https://aspira.ie/open-source-vs-in-house-software/

127   https://blogs.easyequities.co.za/easyequities-capitec-partnership

128   https://www.benjamindada.com/nigeria-thrive-agric-yc-2019/

129   https://www.devex.com/news/agritech-startups-aim-to-lift-nigerian-smallholder-farmers-out-of-poverty-92646

130 https://www.devex.com/news/agritech-startups-aim-to-lift-nigerian-smallholder-farmers-out-of-poverty-92646

131 https://www.businesswire.com/news/home/20191201005232/en/American-Express'-10th-Annual-Small-Business-Saturday®

132 https://store.globaldata.com/report/cscv2003cs--covid-19-case-study-a-shift-toward-localism/

133 https://marketingmagazine.com.my/do-consumers-prefer-global-brands/

134 https://www.businessinsider.com/the-demand-for-local-food-is-growing-2017-4?r=USandIR=T

135 https://www.bbcgoodfood.com/howto/guide/facts-about-food-miles

136 https://www.globenewswire.com/news-release/2019/01/25/1705536/0/en/Global-Organic-Farming-Market-is-Expected-to-Exhibit-a-Growth-Rate-of-8-4-by-2026.html

137 http://www.worldvaluessurvey.org/WVSContents.jsp

138 https://hbr.org/2019/02/how-global-brands-can-respond-to-local-competitors

139 https://www.kantarworldpanel.com/global/News/Colgate-is-the-Most-Chosen-Brand-in-Asia

140 https://www.kantarworldpanel.com/en/PR/2020-edition-of-the-Brand-Footprint-Ranking

141 https://www.mckinsey.com/cn/our-insights/perspectives-on-china-blog/the-real-reason-why-chinese-consumers-prefer-local-brands

142 https://www.statista.com/statistics/1183456/china-preference-of-local-and-foreign-brands/

143 https://www.grandviewresearch.com/press-release/global-craft-spirits-market

144 https://www.cityam.com/uk-distillery-numbers-jump-as-craft-gin-popularity-booms/

145 https://www.businesswire.com/news/home/20200304005274/en/Global-Craft-Beer-Market-2020-2024-Evolving-Opportunities

146 https://www.barkerbrettell.co.uk/popular-piercing-and-profitable-the-growth-of-the-street-food-market/

147 https://www.warc.com/newsandopinion/news/netflix_sources_local_content_for_global_audiences/41881

148 https://www.fool.com/investing/2019/04/17/netflix-drives-global-growth-with-genuine-local-co.aspx

149 https://infed.org/mobi/social-capital/

150 https://knowledge.insead.edu/blog/insead-blog/elon-musk-frugal-engineer-4085

151 https://www.theguardian.com/global-development-professionals-network/2014/sep/29/charles-leadbeater-healthcare-india-mexico

152 https://techwireasia.com/2020/07/why-the-pandemic-will-boost-telehealth-services-across-asia-pacific/

153 https://www.emarketer.com/content/telemedicine-could-be-more-widely-adopted-due-to-the-coronavirus

154 https://www.foxbusiness.com/real-estate/tiny-home-phenomena-the-pros-and-cons-of-living-in-a-micro-home

155 https://www.fastcompany.com/40420576/solar-innovations-means-we-can-bring-power-to-the-1-billion-who-still-live-without-it

156 https://www.oikocredit.ca/k/n3048/news/view/324739/26886/oikocredit-invests-usd-5-million-in-m-kopa-to-support-growth-of-solar-energy-in-africa.html

157 http://www.m-kopa.com/m-kopa-reports-on-savings-inclusion-and-climate-action/

158 Ibid.

159 https://themanifest.com/mobile-apps/popularity-google-maps-trends-navigation-apps-2018

160 https://www.engineering.com/3DPrinting/3DPrintingArticles/ArticleID/20344/New-French-organisation-Covid3D-Creates-24-7-3D-Printing-Factory-for-40-Hospitals.aspx

161 https://massivit3d.com/metropole-set-transform-service-offering-first-dual-massivit-3d-printing-installation-france

162 https://www.cairn.info/revue-journal-of-innovation-economics-2016-3-page-57.htm#

163 https://amfg.ai/2019/07/09/how-mature-is-your-industry-in-its-adoption-of-3d-printing/

164 https://www.popularmechanics.com/technology/infrastructure/a27435078/3d-printed-community/

165 https://www.cnbc.com/2020/09/02/lego-ceo-says-toymakers-digital-future-is-a-10-year-journey.html

166 https://startupgenome.com/article/state-of-the-global-startup-economy

167 Ibid.

168 Ibid.

169 Mark Prensky, 2015, Technology as an 'Amplifier' of practices both good and bad, *Educational Technology*, Vol. 55, No. 5, p. 64. <http://marcprensky.com/wp-content/uploads/2016/12/Prensky-Technology_as_Amplifier-EDTEC-Sep-Oct-2015-01.pdf>

170 For more, see Jeremy Rifkin, 2014, *Zero Marginal Cost Society: The Internet of Things, the Collaborative Commons, and the Eclipse of Capitalism*, New York: Palgrave Macmillan

171 https://www.microsoft.com/africa/4afrika/mkopa.aspx

172 https://www.indigo9digital.com/blog//-jeff-bezos-quotes

173 https://medium.com/build-something-cool/7-ways-to-tell-a-story-like-steve-jobs-pixar-and-netflix-59d6f39c08ba

174 https://b2bstorytelling.wordpress.com/tag/steve-jobs/

175 https://cmxhub.com/achieving-massive-marketplace-growth-how-rover-grew-3500-in-one-year-through-letting-their-community-run-with-the-dogs/

176 https://www.marketingweek.com/uber-ceo-we-need-to-get-better-at-telling-our-story/

177 https://techcrunch.com/2020/02/08/uber-claims-top-spot-in-indian-ride-hailing-market/

178 https://www.nxtbookmedia.com/blog/airbnb-brand-storytelling/

179 Ibid.

180 https://www.thedrum.com/news/2020/05/14/inside-lifebuoy-s-mission-get-the-world-handwashing

181 https://www.unilever.com/planet-and-society/health-and-wellbeing/handwashing-for-life/

182 https://cmxhub.com/achieving-massive-marketplace-growth-how-rover-grew-3500-in-one-year-through-letting-their-community-run-with-the-dogs/

183 https://www.marketingweek.com/uber-ceo-we-need-to-get-better-at-telling-our-story/

184 https://medium.com/the-mission/slacks-epic-marketing-strategy-and-stewart-butterfield-s-thoughts-about-storytelling-c971fcccd8a8

185 https://digital.hbs.edu/platform-digit/submission/uber-medics-and-uber-work-limitless-opportunities-for-uber/

186 https://www.pmtoday.co.uk/spotify-scaling-agile-model/

187 https://www.digitaltrends.com/health-fitness/philips-sonicare-bluetooth-toothbrush-has-a-coaching-app-for-kids/

188 https://www.unilever.com/sustainable-living/improving-health-and-well-being/health-and-hygiene/healthy-handwashing-habits-for-life/

189 https://www.unilever.com/planet-and-society/health-and-wellbeing/handwashing-for-life/

190 https://www.forbes.com/sites/monicamelton/2020/01/14/weight-loss-app-noom-quadruples-revenue-again-this-time-to-237-million/

191 Ibid.

192 https://www.forbes.com/sites/tobyshapshak/2019/06/28/discovery-bank-hopes-to-attract-1000-customers-a-day/

193 https://www.pewresearch.org/fact-tank/2020/01/09/about-one-in-five-americans-use-a-smart-watch-or-fitness-tracker/

194 https://www.alistdaily.com/strategy/how-fitbits-marketing-strategy-has-shifted-to-social-and-community/

195 https://www.marketdataforecast.com/market-reports/fitness-trackers-market

196 The concept of market spaces was first conceived and published by Sandra Vandermerwe, in *Customer Capitalism: Increasing returns in new market spaces*, London: Nicholas Brealey Publishing, 1999

197 https://economictimes.indiatimes.com/industry/healthcare/biotech/health-care/how-philips-is-transforming-into-a-health-tech-trailblazer/article-show/60894455.cms

198 https://www.smartinsights.com/digital-marketing-strategy/online-business-revenue-models/spotify-case-study/

199 https://www.unilever.com/planet-and-society/health-and-wellbeing/handwashing-for-life/

200 https://www.greentechmedia.com/articles/read/a-sneak-peek-at-ubers-electric-vehicle-strategy

201 https://www.nngroup.com/articles/participation-inequality/

202 https://www.forbes.com/sites/kimberlywhitler/2014/07/17/why-word-of-mouth-marketing-is-the-most-important-social-media/#3bc9ca454a8c

203 https://cmxhub.com/achieving-massive-marketplace-growth-how-rover-grew-3500-in-one-year-through-letting-their-community-run-with-the-dogs

204 https://www.freecodecamp.org/news/growth-hacking-lessons-from-the-big-guys-daebb2c791d2/

205 https://blog.markgrowth.com/how-slack-grew-to-8-million-subscribers-in-5-years-2e228bae5082

206 https://www.unilever.com/planet-and-society/health-and-wellbeing/handwashing-for-life/

207 https://www.campaignlive.com/article/why-airbnb-becoming-publisher/1326796

208 https://hivelife.com/business-lessons-fortnite/

209 https://marketingexamples.com/viral/fortnite-changed-marketing

210 https://www.forbes.com/sites/afdhelaziz/2020/06/17/global-study-reveals-consumers-are-four-to-six-times-more-likely-to-purchase-protect-and-champion-purpose-driven-companies/?sh=439aef01435f

211 https://medium.com/@douglas.atkin/how-airbnb-found-its-purpose-and-why-its-a-good-one-b5c987c0c216

212 https://www.drift.com/blog/how-zoom-grew/

213 https://cmxhub.com/achieving-massive-marketplace-growth-how-rover-grew-3500-in-one-year-through-letting-their-community-run-with-the-dogs/

214 For the section on Slack and social media, see https://sumo.com/stories/slack-marketing

215 https://blog.markgrowth.com/how-slack-grew-to-8-million-subscribers-in-5-years-2e228bae5082

216 https://firstround.com/review/From-0-to-1B-Slacks-Founder-Shares-Their-Epic-Launch-Strategy/

217 https://blog.hubspot.com/marketing/social-proof-examples

218 https://www.singlegrain.com/casestudies/growth-study-slack-the-fastest-business-app-growth-in-history/

219 https://gallantway.medium.com/with-over-200m-users-2bn-in-revenue-heres-why-fortnite-may-be-the-ultimate-growth-marketing-e278a3c684d

220 https://www.investopedia.com/tech/how-does-fortnite-make-money

221 https://nationalschoolspartnership.com/initiatives/soaper-heroes/

222 https://www.unilever.com/planet-and-society/health-and-wellbeing/handwashing-for-life/

223 https://www.drift.com/blog/how-zoom-grew/

224 https://www.process.st/freemium-conversion-rate/

225 https://optinmonster.com/free-to-paid-conversion-strategy/

226 https://www.drift.com/blog/how-zoom-grew/

227 https://www.facebook.com/business/success/2-rover
228 https://buildfire.com/app-statistics/
229 https://www.borndigital.com/2017/01/05/fitbit-adds-software-tools
230 https://sproutsocial.com/insights/social-proof/
231 https://marketingexamples.com/viral/fortnite-changed-marketing
232 https://www.successagency.com/growth/2018/10/15/powerful-micro-influencers/
233 https://www.alistdaily.com/social/influencer-marketing-benchmark-report/
234 https://www.businessinsider.com/amazon-global-ecommerce-sales-will-reach-416-billion-in-2020-2020-7?r=US&IR=T
235 https://sproutsocial.com/insights/social-proof/
236 https://www.businessofapps.com/data/whatsapp-statistics/
237 https://www.statista.com/statistics/260819/number-of-monthly-active-whatsapp-users/
238 https://www.hypebot.com/hypebot/2019/05/playlist-manipulation-will-create-a-crisis-in-streaming-says-midias-mark-mulligan.html
239 https://techcrunch.com/2020/11/19/spotify-opens-a-marketplace-for-canvas-looping-artwork-designers/?utm_source=feedburner&utm_mediu
240 https://www.thebrandingjournal.com/2014/10/lego-end-partnership-shell-current-contract-ends/
241 https://inform.tmforum.org/news/2014/11/uber-spotify-partner-car-music-streaming
242 https://www.nytimes.com/2019/12/16/business/media/netflix-commercials.html
243 https://tcrn.ch/3t33kvJ
244 https://timesofindia.indiatimes.com/business/india-business/netflix-focussing-on-pricing-partnerships-to-win-india-market/articleshow/70365972.cms
245 https://tcrn.ch/3nDzn4n
246 https://cmxhub.com/achieving-massive-marketplace-growth-how-rover-grew-3500-in-one-year-through-letting-their-community-run-with-the-dogs
247 https://www.bizjournals.com/bizwomen/news/latest-news/2019/08/pet-sitting-company-Rover-plans-to-expand-grooming.html?page=all
248 https://www.shrm.org/resourcesandtools/hr-topics/technology/pages/slack-zoom-ceos-discuss-remote-work.aspx
249 https://apnews.com/press-release/pr-businesswire/fd2c4981c9d74c20a7a23028f67d40ba
250 https://digital.hbs.edu/platform-digit/submission/ifood-innovation-and-differentiation-for-sustainability/
251 https://pitchfork.com/news/new-spotify-patent-involves-monitoring-users-speech-to-recommend-music/
252 https://econsultancy.com/spotify-2018-wrapped-personalised-data/
253 https://www.linkedin.com/pulse/20130604134550-284615-15-statistics-that-should-change-the-business-world-but-haven-t/

Index

About the authors

SANDRA VANDERMERWE

Sandra is currently an Extraordinary Professor at GIBS (SA) and was previously a Professor at IMD Switzerland and Imperial College Business School, London, having worked on executive programmes at business schools throughout the world. Sandra is a thought leader whose concepts and methodologies are used by corporations worldwide. She works globally with senior leadership to shape future customer-centric strategies, digital innovation and transformation. A prolific best-selling author and speaker, with several awards for her case studies, her work is based on decades of applied research and consulting. Sandra lives in Cape Town.

DAVID ERIXON

After founding the world-renowned digital learning and research institute, Hyper Island—dubbed 'the Oxbridge of Digital'—and digital experience firm Doberman (now part of EY), David spent a decade in senior leadership positions at Vodafone, including five years as global brand director. David has worked on numerous industry projects, corporate accelerators, research initiatives and executive training programmes focusing on customer-centric digital innovation and business transformation. David is an associate of Trinity Business School Dublin and is marketing director at NatWest Group. He lives in Dublin.

VANDERMERWE-ERIXON

The writers have known each other and consulted together globally for 15 years. They have published several articles over the years, like 'Upping the Game to Customer i-centricity' (2015), 'Learning to Compete with AI' (2019) and 'Next Normal Customer post Covid-19' (2020).

Printed in Poland
by Amazon Fulfillment
Poland Sp. z o.o., Wrocław

34936547R00210